Mobilizing Poor Voters

Democracy has provided opportunities for political representation and accountability, but it has also created incentives for building and maintaining clientelistic networks. Why has clientelism consolidated with the introduction of democracy? Drawing on network analysis, *Mobilizing Poor Voters* answers this question by describing and explaining the emergence, maintenance, and disappearance of political, partisan, and social networks in Argentina. Combining qualitative and quantitative data gathered during twenty-four months of field research in eight municipalities in Argentina, *Mobilizing Poor Voters* shows that when party leaders distribute political promotions to party candidates based only on the number of voters they mobilize, party leaders incentivize the use of clientelistic strategies among candidates competing to mobilize voters in poor neighborhoods. The logic of perverse incentives examined in this book explains why candidates who use clientelism succeed in getting elected and reelected over time, contributing to the consolidation of political machines at the local level.

Mariela Szwarcberg is an assistant professor of political science at Reed College. She specializes in the study of democracy, with a geographic focus on Latin America. Her research has been supported and funded by the Fulbright Commission, the Social Science Research Council, and the Mellon Foundation. Her articles have appeared in the *Journal of Comparative Politics*, the *Latin American Research Review, Party Politics, Social Networks, Latin American Politics and Society*, and *Women's Policy Journal of Harvard*. She received her PhD in political science from the University of Chicago.

Structural Analysis in the Social Sciences

Mark Granovetter, editor

The series *Structural Analysis in the Social Sciences* presents studies that analyze social behavior and institutions by reference to relations among such concrete social entities as persons, organizations, and nations. Relational analysis contrasts on the one hand with reductionist methodological individualism and on the other with macro-level determinism, whether based on technology, material conditions, economic conflict, adaptive evolution, or functional imperatives. In this more intellectually flexible structural middle ground, analysts situate actors and their relations in a variety of contexts. Since the series began in 1987, its authors have variously focused on small groups, history, culture, politics, kinship, aesthetics, economics, and complex organizations, creatively theorizing how these shape and in turn are shaped by social relations. Their style and methods have ranged widely, from intense, long-term ethnographic observation to highly abstract mathematical models. Their disciplinary affiliations have included history, anthropology, sociology, political science, business, economics, mathematics, and computer science. Some have made explicit use of social network analysis, including many of the cutting-edge and standard works of that approach, whereas others have kept formal analysis in the background and used "networks" as a fruitful orienting metaphor. All have in common a sophisticated and revealing approach that forcefully illuminates our complex social world.

Other Books in the Series

Mobilizing Poor Voters

Machine Politics, Clientelism, and Social Networks in Argentina

MARIELA SZWARCBERG
Reed College

CAMBRIDGE
UNIVERSITY PRESS

CAMBRIDGE
UNIVERSITY PRESS

32 Avenue of the Americas, New York, NY 10013-2473, USA

Cambridge University Press is part of the University of Cambridge.

It furthers the University's mission by disseminating knowledge in the pursuit of education, learning, and research at the highest international levels of excellence.

www.cambridge.org
Information on this title: www.cambridge.org/9781107534629

First published 2015

Printed in the United States of America

A catalog record for this publication is available from the British Library.

Library of Congress Cataloging in Publication Data
Szwarcberg, Mariela Laura
Mobilizing poor voters : machine politics, clientelism, and social networks in Argentina / Mariela Szwarcberg.
    pages   cm. – (Structural analysis in the social sciences)
Includes bibliographical references and index.
ISBN 978-1-107-11408-1 (hardback) – ISBN 978-1-107-53462-9 (paperback)
1. Poor – Political activity – Argentina.   2. Social media – Political aspects – Argentina.   3. Political participation – Argentina.   4. Voting – Argentina.   5. Argentina – Politics and government – 21st century.   I. Title.
HC173.S99   2015
323′.0420869420982–dc23   2015014378

ISBN 978-1-107-11408-1 Hardback
ISBN 978-1-107-53462-9 Paperback

To my parents,
Dora Psenne and Joel Szwarcberg

Contents

Acknowledgments

I am genuinely indebted to my advisors who supported this project from its inception. Susan Stokes has been a continuing source of thoughtful and constructive criticism. Her analytical and rigorous thinking had an enormous impact on my intellectual development, and for that, and many other things, I owe her an enormous debt of gratitude. John Padgett taught me to see and understand the world through the lenses of network analysis, enriching my professional development. Ernesto Calvo has been following my work since I was an undergrad in Torcuato Di Tella University. Throughout the years, he has patiently guided my intellectual curiosity, pushing me to ask better questions and develop analytical tools to answer them.

This research project benefited from the support and advice of several people and institutions in both the United States and Argentina. I thank the Fulbright Commission, the Tinker Foundation, the Center for Latin American Studies at the University of Chicago, the Social Science Research Council, the Mellon Foundation, the Yale Program on Democracy, the Helen Kellogg Institute for International Studies, and Reed College for their financial support. Some of the findings presented in Chapters 2 and 4 were initially published in "The Microfoundations of Political Clientelism: Lessons from the Argentine Case" in the *Latin American Research Review* and "Uncertainty, Political Clientelism, and Voter Turnout in Latin America: Why Parties Conduct Rallies in Argentina" in the *Journal of Comparative Politics*.

I am particularly indebted to Javier Auyero and Steve Levitsky. Without their works on Peronism and Argentine politics, much of this book could not have been thought, much less written. Their works were a great source of inspiration for my own. I am also indebted to friends and colleagues for their comments and passionate conversations about politics in Argentina and Latin America. I thank Isabella Alcañiz, Luciano Andrenacci, Alyson Benton, Taylor Boas, Valeria Brusco, Eddie Camp, Horacio Cao, Thad

Dunning, Marcelo Escolar, Roberto Gargarella, Carlos Gervasoni, Kenneth Greene, Claudio Holzner, Gabriel Kessler, Joy Langston, Marcelo Leiras, Germán Lodola, Noam Lupu, Luis Fernando Medina, Vicky Murillo, Ana María Mustapic, Marcelo Nazareno, Ana de la O, Ezequiel Gonzalez Ocantos, Virginia Oliveros, Andreas Schedler, Luis Schiumerini, Alberto Simpser, Catalina Smulovitz, Maristella Svampa, Rebecca Weitz-Shapiro, and Rodrigo Zarazaga. Since our time in Chicago, two gifted physicists who share my obsession for politics have enhanced the way I think "analytically" about the problems examined in this book. I treasure those long nights of conversations in Chicago, Istanbul, Italy, and New York with Panos Oikonomou and Ignacy Sawicki about this book and politics in our countries: Argentina, Greece, and Poland.

I am also grateful to the local Argentine journalists, politicians, activists, party bosses, brokers, and voters who spoke with me about their experience and understanding of clientelistic politics. I cannot express in words the debt of gratitude that I have to them. In particular, I want to thank Jorge Ghirardi, Fabián Dominguez, and Alberto Sayus for spending uncountable hours in coffee shops and *asados* (during the electoral campaign), teaching me about the intricacies of the politics of the Conurbano. Most of all, I am truly grateful to those who "do" local politics and who spent hours talking and showing me how they do politics on the ground. Anabella Museri and Sara Niedzwiecki provided great research assistance during fieldwork in Argentina.

In Lima, I benefited enormously from my affiliation with the Universidad Católica. I am indebted to Carlos Melendez, Aldo Panfichi, Cynthia Sanborn, Fernando Tuesta Soldevilla, Martín Tanaka, and Jorge Valladares for their generosity and enthusiasm regarding the project. I also benefited from comments I received in presentations at the Centro de Estudios Políticos y Sociales de Córdoba, Universidad Católica de Lima, Universidad de General Sarmiento, Universidad Torcuato Di Tella, Universidad de San Andrés, University of Utah, the Institute for the Quality of Government at the University of Gothenburg, and the workshops of Comparative Politics at the University of Chicago, Yale University, and the University of Illinois at Urbana-Champaign, as well as conferences organized by the American Political Science Association, the Midwest Political Science Association, and the Latin American Studies Association.

I am also indebted to all of my students who took different versions of my seminar on distributive politics over the years. I want to thank my terrific Reed students, who endured reading the whole manuscript and providing thoughtful comments and criticism: Elaine Andersen, Mariuxi Andrade, Gyulnara Barnett, Ari Galper, Daniel Kallick, Megan Keating, Monty La Salle Hill, Tess Lallemant, G. Luhman, Cristobal Mancillas, Eli Rau, Sydney Scarlata, and Oliver Silverton-Peel.

Robert Dreesen of Cambridge University Press was a dream-come-true editor: thorough and fast. He helped me all the way through the editorial process for first-time authors and found me terrific reviewers. The book is much better because of their constructive criticism and suggestions. Philip Alexander helped me throughout the production process, and Suzette André Costello was a superb copy editor.

My final acknowledgments are to my friends and family. I would have never been able to learn so much about politics were it not for years of long nights and unending weekends discussing and participating in politics with my Argentine *compañeros* and friends. Most still engage actively in politics in various spaces, and we have remained friends despite ideological and geographical differences; I want to thank especially Pablo Pelazzo and Martín "Poca" Tornay.

My best friend since childhood, Paulita Feijoo, shared this long journey with me for many years, and I am grateful for every moment we spent together. I still cannot believe she is gone and unable to "finally see 'the' book." I miss her every single day, but console myself imagining her screaming *"grosa"* as she used to do whenever she saw my name in print (a good sign that she was, indeed, family).

I want to thank my brother, Leandro, and his wife, Eleonora, for sharing with me their sense of humor, which always makes me feel at home in spite of the distance. My parents, Joel and Dora, are my constant and unending source of love and support. Throughout the years they have encouraged me to pursue my goals even when doing so meant long separations. Their strength, courage, and love always push me to do better without forgetting where I come from.

My grandfather arrived in Argentina after escaping the Nazi occupation of his native Poland when he was seventeen years old – without speaking one word of Spanish and without any money. With no time to continue his education, he was unable to finish high school. My father, like my grandfather, needed to work hard to afford basic things and could not afford to go to college. Through his effort, though, he was able to give my brother and me the opportunity to go to college. I did not grow up in a house full of books, but in one of hard-working and curious people who afforded me the chance to pursue my dreams. Many of the activists and voters in this book work as much as my grandfather and father did to give their children a better future. It is in the hope that others can have the opportunities I had that I wrote this book.

1

Mobilizing Poor Voters

One week before the rally, Mario, the local party broker, stopped by Laura's house. Laura is a single mother with three children. After asking her about her children, Mario reminded Laura of the upcoming rally and noted that "a lot of people were waiting to get on a social welfare program like the one she was receiving thanks to him." The message was unmistakable. If Laura wanted to continue receiving benefits from the welfare program, she would have to attend the rally. She asked Paula, her young teenage neighbor, to look after her five-year-old son, her toddler daughter, and her infant Juancito. In exchange, Laura agreed to give Paula some money and whatever she received for attending the rally. When Laura returned home, she realized that Juancito was unusually quiet and unresponsive. Worried, she took him to Mario's house. Mario drove her to the hospital and waited until she spoke with the doctors. Laura's baby had serious brain damage. Years later, Laura would learn that Juancito fell from the bed where his siblings were playing. Scared or inattentive, Paula left him quietly in his cradle. Today, Juancito lives in a special state institution that is paid for by a pension that Mario "helped to get."

Laura's story illustrates the complex relationship between poor voters and party brokers. On the one hand, if Mario had not forced Laura to attend the rally, she would have stayed with her children and Juancito may have never been injured. On the other, if Mario had not taken her to the hospital and secured a pension for Juancito's care, Laura's situation would have been even worse.

This book explores the mechanisms that explain the simultaneous consolidation of clientelism and democracy by studying the relationships between brokers and voters and between brokers and bosses in Argentina. I argue that while democracy has created new spaces for representation and political accountability, it has also created incentives for cultivating clientelistic relationships. Using network analysis to study the nested relationships between party bosses, brokers, and voters, this book reveals a logic of perverse incentives that induces brokers to employ clientelistic strategies to mobilize poor voters. When brokers solve voters' problems by providing them with material and nonmaterial benefits in exchange for participating at rallies and elections, they are using *clientelism* or *clientelistic strategies*. Clientelism is thus defined in this book as "a strategy of *political mobilization* in which politicians solve or promise to solve voters' problems in exchange for their political support."[1]

This book examines the incentives party brokers face in choosing how to mobilize voters to explain why some choose to use clientelism, and why some succeed and others fail in building a party network that uses clientelistic strategies. Studying the construction and maintenance of political, partisan, and social networks at the local level, this book describes and explains how clientelistic networks are built and sustained over time, as well as why some of them succeed in consolidating in new democracies while others fail and disappear.

A detailed description of these networks is an end in itself. As Jon Elster writes, "to explain is to provide a *mechanism*, to open up the black box and show the nuts and bolts, the cogs and wheels, the desires and beliefs that generate the aggregate outcomes" (1985: 5, emphasis in original). I use network analysis to describe the position and strategic decision making of each member within a clientelistic political machine. I study the relationships between and among political, partisan, and social networks, paying attention to the positions of party bosses, brokers, activists, and voters in each network.

In addition to its descriptive component, this book explains why some local politicians choose to use clientelistic strategies to mobilize poor voters and others do not, and why some who choose to utilize such strategies succeed in mobilizing poor voters while others fail. To explain variation in political actors' decisions on whether or not to use clientelism, I focus on the incentives that they face when making strategic choices about how to mobilize voters by considering their capacity to use clientelistic strategies and their individual preferences for or against such strategies within a given social context. I argue that a broker's capacity to build clientelistic linkages with voters is determined by his or her access to particularistic goods and ability to distribute these goods to voters who are likely to turn out and support the party.

I find that brokers who are able and prefer to use clientelistic strategies are more successful overall in mobilizing poor voters than those brokers who are incapable of employing these strategies and those brokers who, although capable of turning to these strategies, prefer not to. I find that the number of *pragmatist brokers* – those who are capable of using clientelism and choose to do so – almost equals the number of *idealist brokers* – those who, although capable, prefer not to use clientelism.

To explain variation in individuals' decision making about using clientelism, it is necessary to investigate the incentives they face and goals they pursue at the time of choosing whether or not to use clientelistic strategies to mobilize voters. Assuming that party brokers seek to win and stay in office, I expect them to pursue political strategies that would enable them to achieve this goal. I find that when party bosses distribute promotions based only on voter turnout, they encourage the use of clientelism among brokers competing for the support of poor voters. This system of rewards and punishments explains the consolidation of clientelism in new democracies. Party brokers learn through experience that clientelistic strategies are effective in mobilizing poor voters, and that their political success hinges upon their capacity to mobilize a larger number of voters.

To shed light on the emergence and consolidation of political clientelism and democracy, I describe and explain the context and mechanisms through which party bosses and brokers decide how to mobilize poor voters. The theory proposed and tested in this book builds a logic of perverse incentives that encourages office-seeking party brokers competing to mobilize poor voters to employ clientelistic strategies. Observing that candidates who use clientelistic strategies to mobilize poor voters are more effective than candidates who reject the use of these strategies, brokers interested in a political career learn about the efficacy of clientelism. Knowing that they will be rewarded with political promotions based solely on the number of voters mobilized and that they are unlikely to be punished for using these strategies by either the courts or political parties, office-seeking brokers are perversely encouraged to use clientelism to mobilize poor voters. This logic of perverse incentives has significant implications for the quality of local democracy.

First, it implies that voters' income inequalities will translate to political representation. A direct consequence of clientelism is that although poor voters can participate in democracy, their preferences are not voiced. When politicians buy voters' participation at rallies and elections, they are muting voters and, thus, precluding themselves from gathering information about voters' policy preferences. As a result, clientelism succeeds in deepening exclusion in democratic practices by inhibiting the ability of the poor to voice their preferences in collective decision making, and political equality suffers.[2]

Second, when only those candidates willing to use clientelism get elected, over time the local party system becomes stable. The political opposition finds it difficult to run against political machines that have the majority of seats in city councils and hold the executive office. I show how low levels of electoral volatility result from the consolidation of machine politics, which induces actors to use clientelistic strategies. Even in such a system, some local politicians are unwilling to use clientelistic strategies, but they are systematically defeated by candidates who do so.

Whereas some scholars accurately point out that clientelism provides voters with solutions that otherwise would not be available to them (Kitschelt 2000; Gay 2006; Kitschelt and Wilkinson 2007; Hilgers 2012), and that it helps avoid party system breakdown and social crises (Mainwaring and Scully 1995; Levitsky 2003), my research describes the costs that clientelism and informal rules have for poor voters. It is the logic of perverse incentives that explains why Mario forced Laura to attend the rally.[3]

Machine Politics, Clientelism, and Social Networks

The bulk of the existing literature on clientelism and clientelistic relationships recognizes the importance of networks in making clientelism work. Networks provide party leaders with information about voters' electoral preferences and likelihood to turn out to vote. Networks also enable party brokers to monitor voters in case they fail to participate and support the party by attending rallies or voting for the party's candidate. Political parties rely on networks of party activists to distribute goods to voters; parties that do not have partisan networks are not able to distribute goods. Networks also enable parties to identify and recruit new community organizers and party activists to work for a party's candidate.

In short, it is networks that make clientelism work. Yet, we do not know how political parties build networks of party activists and followers, nor do we fully understand why some parties are able to sustain and even enlarge the size of their networks over time while others fail. Using network analysis, I study the construction and maintenance of political, partisan, and social networks to explain the causes and consequences of the consolidation of clientelism in new democracies.

"Social network analysis is based on an assumption of the importance of relationships among interacting units ... that is, relations defined by linkages among units are a fundamental component of network theories" (Christakis and Fowler 2009. 4). Using rich ethnographic data, this book describes and explains the emergence, persistence, and decline of political networks by tracing the political careers of candidates at the local level since their origins as community organizers and party activists until their election and reelection – in cases in which they succeed in mobilizing voters.

Whereas most of the literature takes networks for granted without examining their creation and sustainability, this book studies them as theoretical and empirical phenomena. By describing, defining, and explaining their construction, this book advocates for the integration of ethnographic and quantitative approaches to the study of networks.

Network analysis also allows for a closer examination of the context in which actors make their everyday decisions about whom to help (core or swing voters) and whom to ask for help (party brokers affiliated with certain political parties). Networks also provide information about the incentives facing individuals in different structural positions and how these incentives have affected their decision making. Studying the networks in which individuals are embedded and participate daily can help explain party leaders' decisions to use clientelistic strategies and variation in their success and failure in mobilizing voters by employing the same strategies.

Using network analysis, this book focuses on the relationships between party brokers and voters, and party bosses and party brokers. Furthermore, the book also scales up these relationships beyond the local level. While the focus of this book is at the local level where political machines are anchored, network theory enables me to study networks at multiple levels. Indeed, in Chapter 7, I scale up the findings presented at the local level by examining clientelistic networks at the provincial and national level. Hence, whereas most of the book focuses on the relationships between party brokers and mayors, and party brokers and poor voters, Chapter 7 shows how the theory of perverse incentives posed in this book can be scaled up to explain the relationships between and among mayors and governors and presidents.

Without understanding the social context in which individuals build and sustain relationships, the literature fails to grasp the social context in which dyadic clientelistic relationships are cultivated and sustained over time. James Scott's classic study about corruption and machine politics already highlighted the importance of a social context that "encourages the growth of machine-like qualities in ruling parties" (1969: 1145). Indeed, in her own seminal article, Susan Stokes recovered this observation:

> Thirty-five years ago, James Scott (1969) observed that political life of contemporary new nations bore a strong resemblance to the machine politics of the United States in earlier eras. The patronage, particularism, and graft endemic to the Philippines or Malaysia in the postwar decades recalled, for Scott, the Tweed machine in nineteenth-century New York or the Dawson machine in twentieth-century Chicago. Much has happened in the third of a century since Scott outlined "the contours and dynamics of the 'machine model' in comparative perspective" (1143). Many of the new nations that occupied his analysis have undergone transitions to electoral democracy; yet politics in these systems often remains particularistic, clientelistic, and corrupt. We therefore have a larger sample of countries, and a

richer experience on which to draw, to understand the contours and dynamics of the machine. The historiography of the U.S. political machine has also grown, as have historical studies of patronage and vote buying in the history of today's advanced European democracies (see, e.g., Piattoni 2001). Finally, a formal literature on redistributive politics has developed, one in which the political machine plays a central role.

(2005: 315)

Assuming a social context in which poor voters are likely to exchange their political support for goods, this book focuses on explaining variation in politicians' capacity to build a following by taking into account the context in which they build and sustain political networks. Combining quantitative and qualitative data, this book explains the "creation" of local candidates by tracing their political careers at the local level since their origins until their election and reelection (in cases in which they succeed in mobilizing voters and thus get promoted within the clientelistic party).

Beginning from the microfoundations that lead some individuals to build larger networks of followers than others, this book studies individual candidates' decision making by contextualizing their decisions and thus examining the effects that a structure of perverse incentives has on their individual choices. Moreover, beyond enabling the contextualization of the information, network analysis also allows for a focus on the relationships between and among individuals in different (positions within and in) networks. "The fundamental difference between a social network explanation and a non-network explanation of a process is the inclusion of concepts and information on relationships among units in a study" (Christakis and Fowler 2009: 8). Whereas "'standard' social science perspectives usually ignore the relational information" (Christakis and Fowler 2009: 9), this book takes them into account and makes them central in explaining variation among brokers' decision to use clientelism, and their success and failure in mobilizing poor voters by using clientelistic strategies.

Political, Partisan, and Social Networks

To explain the relationship between Laura and Mario, I study the political, partisan, and social networks in which they are embedded and participate daily. Poor voters such as Laura become connected to party brokers like Mario when they look for food to feed their children, construction materials to finish their precarious homes, scholarships to send their children to school, social welfare programs that can help them make ends meet, and jobs. Party brokers such as Mario work to solve voters' everyday problems in exchange for political support to advance their political careers.

Problem-solving networks are anchored in political machines – informal organizations that link party members with voters. Machines consolidate several problem-solving networks in a hierarchical organization, with voters who ask party activists for solutions to their problems at the bottom and a party boss at the top.

Activists begin their political careers when brokers recruit them to represent their candidates and parties in their neighborhoods. Some recruited activists become paid party activists or *brokers*; others who continue mobilizing voters for the party but do not receive a salary remain unpaid party activists. Brokers are paid for daily work in their neighborhoods solving voters' problems and mobilizing them to participate in rallies and elections.[4] Brokers' benefits range from municipal employment to access to welfare programs. Voters at the bottom of the pyramid receive goods of small value, such as construction materials, school supplies, and blankets, and are likely to support and remain in the broker's network as long as they receive something. Otherwise, they will switch their support to another broker who will give them similar goods.

Brokers are office-seeking party activists interested in becoming candidates; therefore, they are motivated to increase the size of their political network to eventually compete for an elected position. Those who succeed in mobilizing voters to turn out at rallies and elections are rewarded with party candidacies, and the most effective get elected as local representatives.

Elected representatives have access to resources and information and are expected to enlarge or at least maintain the size of their political networks. If brokers fail to turn out voters to rallies, they will lose their opportunity to become candidates. Brokers compete first to become candidates, second to get elected, and third to get reelected to the same office or to a higher one.

This book focuses on individuals interested in pursuing a political career within the machine and uses information about municipal candidates who succeeded and failed in getting elected and reelected in Argentina. I chose to focus on local candidates for three reasons. First, to explain why some brokers are able to mobilize more voters than others, I have to make comparisons among individuals who actually manage to turn out voters beyond their family and friends. By examining candidates who succeed in getting elected, I am able to differentiate between those activists who have a party network and those who do not.[5] Second, local candidates are elected representatives, and as such they are in charge of legislating based on the demands of their constituency. Candidates who use clientelistic strategies to mobilize poor voters fail to represent the demands of their constituents. In this way, they seriously diminish the quality of democratic representation and increase the potential for social outbursts from those who feel excluded from the democratic process. Third, in studying elected local candidates, I am able to gather systematic data about their political careers and capacities and preferences to use clientelism.

Political, Partisan, and Social Networks in Argentina

This book takes advantage of the benefits that country studies provide for building and testing theories in comparative politics (George and Bennett 2005; Gerring 2007) while enhancing unit homogeneity (Levitsky and Murillo 2005: 15) to study political, partisan, and social networks in Argentina. Since 1983, the country has seen the consolidation of clientelism in a competitive democratic process that has included the partisan alternation of presidential power and considerable competition at the subnational level where political machines are anchored. Recent scholarship that focus on the Argentine case have done so to build explanations about the pervasiveness and persistence of clientelism in new democracies (see, e.g., Auyero 2000; Brusco et al. 2004; Calvo and Murillo 2004; Stokes 2005; Nichter 2008; Szwarcberg 2009; Weitz-Shapiro 2012; Stokes et al. 2013; Zarazaga 2014).

"Argentina, with its unstable and weakly enforced institutions, is representative of a much larger universe of cases than the handful of advanced industrialized democracies upon which most of the leading theories of democratic institutions are based" (Levitsky and Murillo 2005: 14). In studying politics on the ground in Argentina, I seek to build a theory and draw lessons about the consolidation of clientelism in a democracy that transcend Argentina, and could be applied to understand this phenomenon in other new democracies.

Studying political, partisan, and social networks in eight municipalities in two Argentine provinces – Buenos Aires and Córdoba – I am able to control for historical and cultural variables at the national level that may affect the explanatory variables (Snyder 2001). Focusing my analysis on eight cases has allowed me to carry out the extensive fieldwork necessary for gathering data on individual candidates' capacities and preferences to use clientelism and on the effects of those decisions on their political careers and the political careers of other candidates in their party and in opposition parties. It also enabled me to gather information about each selected municipality.

The selection of these provinces is justified by data availability and regional differences in levels of economic development, demographic characteristics, and electoral patterns. The case selection is based on the differences in population, housing quality, income, partisanship, and incumbency that studies of vote buying and clientelism (e.g., Brusco et al. 2004; Calvo and Murillo 2004; Stokes 2005; Nichter 2008; Weitz-Shapiro 2012) have used to explain variation in parties' selection of mobilization strategies.

In the past two decades, Argentina's historically dominant parties, the Radical Civic Union (UCR) and the Justicialist (Peronist) Party (PJ), achieved different levels of electoral support in Córdoba and Buenos Aires. Both are political parties with stable roots in society and solid party organizations that maintain territorial control over municipalities by combining a recollection of shared watershed historical events with clientelistic inducements (Auyero 2000; Levitsky 2003; Calvo and Murillo 2004, 2005; Torre 2005; Szwarcberg 2009), creating "communities of fate" (Welhofer 1979: 171) and "electorates of belonging" (Panebianco 1988: 267).

The Radical Party governed the province of Córdoba, together with the city of Córdoba and the majority of municipalities in the province since the return of democracy in 1983 until 1999, when the Peronists won the governorship, which they retain today. In contrast, Buenos Aires has been a Peronist stronghold. The predominance of the Peronist Party among the voters of the province of Buenos Aires has been widely documented (Mora y Araujo and Llorente 1980; Ostiguy 1998; Auyero 2000; Levitsky 2003).

Table 1.1 provides socio-demographic and electoral information about the selected cases. The eight cases include municipalities with competitive multiparty elections, competitive two-party elections featuring the Radical Party and the Peronist Party, and elections that are essentially noncompetitive in municipalities dominated by the Peronist Party. Map 1.1 shows the locations of the selected municipalities within the country of Argentina.

Buenos Aires

Buenos Aires is the financial, industrial, and political center of Argentina. Given the size of the province's electorate, voters living in the twenty-four municipalities that border the capital city – collectively referred to as the Conurbano Bonaerense – have the voting power to determine the outcome of national elections. For instance, La Matanza is a municipality that has the same population as six other Argentine provinces combined; similarly, the municipality of José C. Paz contains the same number of voters as some Argentine provinces.

Sixty percent of Buenos Aires's registered voters live in the twenty-four Conurbano municipalities. The importance of the Conurbano for

Table 1.1. *Selected Municipalities in Argentina*

Province	Municipality	Population	Number of low-income households	Local political party system*
Córdoba	Córdoba Capital	1,329,604	369,793	Multiparty
	Río Cuarto	246,393	42,044	Bipartisan
	Villa María	72,162	1,114	Bipartisan
	Colonia Caroya	13,806	4,018	Bipartisan
Total Córdoba	*443 municipalities*	*3,308,876*	*97,405*	
Buenos Aires	José C. Paz	265,981	56,004	Single party
	San Miguel	276,190	65,689	Single party
	Bahía Blanca	301,572	88,260	Bipartisan
	Malvinas Argentinas	322,375		Single party
Total 24 municipalities of Buenos Aires (Conurbano)		9,916,715		
Total municipalities of Buenos Aires without Conurbano		5,708,369		
Total Buenos Aires	*136 municipalities*	*13,827,203*	*508,671*	
Total Argentina	*2,291 municipalities*	*36,260,130*	*1,442,934*	Bipartisan

Note: Population numbers are based on the 2010 national census (National Institute of Statistics and Census of Argentina, INDEC). The number of council members is legally stipulated and varies based on the population of each municipality. By combining educational, occupational, and construction characteristics, the INDEC measures the income levels of Argentine homes. A household that fulfills three of the following five characteristics is classified as low income: (1) a density per room that exceeds three inhabitants, (2) precarious physical conditions, (3) absence of indoor plumbing, (4) children between ages six and twelve who do not attend school, and (5) more than four members per one employed member and a head of household who has not finished primary school.

* *Local political party system* describes the local political administrations that the municipality experienced between 1995 and 2005. *Multiparty* refers to the governing of the municipality by three political parties: UCR, PJ, and New Party (only in the case of Córdoba). *Bipartisan* refers to having had Peronist (PJ) and Radical (UCR) administrations. *Single party* refers to having been governed only by one (Peronist) party.

Argentine politics lies in its combination of poverty levels and number of voters. The Conurbano contains 25 percent (7,173,173 inhabitants) of the country's total population in 1.2 percent of the territory and has the highest percentage of unemployed and illegally employed workers. The proximity between those living in the Conurbano and those living in the city of Buenos Aires constitutes a source of continual tension between citizens and the provincial and local governments of Buenos Aires.

I conducted extensive fieldwork for more than twenty-four months in three municipalities located in the northwest of the Conurbano that, until 1994, constituted the municipality of General Sarmiento. Before being

Map 1.1. Selected cases in Argentina

divided into three municipalities – San Miguel, José C. Paz, and Malvinas Argentinas – General Sarmiento constituted a municipality that was second in electoral importance in the province of Buenos Aires. The division enabled the study of three municipalities that shared a common history but differed in political preferences.

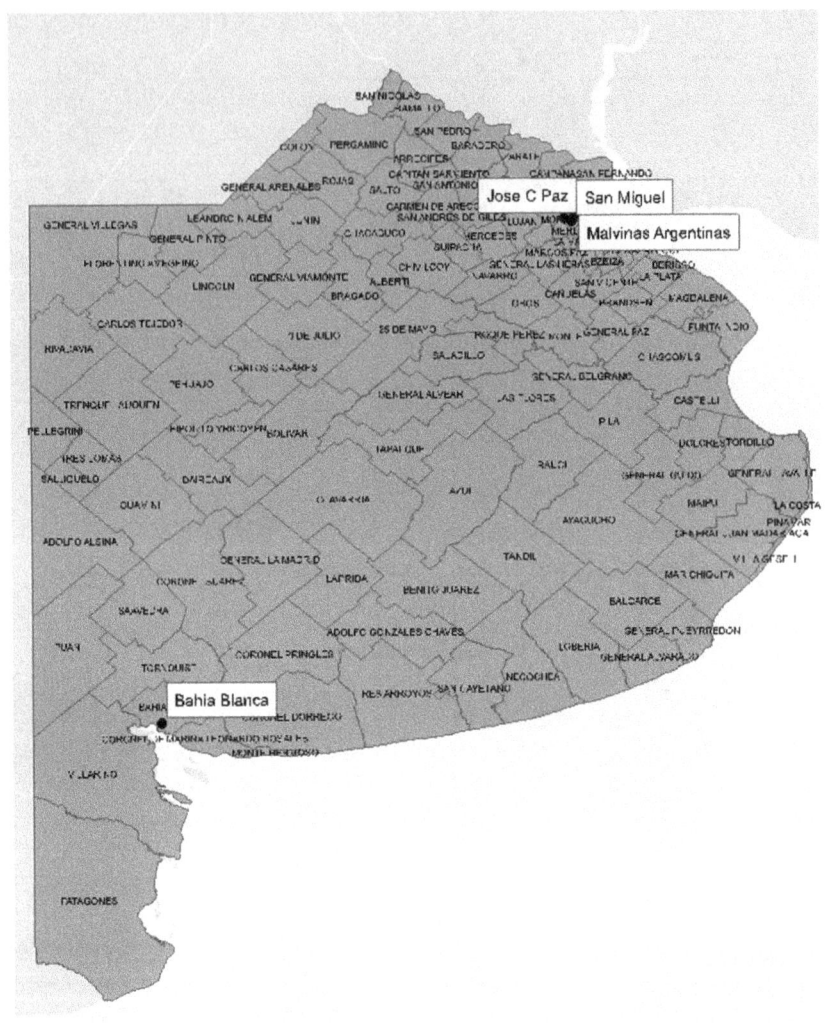

Map 1.2. Selected cases in the Province of Buenos Aires

I also conducted research in Bahía Blanca, a municipality with a population similar to those I studied in the Conurbano, but located in the southern part of the province. The incorporation of this case tests the effects of partisanship and geographical location on party organization and candidates' capacities and preferences in mobilizing voters. Map 1.2

shows the location of the selected municipalities in the province of Buenos Aires.

Córdoba

Córdoba is the third-largest electoral district after the province and the city of Buenos Aires. The case of Córdoba has several comparative advantages. First, in contrast to Buenos Aires, specifically the Conurbano, Córdoba has a bipartisan historical tradition in which both majority parties, the UCR and the PJ, competed at the local level. Moreover, the province was under a series of radical administrations between the return of democracy in 1983 and 1998. Second, the municipality observed changes at all political levels: national, provincial, and municipal. As a result, I can test the effects of changes in party incumbency at different levels. Finally, in examining a previously understudied case, I am making two contributions. First, given that the seminal works of Javier Auyero (2000) and Steven Levitsky (2003) have focused almost exclusively on Buenos Aires, scholars have misinterpreted Argentine politics as the politics of Buenos Aires. Therefore, in also studying a different province, I am contributing to a truly national theory of Argentine politics. Second, in studying the UCR in a political context in which it was as powerful as the PJ, I am able to evaluate existing interpretations about Peronism's uniqueness. As will become clear, more similarities than differences between the two parties appear when they are studied in districts where each had been in power for a considerable period of time.

In Córdoba, I selected the municipalities of Río Cuarto, Villa María, Colonia Caroya, and the city of Córdoba. The city of Córdoba and Río Cuarto are the two largest and most important municipalities in Córdoba, followed by, among others, Villa María. Colonia Caroya is a small municipality located near the city of Córdoba. Map 1.3 illustrates the location of the selected municipalities in the province of Córdoba.

Although the results presented in this book derive from eight municipalities, I interviewed local candidates and voters and attended rallies and political meetings in other municipalities in Buenos Aires, including Avellaneda, Ayacucho, Hurlingham, La Matanza, Merlo, Morón, Pergamino, Quilmes, and Vicente Lopez. I also conducted fieldwork across municipalities in the province of Córdoba, including Mina Clavero, San Francisco, Villa Carlos Paz, and Yacanto. Additionally, in 2009, I conducted fieldwork in several municipalities in the province of San Luis. The information I collected in these municipalities supports the findings presented in this book; thus, I am confident that the selected cases are representative of a larger universe of cases.

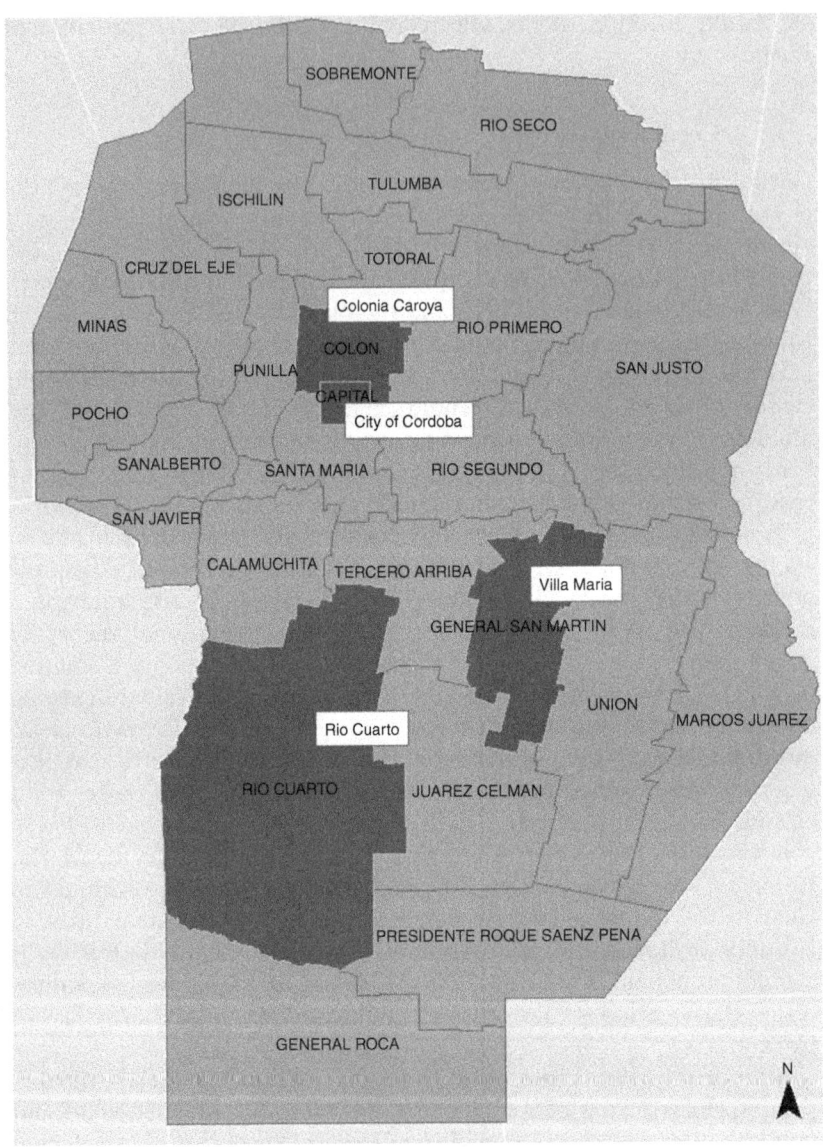

Map 1.3. Selected cases in the Province of Córdoba

Field Research

Research for this book was conducted more than nineteen months between June 2005 and December 2006 in the eight selected municipalities, before, during, and after the national election of October 2005. In this election, voters chose 128 national deputies, 24 national senators, 400 provincial legislators, 55 mayors, and 3,738 councilors. Though a midterm election, October 2005 was in many ways more important than the presidential election that took place two years later. "The 2003 race took place in the aftermath of an unprecedented economic collapse and the massive December 2001 protests that toppled two presidents in a span of ten days. That election – which was won by little-known [Peronist] Justicialist party governor Néstor Kirchner – was held in a climate of political fragmentation and uncertainty" (Levitsky and Murillo 2008: 16).

In 2003, Kirchner won the presidential election with only 22 percent of the votes after former reelected president Carlos Menem decided to abandon the runoff election. It was the crucial support of Eduardo Duhalde, former president and governor of Buenos Aires, that enabled Kirchner to become president. Thus, two years later, when Kirchner decided to challenge Duhalde's control of the Peronist Party in the stronghold province of Buenos Aires by placing his wife, Cristina Fernández de Kirchner, at the top of the Front for the Victory's (FPV) senatorial ballot for Buenos Aires, the province became the center of the battlefield.[6] Duhalde decided to imitate and challenge the Kirchners' response by placing his wife, Chiche Duhalde, at the top of the PJ ballot.

The selected municipalities located in the Conurbano allied with different party factions. José C. Paz's mayor, Mario Ishii, was one of the first local executives of the Conurbano to support Cristina Kirchner's candidacy. Ishii, however, had a long-standing dispute with the former governor, Eduardo Duhalde, who had twice tried, once with success, to impede his election. Still, when Ishii decided to support Cristina Kirchner, it was not obvious at the time who was going to win the election.

San Miguel's mayor, Oscar Zilocchi, opted to support the candidacy of Chiche Duhalde. The Kirchner administration's support of human rights directly challenged Zilocchi's party leader, Aldo Rico, who was involved with the military during the country's dirty war and had led a group of army mutineers, the *carapintada* movement, to rise up against a recently elected democratic government.[7] Hence, it is unclear if Zilocchi's decision to support Duhalde derived from his loyalty to the governor or the impossibility of supporting the president.

Jesús Cariglino, the mayor of Malvinas Argentinas since the foundation of the municipality, was a close friend of Governor Duhalde. Cariglino, who by the end of 2015 would have been in power for twenty consecutive years, remained loyal to his political godfather and was one of the few mayors of the Conurbano who chose not to support the Kirchners.

Conducting field research at a time when the Peronist Party was for the first time so divided that it presented different Peronist candidates in a national election enabled me to interview and talk with several candidates, party activists, and operatives when they themselves were questioning and thinking critically about politics. It was in this context that I did most of my field research in the province of Buenos Aires.

I began fieldwork four months before the election and left the province two months after the election. I arrived in Lima, Peru, in January 2006 to conduct field research during the presidential campaign which took place that year and left the country a week before election day.[8] Before this trip, I had conducted preliminary fieldwork in Lima, Cusco, and Arequipa in 2003. Most of my observations and interviews in Peru served to help me understand how the logic of perverse incentives was present in both countries, despite their differences. I elaborate on this comparison and present the findings in detail in Chapter 7.

I returned to Argentina at the end of March, and moved to Córdoba for six months during 2006 when the UCR was running a campaign to elect its provincial and local authorities. Living in Córdoba Capital, I was able to attend rallies and party meetings before, during, and after the party primary, as well as to participate in Peronist rallies celebrating a variety of occasions, such as the inauguration of the city's remodeled airport, an event attended by President Néstor Kirchner. In addition to party rallies, I spent almost every weekday attending meetings at city hall and the city council. I conducted interviews with almost every candidate on the city council, and interviewed more than forty former candidates, together with party operatives from the UCR, PJ, and New Party (PN). Luis Juez, a former Peronist candidate and provincial anticorruption prosecutor, created the PN to compete for office after being fired by the governor. Competing for votes where the party leadership of the PJ and the UCR was heavily questioned, Juez ended Córdoba's historical bipartisanship, becoming the mayor of the city of Córdoba in 2003.[9] I also spent considerable time gathering and checking information with local journalists, academics, and political consultants.

Beyond Córdoba Capital, I conducted field research in the municipalities of Villa María, Colonia Caroya, and Río Cuarto. I attended city halls meeting in all the municipalities and interviewed mayors and former mayors, as well as the majority of elected candidates.

Each year from 2007 to 2011, I did follow-up field trips to the municipalities of José C. Paz and San Miguel in Buenos Aires, and I conducted additional fieldwork in the municipalities of Villa Mercedes, Potrero de los Funes, and San Luis Capital in the province of San Luis. These follow-up trips were essential for providing further evidence for the argument about the logic of perverse incentives that I advance in this book. For instance, my field research in three municipalities in the province of San Luis during the legislative elections of 2009 enabled me to participate in a dozen party rallies and interview more than twenty candidates in a new case. The information I collected in these follow-up trips to the places that were originally selected as part of my sample, and those that I added during my work for the survey of Argentine political brokers (led by Susan Stokes at Yale University, the findings of which are presented in Stokes et al. 2013), contributed to further test and strengthen my argument.

In addition to direct observations, participation, and interviews, I conducted exhaustive archival research. Newspapers report party rallies, and tend to have features and interviews of candidates from every party before and after elections. They are also an incredible source of information for contextualizing local events. I consulted the archives of three national newspapers: *Clarín*, *La Nación*, and *Página/12*. National newspapers were useful for tracing the daily events that took place in the country and for gathering information mostly from the province of Buenos Aires, as well as interviews with national politicians, party candidates, operatives, and pollsters. Still, national newspapers lack the type of detailed coverage I needed to study local politics. As a result, I decided to visit municipal archives of local newspapers.

In Buenos Aires, I was given generous access to the archives of *La Hoja*, an independent local newspaper that began in May 1995 and ended in September of 2011. The newspaper provided serious and reliable information for the municipalities of San Miguel, José C. Paz, Malvinas Argentinas, and Tigre. Envisioning the financial problems of making an independent municipal newspaper, I digitalized all the information published in *La Hoja* since its creation in 1995 until the end of 2005. It is, to my knowledge, the only archive existing from the paper. I also consulted *La Nueva Provincia,* the most important local newspaper in Bahía Blanca. In Córdoba, I spent more than a month reading the province's two most important newspapers: *La Voz del Interior* and *La Mañana de Córdoba.* While in Río Cuarto, I also visited the archive of the municipality's local newspaper: *El Puntal.*

Before beginning my research and conducting interviews, I did most of the archival research to get familiar with the local context, as well as to identify candidates to interview and key informants. In my field research, I had a great experience with local journalists, who managed a vast amount of information and provided good contacts for setting up interviews. The challenge, however, and not an insignificant one, was to avoid being identified as a journalist.

While most politicians, activists, and voters do not mind expressing their preferences and opinions about the use of clientelistic strategies of mobilization, it is, nevertheless, something they would not like to acknowledge publicly. Hence, I made clear to each of them that the information they provided would remain confidential if they preferred. This also explains why the manuscript identifies some candidates and not others.

Given that I was interested in explaining why some candidates choose to use clientelism to mobilize voters, and why some clientelistic candidates succeed and other fail, I was more interested in finding reasons, causes, and commonalities that enable me to explain the circumstances under which some candidates opt out of clientelism. Beyond descriptive information from their own political biographies, I was not interested in identifying the candidates. On the one hand, allowing them anonymity was the only way to gather reliable information from candidates who decided to use strategies that were illegal. On the other hand, I was not interested in producing a piece of investigative journalism. Indeed, during my time conducting field research, I had two very unpleasant experiences that made me acutely aware of the risks of asking certain questions (mostly about drug trafficking) and of being a young female alone in marginal neighborhoods at night.[10]

Studying political, partisan, and social networks requires amassing significant and substantive data. Using a multi-level research design to build and test the argument about the logic of perverse incentives that explains the consolidation of clientelism in democracy, I combine quantitative and qualitative data. I use quantitative information to learn about a candidate's capacity to use clientelism, and in-depth interviews to understand their preferences to use clientelism. I combine field research observations, in-depth interviews and semi-structured interviews, and archival research to gather information about the size of political, partisan, and social networks over time. And, I use information from closed-party ballots employed in Argentina to observe changes in candidates' positions.

I test the implications of the logic of perverse incentives I developed at the municipal level in Argentina by scaling up the argument to explain the relationships between party mayors and governors, and governors and presidents in the country. I also employ original data collected in Peru, and secondary sources for the case of Mexico to see how the argument travels to explain the consolidation of democracy and clientelism in a democracy without parties (Levitsky and Cameron 2003; Tanaka 2005; Levitsky 2013), in the case of Peru, and one that experienced a single party rule for seventy-one years, in the case of Mexico. Variation in the strength of political, partisan, and social networks between and within these cases and the Argentine case provides further support for the logic of perverse incentives advanced in this book and contributes to discuss scope conditions and alternative explanations.

Contributions

This book makes three contributions to the clientelism literature. First, it increases our understanding of the importance of machine politics in the consolidation of democracy in developing countries. Political machines remain a significant force among long-standing and new democracies alike (Chubb 1981; Piattoni 2001; Kitschelt and Wilkinson 2007; Schaffer 2007; Stokes et al. 2013); therefore, in studying the conditions under which they emerge and persist, as well as the consequences of their rule, this book contributes to our general understanding of machine politics. More specifically, by showing how the extant literature has ignored the role of political, partisan, and social networks in building and sustaining clientelism, it advances a systematic study of clientelistic relationships among political actors at the local level.

Second, by advancing an explanation for the success and failure of Latin American clientelist parties, this study contributes to theory building. It advances a causal argument that explains why, how, and under what conditions political parties encourage candidates to employ clientelistic strategies of political recruitment and mobilization. The insights obtained in examining the dynamics and effects of this system of perverse incentives are not only of interest to scholars studying clientelism, but also to those investigating corruption, transitions from authoritarianism to democracy, democratic consolidation, and the persistence of authoritarianism in democratic countries.

Third, by combining network analysis with both qualitative and quantitative data, this research demonstrates how a creative research design may shed new light on the performance of political machines. This book aims to build a set of testable propositions derived from a theory that other scholars can employ in their own work, as well as to replicate, and hopefully strengthen, the validity of the arguments advanced in this book. These findings and descriptions can be employed by those interested in using formal approaches to study any form of political competition – not just clientelism. For instance, this book shows how the incorporation of party brokers in formal models of distributive politics reveals a nested game among party bosses, brokers, and voters. In formalizing these interactions, existing models can be improved to provide more accurate predictions about political actors' behavior.

Plan of the Book

This book is organized as follows. Chapter 2 examines the microfoundations of machine politics by studying party candidates' decisions to employ or not employ clientelism. The chapter challenges the assumption that parties and candidates with access to material benefits and a party network will always distribute goods to voters in exchange for electoral support. Instead, this chapter claims that a candidate's capacity to turn to clientelistic strategies of mobilization is a necessary but insufficient condition to explain his or her decision to use clientelism. Besides having the capacity to use clientelism, candidates have to prefer to use clientelism to mobilize voters. Drawing on the original dataset collected for this book, the chapter concludes by demonstrating that the number of *pragmatist candidates* who are capable of using clientelism and prefer to turn to such strategies is almost equal to the number of *idealist candidates* who, though capable of doing so, prefer not to use clientelism.

Chapter 3 examines variation in candidates' decisions to use clientelism based on their access to resources and to a network of party activists able to distribute particularistic goods to voters who are likely to turn out and support the candidate. Building on the findings described in Chapter 2, this chapter focuses on candidates who have the capacity and preference to use clientelistic strategies to mobilize voters in order to explain the variation in the size of their political networks. The chapter shows that a party broker's success in mobilizing voters is a combination of what the candidate has to offer, what voters need, and the alternatives that voters have in order to get their problems solved beyond the candidate.

Chapter 4 explains why party candidates distribute material benefits to voters. As party agents who have information about voters' political preferences and their likelihood of turning out to vote, candidates may use the goods and benefits they receive from party leaders to pursue their own personal enrichment at the cost of lost votes for their party. This chapter claims that party leaders force candidates to pursue the party's electoral goals rather than their own material gain by distributing rewards and punishments based on candidates' ability to turn out voters. Using the original dataset employed in this book, the chapter shows how party leaders use information from voter turnout at rallies and elections. By comparing a candidate's ability to mobilize voters, leaders are able to make inferences about *reliable candidates* who will distribute material benefits to voters and *unreliable candidates* who will use party benefits to pad their own pockets.

Chapter 5 argues that by distributing rewards and punishments to candidates based solely on voter turnout, party leaders develop a system of perverse incentives that encourages candidates to use clientelism. Assuming that party candidates are interested in pursuing a political career, their decision about whether or not to use clientelism comes to define their political future. This logic of perverse incentives results in the emergence and consolidation of *mercenary candidates* who distribute money, small goods, and even alcohol and drugs to voters in exchange for political participation. The chapter concludes by examining the implication of this logic of perverse incentives and its unintended consequences for the consolidation and quality of democracy.

Chapter 6 applies the theory of perverse incentives developed in the previous chapter to explain provincial and national politics. Scaling up from municipal to national politics, the chapter shows how governors and presidents employ the same logic of perverse incentives that mayors use in distributing rewards and punishments. Building on a well-researched literature on subnational authoritarianism in Latin America (e.g., Fox 1994; Cornelius et al. 1999; Snyder 2001; Eaton 2004; Montero and Samuels 2004; Falleti 2005, 2010; Gervasoni 2010; Gibson 2005, 2012), this chapter shows the key role that mayors can play in defining strategic electoral outcomes. After applying the analytical and theoretical argument advanced in this book to understand the relationships between mayors and governors and between mayors and presidents, the chapter concludes by suggesting a future research agenda. Only by studying the nested and dynamic political interactions between mayors and governors and between governors and presidents are scholars able to shed some light on the overall strategy politicians pursue to mobilize voters to elect them.

Chapter 7 places the logic of perverse incentives in comparative and theoretical perspective. Drawing on original data for the case of Lima, Peru, and a rich secondary literature for the case of Mexico, I seek to establish the theory's plausibility. The chapter offers some final thoughts about the implications of the consolidation of clientelism in new democracies, both for future research in Latin America and other developing countries and for future research on distributive politics in general. On the one hand, further work is needed to test the theory more rigorously; on the other, finding significant similarities between these cases and the ones studied in-depth in this book provides plausibility for the theory of perverse incentives and its unintended consequences.

Finally, Chapter 8 summarizes the findings and examines the generalizability of the argument to explain the success and demise of machine politics in new democracies. It focuses particularly on the implications that this theory has for understanding the meaning and practice of democracy at the local level in countries with unequal income distributions. It concludes by offering some thoughts about the implications of this study for future research on machine politics, clientelism, and social networks in Latin America and beyond.

2

The Microfoundations of Political Clientelism

The logic of perverse incentives implies that candidates are rewarded based on the number of voters they mobilize regardless of the strategies they employ to achieve their goal. Candidates interested in pursuing a political career have to demonstrate their ability to get votes for the party. The more votes a candidate manages to provide for the party, the more likely he or she is to be promoted. The testimony of Mario, a party candidate in Buenos Aires, explains this logic sharply:

> This is very simple. You are worth as much as the amount of people you can mobilize. You have a prize, a number. Your number is how many people you can carry to a rally and how many votes you can give in an election. I tell you, what you need to do is simple. How you do it, that is strategy.[1]

Building on these incentives, existing explanations assume that all candidates capable of using clientelism will do so and thus fail to shed light on cases in which candidates forgo the use of clientelism. This chapter argues that, beyond being capable of using clientelism, candidates also have to prefer using clientelistic strategies. I claim that a party candidate's *capacity* to turn to clientelistic strategies of mobilization is a necessary but insufficient condition to explain the use of clientelism. Besides having the capacity to employ clientelistic strategies, party candidates have to *prefer* to build clientelistic linkages with voters. In questioning the central assumption in the literature, this chapter contributes to building the microfoundations of clientelism by advancing a distinction between a candidate's capacity and a candidate's preference to use clientelism.

Choosing Clientelism

A candidate's decision to use clientelism to mobilize voters will vary according to his or her capacity and preference to use clientelism.

22

A candidate's capacity to use clientelistic strategies of mobilization varies depending on his or her access to resources and the existence of a network of party activists who contribute to distributing those goods to voters who are likely to turn out and support the candidate.

Incumbent candidates are more likely than candidates affiliated with opposition parties to have access to material goods that enable them to solve voter problems. Incumbents at different levels – national, provincial, and municipal – have different combinations of access to goods. Thus, a candidate from a party that counts on the support of the president (national incumbent), governor (provincial incumbent), and mayor (local incumbent) has more resources than does the one who can count on the support of the president only. It is arguable that local support is as important as national and provincial support, given that municipalities can count on multiple resources to promote political rallies and events and distribute goods to voters. Even so, this chapter focuses on candidates' potential to use clientelism and not on the quantity of resources available to engage in these strategies.

In Argentina, only the Peronist (PJ) and Radical (UCR) parties have had systematic access to public office and large networks of party activists capable of trading favors for votes effectively. Scholars of Argentine politics have consistently highlighted poor voters' loyalty to the Peronist Party (Mora and Araujo 1995; Ostiguy 1998; Levitsky 2003; Calvo and Murillo 2004, 2005; Torre 2005). Ernesto Calvo and Victoria Murillo (2004) show that political parties' access to resources (supply side) and voters' dependence on fiscal largesse (demand side) benefit the Peronist Party because of the geographic concentration of its voters and its linkages with less skilled constituencies. Valeria Brusco and her collaborators (2004: 70–71) show that voters who receive a handout from a Peronist candidate are more likely to vote for the Peronist Party, and the ethnographic and qualitative works of Javier Auyero (2000), Steven Levitsky (2003), and my own (Szwarcberg 2009) found further support for this finding.

In her seminal article about machine politics in Argentina, Susan Stokes describes how party operatives are forced to make choices about how to distribute limited resources:

> Machine operatives everywhere face a version of the dilemma that an Argentine Peronist explains. About 40 voters live in her neighborhood and her responsibility is to get them to the polls and get them to vote for her party. But the party gives her only 10 bags of food to distribute, "ten little bags," she laments, "nothing more."
>
> (2005: 315)

Stokes concludes that the party operative will give the bags of food to swing voters who will support her party only in exchange for a bag. Stokes also argues that the operative will monitor voters who receive the bags to make sure they hold up their end of the clientelistic deal. Building on Stokes, Simeon Nichter (2008) argues that given the constraints of the secret ballot, party operatives will monitor voter turnout instead of vote choice because monitoring electoral participation simply requires observing whether the voters who received bags of food went to vote.

Classical and recent theories of political distribution (see, e.g., Cox and McCubbins 1986; Dixit and Londregan 1996; Schady 2000; Case 2001; Dahlberg and Johanssen 2002; Ansolabehere and Snyder 2003; Stokes 2005; Rosas and Hawkins 2007; Nichter 2008; Díaz-Cayeros et al. 2007; Stokes et al. 2013; Gans-Morse et al. 2014) focus on the types of voters – core or swing – that clientelistic candidates will target. Core voters are likely to support the candidate whether or not they receive goods in exchange, whereas swing voters are likely to support the candidate only if they receive a good in exchange for their political participation.

Despite substantial intellectual progress, these explanations fail to elucidate why a candidate capable of using clientelistic strategies to mobilize poor voters would reject using these strategies. Party operatives in Argentina and elsewhere can prefer not to distribute goods in exchange for electoral support – forgoing the use of clientelistic strategies – as the testimony of an Argentine Peronist candidate in Buenos Aires quoted earlier highlights: "I'll never get 20 bags of food, drive to a neighborhood, and say: 'This is for you to vote for me.' I'll give voters the bags: 'Take this because you need it. *Chau!*'"[2]

Thus, the capacity to use clientelism does not necessarily imply its use. Candidates also have to prefer solving voter problems in exchange for electoral support. As the testimony just quoted illustrates, what distinguishes clientelistic from non-clientelistic candidates is not the use of resources to solve voter problems, but the request that in exchange for material support voters turn out and support the candidate at party rallies and elections:

> If I were using clientelism, I would give voters bags of food only if they would vote for me, but I don't do that, do you understand? I give them the bags because they need them. Of course, I will prefer them to vote for me, but if they need it, I'll give it to them no matter what. Do I explain myself?[3]

I argue that political parties shape politicians' strategies by providing (or not providing) incentives to use clientelism to turn out voters. The theory advanced in this chapter claims that candidates should be distinguished based on the combination of their capacity and preference to employ clientelistic strategies. Table 2.1 categorizes candidates given these combinations. In the upper-left corner, one finds *pragmatic*

Table 2.1. *Candidates' Capacities and Preferences to Employ Clientelistic Strategies of Mobilization*

		Does the candidate prefer to employ clientelism to mobilize voters?	
		Yes	No
Does the candidate have the capacity to access and distribute clientelistic goods?	Yes	Pragmatist	Idealist
	No	Resentful	Utopist

candidates who are capable of using clientelism and of employing these strategies to get promoted. In the lower-left corner are the *resentful candidates* who prefer to use clientelism but are unable to do so. The upper-right corner shows *idealist candidates* who are capable of using clientelism but prefer not to do so, even if this decision works against their interests in getting promoted within the party. Finally, in the lower-right corner are the *utopist candidates* who have neither the capacity nor the preference to distribute goods in exchange for electoral support.

Without observing an explicit choice to forgo clientelistic politics, we cannot be sure whether candidates who do not have the capacity to access or distribute clientelistic goods are resentful or utopist. However, idealist and pragmatist candidates, because they have the capacity to use clientelism, make their preferences known by deciding whether or not to distribute clientelistic goods.

Measuring Political Clientelism

Measuring the use of clientelism is difficult. One cannot go and ask a party candidate: "How many votes did you buy today?" or "How many votes did you buy in the last election?" Given that these practices are illegal and undesirable, one also cannot ask candidates if they deliver benefits to voters in exchange for political support, as candidates are unlikely to recognize using them to mobilize voters. If pollsters – whom the party candidate neither trusts nor has knowledge of or information about – ask candidates these questions, they are unlikely to get honest responses. Hence, survey data is unlikely to provide accurate results about the use of clientelistic strategies. Put simply, candidates would not answer questions about their engagement in an illegal and undesirable social practice truthfully to unknown pollsters.

The same logic applies to voters who sell their votes. Although they engage in clientelistic exchanges, voters would tend to deny selling their vote. Social scientists define this phenomenon as social desirability bias. Respondents wish to present themselves in a favorable light to the interviewer and deny their relationship with practices that have a negative social stigma, given their association with poverty and disjuncture with democratic norms (Gonzalez-Ocantos et al. 2012: 203).

To deal with these problems, scholars interested in using survey instruments have developed innovative research strategies to explain the differences between qualitative research that finds vote buying to be pervasive in new democracies (mostly in Latin America) and individual-level surveys that find otherwise (Gonzalez-Ocantos et al. 2012). Using a survey-based list experiment in Nicaragua after municipal elections, Ezequiel Gonzalez-Ocantos and his collaborators (2012) found that only 2 percent of surveyed voters admitted to receiving a gift or service in exchange for their votes, but in a list experiment, 24 percent admitted such activity existed. Studying party-voter linkages from the perspective of voters, Ernesto Calvo and Victoria Murillo (2013) measured partisan networks using original survey data from Argentina and Chile.

Still, even though innovative empirical strategies may measure clientelism more accurately, they do so in a limited manner. They provide us with a static description of the use of clientelism in a country without explaining variations across places and time. They also fail to explain variations across respondents: Why do some voters in the same poor neighborhood in Nicaragua choose to sell their votes while others do not? Similarly, they fail to explain variations across party candidates who engage in these practices, an explanation of which is the goal of this chapter.

Stokes and her collaborators (2013) employ a multilayered strategy to address these questions. The authors combine sample surveys of voters in Argentina, Venezuela, and India with publicly available individual data on voters' income levels in the case of Venezuela; original experimental research in India; and open-ended qualitative interviews with party leaders, brokers, and voters in all three countries.

The authors enhance our understanding of distributive strategies by examining the nested relationships between party leaders and brokers, and brokers and voters, but they fail to provide a detailed picture of the reasons that lead individual candidates to choose to use clientelism to mobilize voters. Their work ignores the networks in which party activists and candidates are involved and the ways in which these political and nonpolitical networks shape their decision making.

All of these studies share the assumption that poor voters participate at rallies and vote in elections because they receive goods in exchange for their political participation. "This point of view assumes – wrongly – that, because favors, goods, and services circulate one way and support attendance at rallies, and – ultimately – votes circulate the other way, the former are causing the latter, that is, that votes and support come because of goods, services, and particular favors" (Auyero 2000: 23).[4] As Javier Auyero argues, assuming that clientelism causes electoral support is "a serious epistemological mistake" that confuses the circulation of goods with the generative principles of action.

To understand why voters are at rallies, Auyero claims, we need to study the existing informal networks that voters use to solve their every-day problems. Thus, "[s]erious ethnographic work" is needed to explain the persistence of clientelism in new democracies (2000: 209). Auyero correctly claims that our current "analyses do a magnificent job of explaining 'everything,' but' the fundamental elements (or the enigma) of contemporary Peronism, namely, the continuous support that it gets among the poor (despite its electoral setbacks)" (209). Survey opinion polls, he contends, are a "poor substitute" for serious ethnographic work "as if the reasons why some poor people still 'keep memory alive' when voting can be comprehended by the question, 'Why do you vote for X?'" (209). Still, Auyero's focus on a "structure of feeling" (211) fails to provide a substantive and systematic explanation of how clientelism becomes embedded in a political culture of problem-solving networks.[5]

Different from Auyero's contribution, my work explains political par-ticipation by focusing on the relationships between and among all the actors in political, partisan, and social networks. Using ethnographic methods, I was able to build trust with respondents and understand and even problematize their experiences and practices (Gerring 2001; Bayard de Volo and Schatz 2004; Pachirat 2009; Weeden 2009, 2010) with regard to the use of clientelism. Combining ethnographic and quantitative data, I was able to build a substantive and rich explanation of individual candidates' decision making about whether or not to use clientelistic strategies to mobilize poor voters.

Measuring Political Clientelism in Argentina

I consider that a candidate engages in clientelistic strategies of mobiliza-tion if he, she, or a designated party activist takes attendance of voter participation at rallies. I argue that clientelistic candidates who engage in solving voter problems to obtain their electoral support will thus moni-tor their participation. Without monitoring voter turnout, candidates run the risk that voters will follow the political advice of opposition candidates and "take the goods with one hand and vote with the other" (Szwarcberg 2004a: 4).

To monitor voter participation at rallies, candidates simply screen voters by taking attendance. Mabel, the private secretary of a Peronist councilor in the city of Córdoba, explained to me that candidates use rosters "made in Excel and organized alphabetically" with the names of beneficiaries of welfare programs, public employees, and voters who had asked for favors. She updates the rosters "at least once a week, and during elections almost daily."[6]

Classifying candidates by whether or not they take attendance at rallies rather than whether or not they distribute goods to voters enables me to discard a candidate who distributes goods to voters without requesting their electoral support in exchange. Hence, a candidate who does not monitor voter participation at rallies is not classified as clientelistic. Still, it is possible that a candidate monitors voter participation at rallies and not at elections and vice versa. Building on my work (Szwarcberg 2012a), I expect clientelistic candidates to prefer monitoring voter participation at rallies than at elections because rally performance is easier to measure and reward than voter turnout at elections.

In countries where voting is compulsory, as in Argentina, and turnout numbers are considerably high by international standards (Canton and Jorrat 2003), it is not possible to determine if voters turn out because they are mobilized, have strong partisan preferences, or a combination of both.[7] Indeed, I argue (Szwarcberg 2014) that party bosses compare information from voter turnout at rallies and elections to judge a candidate's reliability and dole out rewards and punishments accordingly. Rallies, in contrast to elections, provide party leaders with information that enables them to monitor (a) candidates' capacities to mobilize voters, (b) opportunities for party candidates to display their ability to turn out voters while monitoring voters' responses, and (c) opportunities for voters to display their gratitude to or fear toward candidates. In addition, rallies provide the opposition with a means for gathering information about the electoral strength or weakness of the clientelistic party (Szwarcberg 2014). Reliable candidates who distribute goods to voters instead of pocketing them are rewarded with higher-ranked positions on the closed list, whereas unreliable candidates are punished with lower-ranked positions.

Argentina uses a system of proportional representation with closed-list ballots in which a candidate's position on the party ticket determines his or her chance of being elected. Figure 2.1 displays a party ballot used in the municipality of José C. Paz for the national election of October 2005 for the FPV party. Political parties in Argentina print their own ballots, each listing only their party's candidates. Citizens may then use the ballot to vote for a single party in all races, or they may cut out sections of each ballot for the different races if they wish to vote for different parties (e.g., a voter may vote on the FPV ballot for the first

Figure 2.1. Party ballot of the FPV for the municipality of José C. Paz for the national election of October 2005

three sections – national senators, national deputies, and provincial senators – but cut out the councilors section of a PJ ballot to vote for a PJ candidate in the councilors race).

Party leaders decide a candidate's position on the ticket; by distributing these positions, party leaders are able to effectively reward or punish candidates based on their ability to turn out voters. Consequently, party operatives interested in pursuing a political career are encouraged to mobilize as many voters as possible to secure a higher position on the ticket, which increases their likelihood of getting elected, reelected, or promoted to a higher office. In focusing on municipal candidates, I was able to gather systematic data for a large population of party candidates who vary in their capacity and preference to use clientelism.

To maximize the number of votes that the party obtains, bosses distribute positions based on how many voters each candidate is capable of turning out. Ballot positions, therefore, reflect the value each candidate has for the party. The argument advanced in this book predicts that clientelistic candidates will hold higher positions than candidates who prefer not to use this strategy. However, several candidates who hold middle and lower positions on the ticket will also employ clientelistic strategies, thus canceling out a significant effect. This does not reflect the inefficacy of clientelistic strategies; rather it highlights the differences in the length of candidates' use of them. In fact, the data suggest that the longer candidates use clientelism to build a constituency, the larger their party network and the more likely they are to climb to a higher position on the party ticket.

Comparisons between the strategies pursued by candidates in Buenos Aires whose tenure was going to be renewed in two years and those who were running for reelection and election in 2005 did not show dramatic differences.[8] Nor did the strategies of candidates who were on the top of the closed list, those at the cutoff point where candidates could either succeed or fail in getting elected, and those below the cutoff point where failure to get elected was certain. These findings reinforce the argument that candidates must constantly show their ability to turn out voters if they want to advance in their political careers.

Explaining Variation in Party Candidates' Selection of Strategies of Political Mobilization

I combine information from quantitative and qualitative observations of elected municipal candidates in Argentina to measure their capacities and preferences to use clientelism. I focus on the 137 candidates who held elected positions as council members in 2005 in the seven selected municipalities for this study.[9] I conducted 101 in-depth interviews and

36 semi-structured interviews with elected candidates in their municipalities to learn about their preferences to use clientelism. The length of the interviews ranged from two to several hours, even several hours over several weeks, during which candidates reflected on their decisions to use clientelism.

As the qualitative section of this chapter shows, candidates talked very openly about their capacities and preferences. While conducting the interviews, I remember finding candidates who preferred not to use clientelistic strategies to mobilize voters, although they were able to. I did not, however, think that the finding was going to be significant, and thus, I did not have a systematic way to determine the reasons for their choices. I still find the decision to reject using clientelism surprising, as it definitely challenges our understanding of office-seeking candidates.

If I could not interview the candidates directly, I relied on information provided by key informants – mostly advisors who had known and worked for the candidates for several years, even decades, and were thus able to provide knowledgeable and reliable information about candidate preferences. By combining observations made in more than forty rallies during the 2005 national election in Buenos Aires, five rallies and a primary election in Córdoba in 2006, in-depth and semi-structured interviews with candidates, and interviews with key informants, I classified the mobilization strategies of 137 candidates. The first three columns on Table 2.2 describe the provinces (column 1), municipalities (column 2), and number of council members elected in each municipality (column 3). The remaining four columns provide information about the number of in-depth interviews (column 4), semi-structured interviews (column 5), and interviews of key informants (column 6) that I conducted.

Table 2.2. *Data Gathered by the Author during Field Research, June 2005–December 2006*

Province	Municipality	Number of council members	Number of in-depth interviews	Number of semi-structured interviews	Number of key informants interviewed
Buenos Aires	José C. Paz	20	20	0	5
	San Miguel	24	17	7	3
	Bahía Blanca	24	15	9	4
Córdoba	Córdoba Capital	31	20	11	5
	Río Cuarto	19	15	4	2
	Villa María	12	9	3	3
	Colonia Caroya	7	5	2	2
Total		137	101	36	24

Table 2.3. *Incumbency and Partisanship*

Incumbency	Partisanship			Total number of candidates
	Other party	Radical Party	Peronist Party	
No incumbent support	8 (5.84%)	16 (11.68%)	–	24 (17.52%)
Local incumbent support	18 (13.14%)	10 (7.30%)	69 (50.36%)	97 (70.8%)
Provincial incumbent support	–	–	66 (48.18%)	66 (48.18%)
National incumbent support	–	–	85 (62.04%)	85 (62.04%)
Combinations				
National and local incumbent	–	–	19 (13.87%)	19 (13.87%)
Provincial and national incumbent	–	–	16 (11.68%)	16 (11.68%)
National, provincial, and local incumbent	–	–	50 (36.50)	50 (36.50%)
Total	26 (18.98%)	26 (18.98%)	85 (62.04%)	137

Note: "–" indicates cases with no observations.

To distinguish candidates who were capable of using clientelism from those who were not, I employ two necessary conditions. The first was party affiliation. I distinguish candidates who were affiliated with parties that held one or more executive offices in 2005. Column 5 in Table 2.3 provides descriptive statistics about candidates who ran with the support of the local government (70.8 percent); national and local governments (13.87 percent); provincial and national governments (11.68 percent); and national, provincial, and local governments (36.50 percent). Only twenty-four candidates (17.52 percent) did not have any governmental support and so were unable to use clientelism. Incumbent candidates, despite their having governmental support, might still be unable to distribute goods in exchange for support. To be effective in using clientelism, candidates need to have access to resources as well as a network of party activists to distribute those goods to the voters who are likely to turn out and support the party in exchange for receiving goods.

Building on this criterion, the second condition implies that only those candidates who had either access to an organization capable of distributing particular goods and monitoring voters' electoral support or their own party network were able to employ clientelism.[10]

Table 2.4. *Partisanship and Clientelism*

		Candidates' partisanship			
		Other party	Radical Party	Peronist Party	*Total*
Does the candidate take attendance of voter participation at rallies?	No	22 (16.06%)	19 (13.87%)	33 (24.09%)	*74 (54.01%)*
	Yes	4 (2.92%)	7 (5.11%)	52 (36.96%)	*63 (45.99%)*
	Total	*26 (18.98%)*	*26 (18.98%)*	*85 (62.04%)*	*137 (100%)*

Table 2.4 shows that only 22 candidates (16.06 percent) were unable to use clientelism: the remaining 115 candidates could turn to these strategies. Of the candidates who could use clientelistic strategies, 62.04 percent were affiliated with the Peronist Party, and 18.98 percent with the Radical Party and other parties. Whereas Peronist candidates could count on the support of the national, provincial, and local governments in José C. Paz, Bahía Blanca, Villa María, and Colonia Caroya, non-Peronist candidates could count on the support of the municipal executive in Río Cuarto (UCR) and in the city of Córdoba (PN). The majority of the eighteen elected candidates affiliated with the PN lacked a network of activists and thus were unable to use clientelism. Yet, as I examine later, candidates who participated in politics with either the Peronist or Radical Party before joining the New Party (PN) did possess networks of activists and the know-how to use clientelism, and some of them did indeed continue exchanging favors for votes as in the past. Likewise, ten Radical and eighty-five Peronist candidates had the capacity to engage in clientelistic strategies of mobilization.

The findings in Table 2.4 suggest that Peronist candidates were more capable of using clientelistic strategies than Radical candidates, but they do not provide information on candidate preferences. Are Peronist candidates more likely than Radical candidates to prefer using clientelism under similar circumstances? To answer this question, I compare the strategies employed by Peronist and Radical candidates who had the same capacity to use clientelism when competing for the same voters.

My theory predicts the existence of four types of candidates based on the combination of their capacities and preferences to use clientelism. Table 2.5 includes comparative data from Argentina to categorize candidates based on this schema, showing not only the existence of idealist candidates but also the almost even number of pragmatists (fifty-nine candidates) and

Table 2.5. *Municipal Candidates' Capacities and Preferences*

| | | Does the candidate prefer to employ clientelism to mobilize voters? | | |
		Yes	No	*Total*
Does the candidate have the capacity to access and distribute clientelistic goods?	Yes	Pragmatist 59 (43.07%)	Idealist 52 (37.96%)	*111 (81.02%)*
	No	Resentful 4 (2.92%)	Utopist 22 (16.06%)	*26 (18.98%)*
	Total	63 (45.99%)	74 (54.01%)	*137 (100%)*

idealists (fifty-two candidates). In failing to consider that 52 out of 111 candidates preferred not to use clientelism, the literature both miscalculates the extent of clientelism and misinterprets candidate preferences. First, in ignoring candidate preferences, the literature assumes that in these cases, 111 candidates will use clientelistic strategies when only 59 actually did so. Second, in advising policy makers of both the existence and the significant numbers of candidates who prefer not to use clientelism, the current work will help make a successful case for designing institutional incentives that will promote the political careers of idealist candidates.

Candidate testimonies highlight the importance of having access to material resources to turn out voters and how this capacity induces candidates to prefer to use clientelism: "Money is fundamental. If you don't have money, you can't do anything in politics. You can't solve voter problems; you can't mobilize people [*no podes tener gente*]."[11]

Table 2.5 also shows that although not even, the division between candidates who distributed goods in exchange for participation and those who did not was uniform: sixty-three candidates used clientelism (45.99 percent), and seventy-four candidates (54.01 percent) did not. In linking access to material resources with the possibility of solving voter problems, candidates' partisan affiliation becomes a key variable in explaining variation in candidates' preferences. Table 2.6 shows that among the seventy-four candidates who did not use clientelism, thrity-three were affiliated with the PJ, nineteen with the UCR, and twenty-two with other parties. Among those who engaged in clientelistic strategies, fifty-two candidates were affiliated with the Peronist Party and seven with the Radical Party; four candidates were former Peronist candidates who had ties to networks of party activists now affiliated with the New Party. Most candidates affiliated with the New Party preferred not to use clientelism, but these four candidates chose otherwise.

Table 2.6. *Candidates' Capacities, Preferences, and Partisanship*

Candidates	Other party	Radical Party	Peronist Party	Total
Pragmatist	0	7	52	59
	(0%)	(5.11%)	(37.96%)	(43.07%)
Idealist	0	19	33	52
	(0%)	(13.87%)	(24.09%)	(37.96%)
Resentful	4	0	0	4
	(2.92%)	(0%)	(0%)	(2.92%)
Utopist	22	0	0	22
	(16.06%)	(0%)	(0%)	(16.06%)
Total	26	26	85	137
	(18.98%)	(18.98%)	(62.04%)	(100%)

To explain why fifty-two candidates who were affiliated with majority parties and who had the capacity to use clientelism preferred not to turn to these strategies, I combine descriptive statistics with life histories and in-depth and semi-structured interviews. I also examine the preferences of candidates affiliated with other parties who opted out of pursuing clientelistic strategies.

To evaluate the effect of partisanship on candidates' preferences, I compare candidates affiliated with the same party running in the same election under similar circumstances. Opposition parties' lack of access to government resources mostly prevents them from turning to clientelistic strategies of mobilization; thus, I focus on the PJ and the UCR. I also study the unique case of the PN, which succeeded in winning a local election by using programmatic linkages with voters.

To make comparisons among candidates affiliated with the PJ in José C. Paz, the UCR in Río Cuarto, and the PN in the city of Córdoba, I conducted interviews with every elected candidate during their participation in several political mobilizations and activities. In comparing the strategies chosen by candidates affiliated with the same party, who were competing for the same voters and had the same capacity to use clientelism, I was able to hold constant variables such as age, gender, education, and income, as well as capacity to use clientelism and focus on variation in candidates' preferences.

As one of the poorest municipalities in Buenos Aires, José C. Paz could easily be described as a giant shantytown. Socioeconomic indicators collected during the 2001 national census found that 44 percent of the households in the municipality lived in poorly built homes, and 7.7 percent of those households experienced critical overcrowding (*hacinamiento crítico*). More than a quarter of the municipality's 230,208 residents could not meet their basic needs (*necesidades básicas insatisfechas*, NBI), such as indoor plumbing, employment, and education, and 63.2 percent of the residents did not have health insurance. More than half of the population had not finished high school, and fewer than 10 percent attended college.

The municipality has 160 soup kitchens and 6,400 unpaved roads (*calles de tierra*). Local authorities delivered between 4,000 and 5,000 bags of food daily during the economic crisis in 2001, and almost 50 percent of the population received state aid, mostly in the form of welfare programs. During that time, 80 percent of the economically active population was unemployed.[12] Under these conditions, incumbent candidates could easily mobilize voters by simply distributing bags of food, a strategy that several of them pursued. In explaining or justifying their decisions, pragmatist candidates referred to a more or less explicit conception of *realpolitik* (a system of politics or principles based on practical rather than moral considerations) to explain their decision to use clientelism:

> The only thing to eat is shit, and there isn't enough for everyone. Under these circumstances, one cannot think of an ideal world. Either you go home or you stay in a coffee shop philosophizing about how it should be. It is messed up, but the rest of the reasoning is immature because it confuses what should be with what is. The activists have to stay true to their principles every day. Yeah, that is wonderful, you know, but if I think like that, I'm a romantic without practical consequences.[13]

Beyond, their pragmatic view, the dynamics of intraparty competition also induce candidates to engage in clientelism. Thus, if candidates do not exchange goods for support, someone else from their party will, and that person will get the political promotion:

CANDIDATE: In that election, they brought our voters [to the polls] in the bus we had rented to mobilize people.

AUTHOR: Dirty?

CANDIDATE: Dirty or not, that's politics. You can be the Mother Teresa of Calcutta, but in politics you don't go anywhere if you don't know how to play these games. When the definitive moment comes, you have to show what you've got [*poner la carne en la parrilla*]. There are always those who believe they are better than you are, and they are convinced that you are trash, that you're completely unworthy. There is always someone competing with you, ready to cut your throat [*serruchándote el piso*] because he wants to be in your position. And instead of being happy because you have been elected, he still wants to be elected even though he doesn't have the capacity to be an elected official [*aunque no le de el cuero*]. The worst among politicians are never those who are in front of you, but those who are by your side. The ones who are in front of you compete against you by using another image, with another program. But those who are supposed to be with you, those are the worst of all.[14]

Then there are idealist candidates who have the capacity to use clientelism but prefer not to use it even when that choice results in political suicide. Candidates who prefer not to use clientelism do not mobilize voters and fail to send party leaders the signal that they are willing to do whatever it takes to remain in power. Idealist candidates are neither naïve nor inept. They understand well how clientelism works, yet they prefer not to use the strategies that would secure their tenure in office. Peronist idealist candidates in José C. Paz as well as Radical idealist candidates in Río Cuarto believe that political action should be guided by a normative commitment to social justice.

By comparing the preferences of candidates competing for the same voters under the same conditions in José C. Paz, I am able to examine why some candidates prefer to use clientelism while others do not. Out of the twenty elected candidates in José C. Paz, all but one, Sergio, were affiliated with the Peronist Party. Sergio, who is affiliated with the Federalist Union Party (PAUFE), will be examined later as a representative of a resentful candidate.[15] Now, though, I will focus on three Peronist candidates who are affiliated with the mayor's political network (*agrupación*) and who worked in poor neighborhoods that are comparable in terms of size, voter partisanship, and propensity to turn out. I chose these cases for two reasons: (a) they allowed me to learn about candidates' preferences – the candidates made different choices about using clientelism despite facing the same opportunities, and (b) they provided an opportunity to understand why candidates opt to commit political suicide (two of the three candidates preferred not to use clientelism).

The first candidate, Néstor, exemplifies the idealist candidate who is aware of the consequences of rejecting clientelism and yet prefers to pursue this path. Candidates from his own and rival parties, key informants, and party strategists agreed on highlighting Néstor's political potential. In the words of one activist, "He could have been reelected easily if he was a little bit more flexible,"[16] referring to Néstor's well-known rejection of the use of clientelism to get political support. When I asked Néstor why he rejected using a strategy that he knew would allow him to be reelected, he replied: "I just don't believe in a clientelistic political construction. It's that simple. I believe that supporters have to choose to become part of a political project after discussing ideas and policies, not salaries."[17]

Although he obtained a significant number of votes, Néstor could not compete against the political machine of the mayor of José C. Paz, who had a personal grudge against Néstor and thus deployed additional money to make sure his poor supporters had a hard time getting to the polls to support his candidacy.[18] At the time of the interview, Néstor was selling acrylic paint while still participating in afternoon political meetings in his neighborhood. In those meetings, voters discussed political issues such as: Who should be taxed in the municipality? Who should have a right to receive state aid? How should that aid be distributed to guarantee that voters take those goods as rights and not as political favors with conditions attached? The political meetings Néstor attended were significantly different from the meetings of other Peronist *agrupaciones* in the municipality, where the majority of the attendees showed up to avoid the loss of state aid threatened by clientelist brokers, and where there the discussion centered around logistics rather than politics: Who is going to mobilize voters in each neighborhood? Who is going to go house-by-house to inform voters about an upcoming party rally?

Neighboring candidate Juan Carlos, whose tenure was going to expire in two years, echoed Néstor's preferences as well as his awareness of the consequences of rejecting the use of clientelism. During our conversations before the 2005 election, Juan Carlos acknowledged that if he wanted to boost his turnout numbers, he had to threaten voters who were receiving benefits and those whose problems he had solved; otherwise, it was likely that those voters would support another candidate from his party: "Voters are not bad people. They just have dire needs, and so they will support whoever helps them solve their problems. It's simple, even understandable, and straightforward."[19]

Juan Carlos also informed me about the effects that his preference not to use clientelism had on candidates from his party who made the opposite choice. "They won't forgive me," he said, as his tone of voice began to change and his eyes got wet:

AUTHOR: You got emotional . . .
JUAN CARLOS: No. It's that I have my ideals, right? And there are things that I will not accept because they go against what I think. And I say it, I make it known.[20]

It was a difficult moment, and he asked me not to keep on talking about this issue. A long silence followed. Juan Carlos had been raised in a popular *machista* culture where men do not cry at all, much less in public and in front of a woman. Juan Carlos's tears captured the impotence a candidate must feel when choosing not to use clientelism. At the end of our interview, Juan Carlos conceded, "This is how politics works."

An understanding of how politics works explains why candidates who prefer to use clientelism, such as pragmatist candidate José, make certain choices. José envisions politics as a boxing match without referees:

I get up to the ring to box with gloves, but if you kick me in the knee, I'll kick you back. If I don't kick you, I'll lose, you'll win, and there won't be a judge to tell me: "You, sir, are correct." You are kicked out and left alone, crying, and that's a pretty thing about politics. There are no untouchables. No one will look for you. No matter how much they respect you and tell you that you are great, no one is going to make an effort for you. This isn't bad; it's just the rules. One cannot take things too personally, but one must use the rules of the game. Either you get used to it, or you go crazy, or you leave.[21]

In José C. Paz, Peronist and not-Peronist candidates observed that those who engage in clientelism succeed in their political careers without being effectively penalized by either the party or the courts. As a result, candidates interested in pursuing a political career who have the capacity to employ clientelistic strategies are strongly encouraged to turn to these strategies.

Radical candidates in Río Cuarto, a municipality that has had a Peronist government only once since the return of democracy, experienced the tension between an idealist campaign and a pragmatist campaign during the Radical Party primary in 2000. At the time, two former reelected mayors, Miguel Angel Abella and Antonio Benigno Rins, took different approaches to recover the local administration for their party: Rins favored building an electoral alliance with the PN to secure the UCR's electoral victory, whereas Abella openly rejected such a strategy and campaigned against compromising the UCR's principles by building pragmatic alliances. Rins won the highly contested primary to once again become mayor of Río Cuarto by joining forces with More for Río Cuarto (MRC), the electoral coalition between the UCR and the PN.

When I asked Abella what he had learned from the experience, he replied that he still held the same convictions and would have acted exactly the same no matter what. I asked if he felt like David fighting against Goliath for trying to compete using ideals, and he replied that he envisioned himself rather as Moses walking in the desert – he and other idealist activists believed that they were training a new generation of politicians who would eventually get elected based on programmatic rather than clientelistic appeals.

Utopist candidates' beliefs mirror those of idealist candidates, but their inability to distribute goods makes them ineligible to commit political suicide. Opposition candidates affiliated with parties with limited resources are unable to turn to clientelism. In practice, this means that neither resentful nor utopist candidates will employ clientelistic strategies, but for significantly different reasons. Resentful candidates are unable to use clientelism because they do not have access to material goods, whereas utopist candidates would not use clientelism even if they had access. Resentful and utopist candidates comprise 19 percent of the sample, and it is worth noting that there were 13.14 percentage points more; approximately 5 times as many utopist than resentful candidates.

Resentful candidates constantly refer to what they define as unfair competition, that is, competing to mobilize poor voters in situations in which some candidates – those affiliated with incumbent parties – have more access to resources than other candidates – those affiliated with nonincumbent parties. This was the reasoning of Sergio, a candidate affiliated with the PAUFE who was competing to mobilize the same voters targeted by Peronist candidates in José C. Paz, a municipality where Peronist candidates could count on the support of the national, provincial, and municipal governments.

> In reality, there is less conspiracy than it seems. For instance, in the 2001 election, an election of which we are very proud, I went to the neighborhoods of very poor people, people with whom I had worked a lot, people who knew me and liked me. Nevertheless, one of the guys who had helped me came to ask me for money because he needed to buy some construction material to repair the roof of his house. He told me that he was not asking for money to vote for me; he said that it was OK if I didn't have the money, but he wanted me to understand that people needed money. Today you can't mobilize 20 voters if you don't buy them.[22]

Following this reasoning, if Sergio had been able to distribute construction materials, he would have been able to get voters' support. Candidates, such as Sergio, who were unable to solve voter problems, constantly pointed out their incapacity as the reason for their failure to mobilize voters. This was the case of a party candidate in Córdoba who told me:

> Voters listen to you, they are interested in you, but unfortunately they need things. If you don't have money, if you can't give them things, they can't support you. They support whoever has things to give away, no matter who she or he is.[23]

As shown in Table 2.6, which describes the partisan affiliation of each type of candidate, there is a strong relationship between Peronism and clientelism, as the majority of pragmatist candidates were affiliated with the PJ. Still, the number of idealist candidates within the Peronist Party was significant. Partisanship differences also highlight the fact that Radical candidates were less prone to use clientelism than Peronist candidates. The large number of utopist candidates is driven mostly by the emergence and success of the New Party in Córdoba. Four out of eighteen candidates affiliated with the PN did not distribute particularistic inducements to voters. The majority of the PN candidates were successful businesspeople, professionals, and professors who decided to participate in politics for the first time and thus had neither the know-how nor the network of activists that would have enabled them to use clientelism. Indeed, it is plausible to suppose that Juez selected these candidates precisely because they were new to the existing political establishment and thus unfamiliar with the old clientelistic strategies used to turn out voters. In contrast, the four candidates who resorted to clientelism were former Peronist (three candidates) and Radical (one candidate) Party members. Placed in lower-ranked positions on the party ticket, these candidates continued to mobilize voters by exchanging favors for votes.

Conclusion

Political parties are organizations that seek to win elections; to achieve this goal, they try to turn out as many voters as possible. By distributing rewards to candidates based only on the number of voters they mobilize, parties encourage the use of clientelistic strategies. Candidates who are capable of and prefer to use clientelism are encouraged to employ these strategies by a perverse system of incentives that promotes the careers of clientelistic candidates to the detriment of candidates who are either unable or unwilling to use these strategies. Hence, it is not the case that candidates are always willing to use clientelistic strategies but, rather, that those who refuse to engage in these practices are unable to advance in politics.

In the Argentine case, I suspect that candidates' political activity and involvement in the resistance and/or their political exile (James 1988) during the dictatorship have an important effect on their future decisions about how to do politics. Most of the interviewees who had been persecuted during the dictatorship had a hard time adapting to the use of clientelistic strategies – I did not find significant gender or age differences.

When only candidates who use clientelism are promoted within the party, office-seeking candidates are indirectly, but successfully, encouraged to use clientelistic strategies. In examining the causes and consequences that induce individual candidates to prefer clientelism, this chapter contributes to the literature by improving our understanding of causal mechanisms. The perverse logic of incentives that induce candidates to use clientelism becomes evident only if we focus on the conditions under which candidates make decisions about how to mobilize voters.

A candidate who solves voter problems and does not mind if that voter is not loyal to him or her is committing political suicide. Yet, the logic of an alternative, non-clientelistic political construction is based on building trust with voters. Non-clientelistic candidates tend to believe in the importance of building relationships of mutual trust and respect between voters and candidates as the foundation of stronger and healthier relationships of representation.

Understanding the mechanisms by which candidates are promoted at the local level enables scholars and policy makers to study the effects of these strategies on democratic representation and to design effective political reforms. The systematic promotion of pragmatic over idealist candidates poses a potential challenge to the effective representation of poor voters. When pragmatist candidates prefer to pursue their reelection by silencing voters' demands, the voices of poor voters in the decision-making process are effectively muted. Only by comprehending how political promotions actually work will policy makers be able to modify the existing system of incentives to favor the promotion of idealist candidates.

Whereas economic growth and, more importantly, the distribution of wealth are directly related to the transition away from clientelism, this chapter contributes to the understanding of the effects that the combination of candidates' capacities and preferences have on candidates' decisions to mobilize voters. By taking individual candidates' preferences into account, policy makers can find ways to reward idealist candidates who would otherwise abandon politics.

3

Building a Party Network: Political, Partisan, and Social Networks in Argentina

> Let me tell you: I have a cousin, a young man who didn't take any particular interest in politics. I went to him and said: "Tommy I'm going to be a politician, and I want to get a followin'; can I count on you?" He said: "Sure, George." That's how I started in business. I got a marketable commodity – one vote.
>
> George Plunkitt (Riordon 1995: 8–9)

George Washington Plunkitt, a long-time state senator from New York's Fifteenth Assembly District and Tammany Hall boss for forty years, knew how to build and run a political machine. His strategies for gaining long-lasting success in politics are followed today in old and new democracies alike. Still, politicians around the world who share Plunkitt's ambitions have not always been successful in their attempts to mobilize voters. In Argentina, for instance, some party brokers are incapable of garnering much support beyond that of their family and friends (and in some cases not even that), whereas others manage to get the support of their entire neighborhood.

A party broker's success in mobilizing voters is a combination of what he or she has to offer, what voters need, and the alternatives that voters have to get their problems solved without the aid of the broker. In my investigation, I chose to focus on candidates who, like Plunkitt, are able to build a party network by mobilizing voters in poor neighborhoods and found that candidates' decisions to use clientelism in order to mobilize voters vary based on their capacity and preference to use this strategy. My study of candidates who have the capacity and preference to use clientelism explains the degrees to which they are able to build a party network.

I argue that the existing opportunities for candidates at the time of mobilization are crucial to explaining (a) candidates' capacities to effectively use clientelism and (b) their preferences to use these strategies as a means of mobilizing voters. Candidates who build clientelistic linkages with voters – exchanging goods and services for political support – at the beginning of their political careers are not likely to stop using clientelism once in office. That makes sense given that candidates who want to get promoted must display their ability to mobilize voters, and in geographical locations with a concentration of poor voters, preferring not to distribute goods could be a risky strategy. If voters fail to participate or choose instead to participate with another candidate, former clientelistic candidates will lose political support.

The logic of my argument echoes Martin Shefter's (1977) seminal study about parties and patronage (i.e., distributing public employment to voters in exchange for political support) in England, Germany, and Italy. Shefter argues that enjoying access to and utilizing patronage the first time a party undertakes the mobilization of a popular base is character forming, and the decision has enduring implications for future party strategies. Assuming that party activists seek to get elected or remain in office, variation in their levels of success can be explained by the combination of their capacities and preferences to use clientelism. Office-seeking party activists learn early on that only activists who have the capacity to solve voter problems have a chance to mobilize poor voters.

This book argues that the way in which candidates prefer to mobilize voters at the beginning of their political careers has enduring effects on the strategies that they employ to mobilize voters later in their careers. Candidates who begin their careers from the bottom up and prefer to be paid in exchange for their mobilizing of voters are more likely to engage in clientelism than candidates who do not start as paid party activists or brokers, terms that I use interchangeably. Current elected officials who were brokers in the past seem to find no reason to abandon the strategies that contributed to their election. In contrast, councilors who succeeded in mobilizing voters without employing clientelistic strategies are less likely to engage in clientelism later on in their careers.

By studying candidates' participation – embeddedness – in political, partisan, and social networks, I am able to examine the constraints and possibilities that party activists face based on their positions in these networks. It is only by describing and examining these networks, as well as the connections between and among them, that we can "identify the sets of incentives that make political clientelism and patronage into viable and acceptable strategies" (Piattoni 2001: 2–3).

Political networks connect voters, party activists, candidates, and party leaders in an informal hierarchical organization that provides voters with benefits in exchange for political participation, and candidates with political promotions in exchange for mobilizing voters. Political networks define the informal hierarchical structure of political machines and are thus identical among all clientelistic parties. This implies that political networks are not partisan, as they share the same logic across political parties. Political networks inform voters that in order to receive benefits they have to provide political support. These networks also supply information to candidates interested in a political career: the larger the size of their network of followers, the more likely they will get promoted within the party.

Partisan networks provide access to material and nonmaterial resources and determine activists' capacity to solve problems and build a party network. Activists interested in pursuing a political career seek central positions in partisan networks to be capable of solving as many voters' problems as possible. Centrality in the network implies being connected with the largest number of party candidates and leaders that provide activists with access to material and nonmaterial resources that enable them to solve voters' problems. It is through their access to welfare benefits, or contacts with public employees and officials at city hall and a local hospital that activists are capable of solving voters' problems in exchange for their political participation. Without access to material and nonmaterial goods, activists are unable to solve voters' problems and thus to build a following.

Social networks, in contrast, refer to the relationships among political actors that are not centered on solving political problems, but on building nonpolitical social relationships. My study of how political actors build friendships and trust in their communities shows that these networks have the potential to supplement or challenge existing relationships in political and partisan networks.

This chapter describes and analyzes political, partisan, and social networks to demonstrate how candidates' positions in these networks shape their opportunities to use clientelistic strategies to build a party network. By studying Peronist networks, I am able to describe and explain the connections between and among nested political, partisan, and social networks in Argentina. Using process tracing, I analyze the decisions of unpaid and paid party activists, and elected and reelected local candidates. The chapter concludes by examining the implications of using political, partisan, and social networks to build a party network.

Political Networks

Political networks connect party leaders, candidates, activists, and voters through an informal hierarchical structure. In studying the morphology of these networks, it is easy to observe that the many links among actors are arranged in a pyramidal structure, with the party leader on the top and voters at the bottom. To describe and explain the organized disorganization (Levitsky 2001) of these networks, I study the political trajectories of party candidates who begin their careers as activists charged with mobilizing voters in their own communities. Following these activists' careers enables me to describe the structure of political networks and illustrate their pyramidal shape.

Just above voters at the bottom of the pyramid are party activists who lead groups of poor voters. What distinguishes activists from voters in poor neighborhoods is their access to partisan networks that provide them with material and nonmaterial resources. Without access to these networks, party activists would not be able to find solutions to voters' problems. Activists are no wealthier than the voters whose problems they solve; indeed, most live in the same poor, high-density-per-room neighborhoods, in precarious homes with no access to indoor plumbing.[1] Activists also share the same educational level as their neighbors, which in the cases studied in this book is less than high school graduation, on average. Yet, despite sharing similar levels of economic and human capital, activists significantly surpass their fellow neighbors in social capital.

"The core idea of social capital theory is that social networks have value" (Putnam 2000: 18–19). Activists know more people than voters, and it is this knowledge that enhances their value vis-à-vis poor voters. More importantly, activists do not only know more people than poor voters, but they also know more people who have access to material and nonmaterial resources which enable them to solve problems. In short, activists have more "connections among individuals" (Putnam 2000: 19) than voters and, equally important, those connections are with politicians who are likely to have access to the resources that enable activists to solve voter problems.

Building on this theory, we would expect to distinguish voters from activists by comparing the number of connections (linkages) they have with political candidates, not based on where they live or where they went to school. Empirically, activists would have more connections with poor voters and with party candidates that provide them with material and nonmaterial goods to exchange or order to entice voters to come to their rallies and to vote for their party in elections. Party activists are keenly aware that without their connections with party candidates, they would be no different than the poor voters they mobilize:

> Politics here gives you a lot of power, and you think that you're God, that you can get anything. A neighbor told me the other day: "Four months ago you were able to put water pipes in the front of my house." I asked the mayor – I can talk to the mayor, which is worth a lot – I don't have to go through all the municipal bureaucracy. The mayor said to a delegate: "Go and do what he's

asking." . . . The next day five water pipes were up! They did it by noon. That guy still – even to this day – thanks me for it. "I've been struggling with that for five years, and you solved the problem for me in a day," he told me.[2]

As this testimony from a party activist in San Miguel shows, it is the activist's position between political and partisan networks that enables him or her to know on whom to call to solve a voter's problem. Without being able to talk with the mayor – or, more realistically, to talk with someone who could talk with the mayor directly – the activist would have been unable to deliver the water pipes. Activists hold central positions in political networks that provide them with access to resources (Knoke 1990; Auyero 2000; Szwarcberg 2012a).

Still, not every party activist is interested in pursuing a political career, and not all of them engage in the mobilization of voters. Among those who are interested in having a career in politics, however, the competition is brutal. There are always fewer positions than individuals seeking them, and activists face constant competition to mobilize voters from those in their own party as well as those in opposition parties. Activists who succeed in mobilizing voters are rewarded with nonelected offices in the municipality that provide them with access to resources and, of equal importance, a stipend to do politics.

Paid party activists or brokers are nonelected party representatives who receive a salary, usually paid with public funds, in exchange for mobilizing voters in their neighborhoods to attend rallies and vote in elections for the party that the broker works for. Party candidates seeking local representation in poor neighborhoods are constantly trying to recruit activists working at civic associations (*sociedades de fomento*), school cooperatives, soup kitchens, churches, and primary care community health clinics (*salitas*), as in the case of Marcelo. After meeting him at the health clinic for the working-class neighborhood of Sargento Barrufaldi in San Miguel, I simply asked him if candidates came to the clinic to ask him to work politically for them:

MARCELO: Of course, there are many candidates interested in Barrufaldi. After all, it is in neighborhoods with unpaved streets [*calles de tierra*] where they get the vote. It is here where they fill the buses to go to rallies and to go to vote.

AUTHOR: How many people, more or less, live here?

MARCELO: I calculate that there are between 7,000 and 8,000 people, and since there were no strong leaders here, the right-hand man of the mayor called me and told me: "Look, from now on I want you to work politically for me. What do you want?" "What do you offer me?" "I will give you a salary and the opportunity to solve voter problems. In the future, we will talk." "Great," I responded. It was

that simple. Since that moment, I have been a party broker and work for
him in this neighborhood.

AUTHOR: What does he give you?

MARCELO: He just pays me to do politics. I receive a salary as the director
of the primary care community health clinic, and I have all day to solve
voter problems.[3]

Marcelo's salary came from his appointment as director of the primary
care neighborhood health clinic. In Argentina, activists who carry out
political work for a candidate and receive a political appointment with a
paycheck from the municipality are called *ñoquis*. *Ñoquis* are a pasta dish
traditionally eaten the twenty-ninth day of every month. The name is
currently used to describe public employees who only show up at city
hall at the end of the month to get their paycheck. Although *ñoquis* are
portrayed as parasites, some may actually work harder than many municipal employees.

During my field research, I met several activists who, like Marcelo,
wake up at dawn and work until midnight to solve voters' problems. In
commenting on the job of an activist, one of them told me, "We are like a
gas station: open 24/7."[4] Interestingly, this fact is also acknowledged in
the savvy political lessons of George Washington Plunkitt when he
describes "the strenuous life of the Tammany district leader":

> No other politician in New York or elsewhere is exactly like the
> Tammany district leader or works as he does. As a rule, he has
> no business or occupation other than politics. He plays politics
> every day and night in the year, and his headquarters bears the
> inscription, "Never closed."
>
> (Riordon 1995: 90)

Day and night, every day of the year, paid party activists engage in
solving voters' problems in exchange for a salary, a fact that was explicitly
written on a bumper sticker Javier Auyero spotted while conducting fieldwork in Villa Paraiso: "I don't work; I do politics." Shantytown leaders
(*líderes villeros*), whose key role in mobilizing voters has been described in
ethnographical works of the Conurbano in the municipalities of Lomas de
Zamora (Frederic 2004) and Lanus (Auyero 2000), are systematically
offered a salary after showing their capacity to mobilize voters. Indeed,
this is the story of Pino, a shantytown leader who is now a councilor in
José C. Paz.

Pino became the leader of the poorest neighborhood in José C. Paz, the
shantytown El Ceibo, as a result of his commitment to solving voters'
problems. During the period of hyperinflation in 1989, when neighbors
were starving (*la gente se estaba muriendo de hambre*), Pino organized
soup kitchens (*ollas populares*) that remained active after the crisis.

Emerging as a natural leader for his charismatic appeal and organizational capacities in a time of need, Pino became involved in multiple community activities, chief among them the organization of three soup kitchens and an athletic club:

> I funded three soup kitchens and a social and athletic club that is still here. How did I do it? I dropped a soccer ball and became a referee. Who then would set up a tournament? Pino. Let's go to Pino's tournament. And then Pino is in the municipality. Pino is giving out goods. Pino is solving problems. You become a little bit the leader, the one who represents the neighborhood.[5]

As a result of these activities, Pino's name was constantly repeated in local political associations and city hall corridors. For instance, the soccer tournaments that took place every weekend mobilized the families of the entire shantytown, clearly displaying Pino's popularity and leadership:

> At first, I went to the municipality and waited for my number to be called so that they would give me a can of tomatoes, preserves, and pasta to cook at the soup kitchen. Then ... I got a hold on things and I began to grow. One day when I was at city hall, Ortega [a councilor in José C. Paz] told me: "I believe you do a great job. Why don't you work for me?" "What will you give me?" "A job in the municipality [*un nombramiento*]."[6]

Ortega recruited Pino to mobilize voters for his party in exchange for full-time work in politics. Since his appointment, Pino has worked full time to solve voters' problems, mobilizing them to participate at rallies and support Ortega's party in elections.

Brokers interested in becoming elected candidates need not only to continue mobilizing poor voters but also to increase the size of their party network in order to compete and win the numbers battle with fellow party brokers. Moreover, regardless of whether brokers seek to move forward in the political network, the possibilities of continuing to get paid for doing their political job are enhanced if they show that they are capable of not just mobilizing the same number of voters as in the past, but of increasing the size of their party network.

The reasoning behind these enhanced expectations is that once party activists are recruited as brokers, their new position provides further access to material and nonmaterial resources; as such, they should be able to solve more voters' problems and thus mobilize more voters than in the past. As the testimony of a party broker quoted here illustrates, as a result of their position within political networks, brokers are able to provide employment opportunities to their followers by furnishing them information before it becomes publicly available:

Given your position, you get information first. For instance, if the municipality needs people to work, you can tell your friends to apply for the position before it becomes public; you can get an appointment with a doctor. I know it's terrible what I am telling you, but this is the way things are.[7]

Brokers' positions in political networks not only provide them with access to material goods, but also to information that translates into access to material and nonmaterial benefits. Running for elected positions on the ballot is a reward for successful party brokers who effectively manage the distribution of resources and mobilize a larger number of voters than they did before getting paid for their political work.

Party leaders promote the most effective brokers to be candidates. Promotions are simply based on the number of voters that brokers succeed in mobilizing for the party. The logic, as succinctly described by Auyero, is straightforward:

Politics means "to have your own people," your own faction. The bigger the faction, the greater the renown, as with the Melanesian big man analyzed by Sahlins (1977). The greater the renown, the greater the access to resources. The greater the access to resources, the greater the brokers' capacity to solve problems, and the better their chances of getting a public post (whether elected or appointed).

(2000: 102)

There are, however, consequences of measuring and rewarding brokers based only on the number of voters they mobilize. As I explain in the following chapter, rewarding brokers based only on outcomes regardless of how those outcomes are achieved encourages brokers who compete to mobilize poor voters to turn to clientelism. Over time, this logic of perverse incentives explains the consolidation of clientelism.[8] Figure 3.1 illustrates the ascending movement in political networks from party activists to elected candidates.

To be effective in mobilizing poor voters in exchange for political support, party activists, brokers, and candidates require access to material and nonmaterial resources to solve voter problems. Partisan networks enable access to these benefits and are thus essential in understanding how party agents build and sustain a party network.

Partisan Networks

Partisan networks provide candidates with access to material and non-material resources such as food, medicine, wheelchairs, welfare programs,

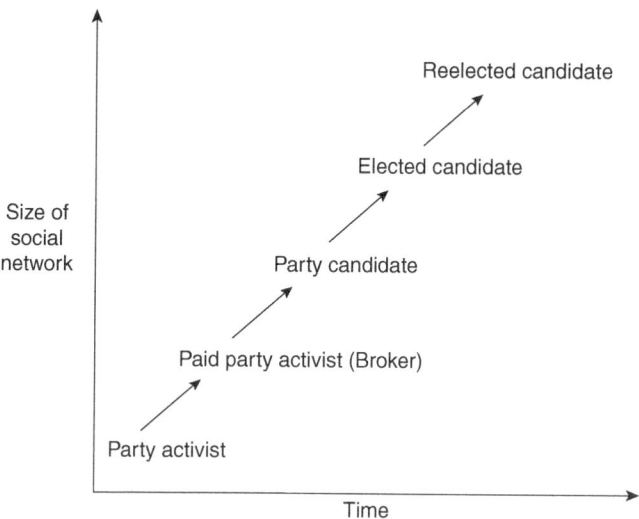

Figure 3.1. The political careers of bottom-up candidates

housing titles, public employment (temporary and permanent) in the municipality, and information about how to obtain benefits and services.

Beyond partisan networks, candidates can have access to resources from religious organizations, businesses, and even illegal organizations such as drug cartels. In this book, I focus on the linkages between and among political, partisan, and social networks only. Whereas the existence of other networks is certainly undeniable, they are, however, inconsequential in understanding and explaining candidates' strategic choices to use clientelism. Even when I did observe the increasing penetration of networks involved in illegal activities, especially narcotic networks at the municipal level, only one councilor served as a representative of these organizations in the city council. My belief is that most illegal businesses do not need – or at least they do not actively seek – political participation at the local level.

Candidates' access to different sources and amounts of support varies based on their location among national, provincial, and local partisan networks. I examine the nested relationships between and among different levels of government and incumbency in Chapter 6; here I focus on how partisan networks and specifically municipal incumbent networks determine a candidate's capacity to solve problems. Candidates affiliated with the municipal incumbent have access to a local network of material and nonmaterial resources that are inaccessible to opposition candidates. For instance, local incumbents can easily use the resources and bureaucratic apparatus of the municipality to promote their party's local rallies, as is illustrated in the dialogue that follows between an investigative journalist and the communications director of a municipality in the Conurbano. While looking at the signs posted inside the municipality that invited voters to participate in a Peronist Party rally, the journalist asked the director who had paid for the posters:

DIRECTOR: Who do you think is going to pay for them? The municipality.
JOURNALIST: And do you think that is appropriate that the municipality pays for a party expense?
DIRECTOR: Of course, why not? It has always been like this. This is historic.

(Otero 1997: 32)

Candidates who do not count on the support of the local incumbents can, nevertheless, have access to significant amounts of resources from the provincial and national governments. During the national election of October 2005 in Argentina, the mayor of San Miguel, Oscar Zilocchi, supported the candidacy of Chiche Duhalde, the wife of former president and governor of Buenos Aires Eduardo Duhalde, who was running for the senate seat of the Peronist Party's stronghold, the province of Buenos Aires, against Cristina Kirchner, who was at the time a national senator for the province of Santa Cruz and wife of President Néstor Kirchner. Given the importance of the election and the need to secure the support of San Miguel's voters, Kirchner enabled Franco La Porta, the Director of the Lottery of the Province and a party operator, to use as many resources from his office as needed to support the candidate of the party, Joaquín de la Torre, in the municipality. Running with a Peronist Party label, and having the support of a resource-rich sponsor, de la Torre was able to quickly mobilize a considerable number of voters in support of Kirchner.

Assuming that partisanship contributes to candidates' access to resources, the question is whether candidates distribute these resources differently depending on their partisan affiliation. If partisanship simply signals candidates' probability of solving problems given their access to resources, we should not expect to observe variation in how brokers distribute and solve voters' problems.

In his study of problem-solving networks in the poor neighborhoods of Buenos Aires, Javier Auyero (2000) claims that there is a Peronist culture of solving poor voters' problems. Defining political clientelism as "personalized political mediation," he focuses on "the embeddedness of political culture in problem-solving networks" (26). Using ethnographic observations, he describes "how politics intermingles with people's everyday lives, becoming their reality" (177) with the interest of explaining how, but not why, poor voters engage in clientelistic relationships with Peronist brokers. Despite the centrality that they have in his account, Auyero never provides an explicit definition of problem-solving networks. In this book, I define them as networks that enable candidates to solve voter problems; thus, they have the potential to be used as an electoral strategy to mobilize voters. In cases in which candidates only solve the problems of voters or groups of voters that are likely to support them, problem-solving networks are clientelistic. Yet, in cases in which candidates use them to generate "goodwill among constituents who receive assistance," allowing themselves "to build a reputation for fairness and competence" (Stokes 2009: 13), these networks imitate other non-programmatic electoral strategies. As the previous chapter demonstrates, candidates not only require access to problem-solving networks, they also have to prefer to use these networks to solve problems in exchange for political support. In cases where candidates solve voter problems without requesting voters' support in exchange, problem-solving networks emulate constituency services.

I argue that differences in access to resources over time translate into significant partisanship advantages that become – formally and informally – institutionalized and ultimately embedded in political culture. In Argentina, the Peronist Party has historically benefited from these differences by building and sustaining a network of core party supporters through what Juan Carlos Torre (2005) sharply described as the organization's two pillars: "The first is a party identification grounded in a dense web of historically grounded ties of solidarity. Second, this party's identification is cemented by clientelistic political machines that give the Peronist Party a significant advantage in maintaining territorial control" (178).

Scholars of Argentine politics have consistently highlighted the loyalty of poor voters to the Peronist Party (Ostiguy 1998; Levitsky 2003; Brusco et al. 2004; Calvo and Murillo 2004, 2005; Torre 2005). In their study of vote buying in Argentina, Valeria Brusco and her collaborators (2004: 70–71) show that voters who receive a handout from a Peronist candidate are more likely to vote for the Peronist Party. Ernesto Calvo and María Victoria Murillo (2004) find that the Peronist Party benefits more from using patronage as an electoral strategy to mobilize voters than do non-Peronist parties because the former is most popular and most institutionalized in provinces with a concentration of working and lower-income voters. The party is able to take advantage of the geographical concentration of these voters as a function of its capacity to provide significant salaries to the otherwise low-income workers to whom it provides public sector jobs through the use of patronage. The Peronist Party thereby benefits more from providing jobs to voters than do other parties that do not share its resources, its level of institutionalization, and its dominance in locations with a concentration of low-skilled workers.

Focusing on "the continuous presence of the [Peronist] party as a problem-solving center at the grassroots level," Auyero (2000) provides sound evidence that "problem-solving networks are the long-term product of regular interactions that, although usually inaugurated by a foundational favor, must be continuously cultivated" (210). Based on careful ethnographic work, Auyero examines both the clients' point of view and the context in which this view is constructed in order to explain "the fundamental elements (or the enigma) of contemporary Peronism, namely, the continuous support that it gets among the poor (despite its electoral setbacks)" (209).

One of the testimonies that Auyero shares in his ethnographic work is the experience of Juana, a poor voter from Villa Paraiso who attended a rally for the launching of President Carlos Menem's (1989–1999) presidential campaign in the summer of 1989: "The party paid her bus fare to Mar del Plata (Buenos Aires's main beach resort) and put her up at the Transport Union's hotel, where, Juana marveled, 'they even have hot water.' On this trip, at age thirty-four, Juana saw the sea for the first time" (163). Certainly, in consideration of the experience that she was able to have in exchange for participation, we cannot blame Juana for attending the rally in exchange for the trip. We can also understand why, after such an experience, Juana would feel gratitude toward the party broker who invited her, as well as toward the party that paid for her vacation.

Assuming that Juana continues to receive benefits from the party, even sporadically enough so as to simply remind her of the unforgettable experience, we can get a sense of how party loyalties or core voters are cultivated. The support of contemporary Peronism is to be found in the historical experiences of participants such as Juana in problem-solving networks, and in the experiences of new activists who join these networks with the hope of getting their problems solved in the future.

Social Networks

Social networks refer to nonpolitical problem-solving networks that enable voters to solve everyday problems. I argue that social networks provide voters with services and personal support that is not available through political and partisan networks but is, nevertheless, important for their well-being, and that most definitely contributes to the cementing of political loyalties.

While conducting research in Villa Angel, a densely populated working-class neighborhood located on the outskirts of Buenos Aires City, I observed how brokers' central positions in nonpolitical networks such as babysitting, money lending, and counseling services explain their abilities to influence vote choice (Szwarcberg 2012a). In a context in which no one seems to listen to voters' problems and feelings, candidates who supply this simple but key service are able to build significant and enduring relationships with voters, as this testimony from a candidate in San Miguel suggests: "At least I can give people a sense of protection. They know they can come and talk to me; they know that I will listen to them."[9]

Many brokers also mentioned how problem solving sometimes does not involve material goods, but simply relationship advice:

> I'm going to tell you about another case. A lady came up to me and told me she had a problem and that she wanted to talk to me. "You know, my husband didn't come home last night." They'll tell me anything. "I went to the little room [*piecita*] that we had next door, and he was laying with another man." I didn't know if I should have laughed. "Yes, it was three in the morning." And I said, "But was he drunk?" "Yes, but in my opinion he slept with another man," she said to me. "And what do you want me to do with that?!" I asked her. She wanted a lawyer for the separation papers. She wasn't married but they were living together [*juntada*]. Nonetheless I got her a lawyer. Later she came up to me and apologized, and said that he was drunk. How can they tell me such a thing?[10]

Voters share their personal problems with brokers from a combination of isolation, desperation, and trust. Many of them have been separated from their families and friends since coming to the city and find the brokers to be understanding individuals who are trying to help them. In a sense, voters who are grateful to brokers and believe that they are there to offer help are also likely to share some intimate problems with them.

Nested Networks

Studying municipal-level Peronist Party organizations, or *agrupaciones*, enables me to observe and analyze connections between and among political, partisan, and social networks at the local level. Peronist *agrupaciones* cluster neighborhood-level organizations, or *unidades básicas* (base units), which "tend to be run by either a small group of activists or a single *puntero* (neighborhood broker) and her inner circle of friends and family" (Levitsky 2003: 66). Levitsky's 1997 survey of 112 *unidades básicas* in the city of Buenos Aires and in two municipalities in the Conurbano – La Matanza and Quilmes – found that "96 percent of *unidades básicas* engaged in some form of social assistance" (187). Data collected for this study suggests that base-level units continue to engage in the same welfare-providing activities: direct distribution of food and medicine, regular delivery of particularistic favors, programs for children, neighborhood social and cultural events, neighborhood improvements, programs for the elderly, legal assistance, and provision of government jobs (188).

I focus on *agrupaciones* instead of *unidades básicas* because I am interested in the strategies by which party brokers build a political network that enables them to get promoted and eventually elected within the party – a process that occurs at the level of the *agrupación* and not at the *unidad básica*. Describing the disorganized organization of Peronist networks, Levitsky claims:

> Political careers are channeled through *agrupaciones*. Because leadership recruitment and candidate selection [are] done almost entirely by the *agrupaciones*, emerging politicians invest in *agrupaciones* rather than build careers in the party bureaucracy. *Punteros* work their way up through *agrupaciones* by building up territorial bases and exchanging votes for candidacies or government posts. Once in office, they use patronage to sponsor new *unidades básicas* and build their own *agrupaciones*.
>
> (2003: 72)

The distribution of employment and social welfare programs constitutes the clientelistic glue of *agrupaciones* as illustrated by the testimony I collected from the daughter and elected candidate of José C. Paz's party leader of the *agrupación* Por la Ruta de Perón [Following Perón's Road]: "When we began with this *agrupación*, we only had 25 paid workers [*nombradas*] in the municipality, who received 250 pesos [41 dollars] per month. And later, we had people that received the Plan Bonaerense who got 120 pesos [20 dollars]."[11]

Leaders of political *agrupaciones* also distribute rewards and punishments to party activists and candidates, defining their political future. *Agrupaciones* are allotted a number of elected and unelected positions on party lists that they distribute among party activists based on the number of voters they are able to mobilize for the *agrupación*. The more voters a broker is able to mobilize for the *agrupación*, the more likely that he or she will be rewarded with a *nombramiento* (paid job) from the municipality, and eventually even with an elected position on the city council. The goal, therefore, is to understand why some brokers are more effective than others at building a party network that enables them to get promoted within the organization.

Building a Network

Before they can mobilize voters to participate at rallies and elections, party brokers must first solve their problems. Every voter who comes to

DNI	APELLIDO	NOMBRES	PROFESION	DOMICILIO CALLE	NRO	DOC TIPO	A	ORIG-DUP-TRIP	CIRCUITO	SEXO
██	██	HECTOR	TRAB.IN	9 DE JULIO	1578	DNID		3	3009	M
██	██	JOSE RICARDO	COMERCI	9 DE JULIO	1648	DNID		3	3009	M
██	██	RAMON FACTOR	MILITAR	9 DE JULIO	1607			3	3009	M
██	██	HUMBERTO LUIS	EMPLEAD	9 DE JULIO	153	DNI		3	3009	M
██	██	VENTURA	CHAPIST	9 DE JULIO	1620			3	3009	M
██	██	JULIO CESAR	EMPLEAD	9 DE JULIO	1211	DNI		3	3009	M
██	██	JESUS HUGO	TRAB.IN	9 DE JULIO	1566	L		3	3009	M
██	██	ARMANDO DOMINGO	MECANIC	9 DE JULIO	1620	DNI		3	3009	M
██	██	LUIS HECTOR	EMPL.A	9 DE JULIO	1401			3	3009	M
██	██	MARTIN	COMERCI	9 DE JULIO	1494	DNID		3	3009	M
██	██	ISIDRO RAMON	EMPLEAD	9 DE JULIO	1578	DNIT		3	3009	M
██	██	RUBEN VICENTE	ESTUDIA	9 DE JULIO	1570			3	3009	M
██	██	ENRIQUE HUGO	MEDICO	9 DE JULIO	1288			3	3009	M
██	██	HECTOR OSCAR	EMP	9 DE JULIO	1372			3	3009	M
██	██	MIGUEL ANGEL	EMPLEAD	9 DE JULIO	1377			3	3009	M
██	██	OSCAR ALFREDO	JORNALE	9 DE JULIO	1329	DNID		3	3009	M
██	██	EULOGIO SAUL	EMPLEAD	9 DE JULIO	1570	DNID		3	3009	M
██	██	JOSE ANIBEL	EMPLEAD	9 DE JULIO	1510			3	3009	M
██	██	NELSON JUAN CARLOS	EMPLEAD	9 DE JULIO	1365			3	3009	M
██	██	RAUL OSVALDO	EMPLEAD	9 DE JULIO	1565	DNIT		3	3009	M
██	██	DIEGO FERNANDO	ESTUDIA	9 DE JULIO	1899	DNIT		3	3009	M
██	██	JUAN ERNESTO	JUBILAD	9 DE JULIO	1502			3	3009	M
██	██	MIGUEL ANGEL	ESTUDIA	9 DE JULIO	1399			3	3009	M
██	██	DIEGO DARIO	ESTUDIA	9 DE JULIO	1765			3	3009	M
██	██	RAMON FERNANDO	EMPLEAD	A ORIGONE 331				3	3009	M
██	██	JORGE AUGUSTO	EMPL.	ARENALES	105			3	3009	M
██	██	FRANCISCO	EMPLEAD	ARENALES	530	DNI		3	3009	M
██	██	ALDO OSCAR	EMPLEAD	ARENALES	212			3	3009	M
██	██	HECTOR OSMAR	CHOFER	ARENALES	520			3	3009	M
██	██	GUILLERMO SANTOS ANTONI	MEDICO	ARENALES	386			3	3009	M
██	██	ROLANDO SALVADOR	ELECTRI	ARENALES	105			3	3009	M
██	██	ERNESTO OMER	EMPLEAD	ARENALES	277			3	3009	M
██	██	JULIO ARGENTINO	COMERC	ARENALES	497	DNID		3	3009	M
██	██	JUAN BAUTISTA	EMPLEAD	ARENALES	443			3	3009	M
██	██	JORGE DOMINGO	EMPLEAD	ARENALES	529	DNID		3	3009	M
██	██	ALEJO JOSE	EMPLEAD	ARENALES	460	DNIT		3	3009	M
██	██	RICHARD CEFERINO	EMPLEAD	ARENALES	481			3	3009	M
██	██	JORGE ENRIQUE	EMPLEAD	ARENALES	137	DNIT		3	3009	M
██	██	DIEGO MARTIN	ESTUDIA	ARENALES	328	DNID		3	3009	M
██	██	ADOLFO	EMPLEAD	ARENALES Y BOLIVIA				3	3009	M
██	██	AUSBERTO ELVIO	COMERCI	ARENALES Y BOLIVIA				3	3009	M
██	██	OMAR MARIO	COMERCI	ARENALES Y SUIPACHA		DNI		3	3009	M
██	██	ROSARIO ARTURO	AUTONOM	AV. AVIADOR ORIGONE	433	DNI		3	3009	M

Figure 3.2. Party list

Note: This list, given to me by a party candidate, shows the number of the DNI (*documento nacional de indentidad* [national document of identity], which Argentine citizens need to have to vote), last name, first name, profession, street address, street number, type of document, if the document is an original or duplicate or triplicate, the number of the electoral circuit in which the voter is registered, and the voter's gender. Voters' DNI and last names are blocked out to protect their identities.

ask for help or who has been offered assistance is registered on a party broker's list. Information collected from lists that candidates use in several municipalities located throughout different provinces in Argentina suggests that while there is variation in the level of detail that each list provides, all lists share the same basic information: a voter's first and last names, address, age, employment, marital status, and his or her federal identification number [*documento nacional de identidad*], a unique number that is used for voting purposes and to receive state aid.[12]

During the political campaigns for legislative elections in 2009 in the province of San Luis, I was able to make copies of the party lists, shown in Figure 3.2, elected candidates used to mobilize voters in the municipality of Villa Mercedes. The lists have more than a dozen columns, including the voter's federal identification number (needed to vote in elections), profession, address, the number of the electoral circuit in which the voter is registered, and his or her gender.

Candidates also ask voters about employment and whether or not they are receiving state benefits in order to gather information about current and potential beneficiaries. Beneficiaries are voters who already receive small goods or services such as wheelchairs, medicine, bags of food, construction materials, and welfare programs or who are employed, temporarily or permanently, at the municipality. These beneficiaries are expected to attend rallies and vote in elections to continue enjoying their benefits and to guarantee future benefits for their family and friends. Potential beneficiaries are voters who attend party rallies without receiving anything in exchange, but who hope to get material rewards after publicly displaying their support for the party. While conducting fieldwork across municipalities in Argentina, I discovered that the majority of voters on these lists were potential beneficiaries.

Once a voter has asked a broker to solve a problem, he or she has to wait until receiving an answer before asking other brokers for solutions to the same problem. If a broker discovers that a voter has been asking another broker for a solution to the same or other problems, both brokers are likely to abstain from helping the voter – brokers, more or less explicitly, demand loyalty. Certainly, there is variation in the time it takes to reply to a request based on the type of favor: getting medicine for someone with a terminal condition and getting someone out of jail may elicit immediate responses, as opposed to getting construction materials for a housing project. It is worthwhile to note that most problems are of a pressing nature for poor voters; thus, brokers solve urgent and time-sensitive problems daily.

This implicit agreement shows that voters act strategically in deciding from whom they should ask for assistance. In making their decisions, voters take into account a broker's capacity to solve problems and the time the broker is likely to take in providing solutions. As a result, brokers who have built reputations as effective problem solvers are likely to have more voters willing to wait longer to get their problem solved than are brokers whose problem-solving reputation is unknown or unfavorable.

"Waiting," writes Pierre Bourdieu in *Pascalian Meditations,* "is one of the ways of experiencing the effects of power. Making people wait … delaying without destroying hope … adjourning without totally disappointing" are, according to Bourdieu, "integral parts of the working of domination" (2000: 228). Studying poor people's waiting experiences, Auyero notes how the welfare bureaucracy "introduces economy and order (i.e., government, in Foucault's sense) by manipulating poor people's time" (2012: 25). The welfare offices thus reproduce the same conditions found at local political organizations, city council, city hall, and at the municipality: "sites of intense sociability amid pervasive uncertainty" (6).

As a result of his ethnographic fieldwork performed in the waiting area of the main welfare office in the city of Buenos Aires (Ministerio de Desarrollo Social) between August 2008 and January 2009, Auyero finds that:

> to be an actual or potential welfare recipient is to be subordinated to the will of others. This subordination is created and re-created through innumerable acts of waiting (the obverse is equally true; domination is generated anew by making others wait). In those recurring encounters at the welfare office, poor people learn that, despite endless delays and random changes, they must comply with the requirements of agents and their machines.
>
> (2012: 24)

While waiting for solutions, voters are, nevertheless, expected to participate in politics. Studying how voters envision clientelistic exchanges, Auyero finds a combination of gratitude and pragmatism in voters' responses to the question of why they participate at rallies. Beyond the testimonies that demonstrate voters' heartfelt gratitude, Auyero also presents testimonies of voters who turn out because they believe that failing to participate will affect the flow of goods and services and their ability to get their problems solved in the future:

> I know that I have to go with her [the party broker] instead of with someone else. Because she gave me medicine, or some milk, or a packet of yerba or sugar, I know that I have to go to her rally in order to fulfill my obligation to her, to show my gratitude. Because, if I do not go to her rally, then when I need something, she won't give it to me. [She would say,] "Go ask the person who went to the rally with you."
>
> (2000: 160)

While studying the strategies that female party activists employ to distribute goods for a food program in Buenos Aires (Szwarcberg 2011), I became aware of the use of promises and the rotation of benefits to enlarge the size of a broker's network beyond that allowed by the actual amount of benefits. I spent a couple of weeks with Rosa Acevedo, a paid party activist for the Peronist Party who ran an *unidad básica* and a soup kitchen that fed approximately 50 children daily. Most of the resources that she used to prepare the meals came from the municipality. I asked Rosa about the women who helped her in the soup kitchen, and she responded with Alicia's story:

One day this woman came crying to see if I could help her. "I will wash the dishes, clean, do whatever you want if you can just give me two coupons for food. I do not have enough and my father is taking a very expensive medicine." I said, "Of course, miss, there is no problem." This is how she came to work for me, and she stayed for four months. After that, when she finished paying the bills and things began to get better, I asked her to leave because there were people that needed this job more than she did.[13]

Alicia's relationship with Rosa began with a favor, and although Alicia does not work for Rosa, she still participates in all the political events that Rosa organizes. In my follow-up interview with Alicia, I was told that she did not care "at all" about politics, but she participated simply because that was "Rosa's business." However, Alicia did not want to contribute to Rosa's political promotion; on the contrary, she despised Rosa, but followed her because she "had no alternative":

Rosa is bossy, arrogant, and treated me badly every single day I worked there [at the soup kitchen]. She knew that the girls [other workers at the soup kitchen] and I needed the job, so she exploited us and then she asked me to leave. What can I do? I know that I will have to wait, and when I cannot make ends meet, I will go crying to her again.[14]

Moreover, Alicia thought that Rosa purposefully made promises to everyone in the soup kitchen to solve their problems, but she rotated fulfilling those promises among the women of the neighborhood so as to save resources and still "have us all under her thumb."[15] By rotating favors among voters, Rosa guaranteed their obedience without providing solutions to all of their problems.

This dynamic use of promises and rotation of favors contributes to an explanation of why some candidates are able to build political networks that are larger than the corresponding amount of resources that they have. It also explains why voters are less likely to switch networks once they are actively participating in one that has succeeded in solving their problems in the past.

In short, some clientelistic brokers have a deep understanding of how to manage scarcity and the hope of their clients in order to build larger political networks than their resources actually allow; these are the brokers who can cultivate the largest networks and use clientelistic methods to increase participation and partisan support to the greatest extent possible. Skillful management of scarcity and hope can also be seen in Palermo, Italy, where "the system works less through the mass distribution of benefits to all comers than through the astute management of scarcity and, above all, the critical element of hope. The key to the successful politician is not mass patronage but the maintenance of the maximum clientele with the minimum payoff in terms of actual benefits" (Chubb 1981: 114). Thus, an understanding of the strategic management of scarcity and hope through patronage and clientelism contributes to an account of the relative success of political organizations.

In addition to making promises and solving everyday problems, incumbents have the capacity to distribute welfare programs and public employment. In many developing countries, jobs in the public sector are the only source of employment in the formal sector for low-skilled workers. This is the case in India, where "the state monopolizes access to jobs and services, and in which elected officials have discretion in the implementation of laws allocating the jobs and services at the disposal of the state," leading Kanchan Chandra to define the country as a "patronage democracy" (2004: 6).

Patronage, however, is not unique to developing countries, as Judith Chubb's study of political machines in Palermo, Italy shows. In Palermo, Chubb argues, politics is the only road to stable employment, and "a job signifies a vote and vice versa." She continues, "in an economic context like that of Palermo, where a stable job is a rare commodity, employment in the public sector, however lowly, has become a universal aspiration – the dream of stable and dignified employment, of a regular salary and fringe benefits, in sum, of security" (Chubb 1981: 112).

In Argentina, public employment also provides security for voters with low skills. As stated earlier, the geographical concentration of these voters in politically significant provinces provides an important electoral advantage to the Peronist Party – a phenomenon that further explains why parties obtain varying degrees of electoral benefits from using patronage to get votes (Calvo and Murillo 2004). Most politicians prefer to provide voters with untenured (*temporario*) public jobs that are easy to withdraw than with tenured (*permanente*) public jobs that are almost impossible to revoke.

Untenured jobs enable candidates to end the contract of a voter who fails to participate and support the party, whereas tenured public jobs render candidates effectively unable to punish a voter regardless of his or her electoral behavior. As a result, the interesting and pressing question concerning patronage regards commitment: Why will a voter who receives a job that is effectively irrevocable continue voting for the candidate who appointed him or her?

The works of Judith Chubb (1981) and Virginia Oliveros (2012) concerning public employees in Italy and Argentina, respectively, provide interesting insights about why tenured public employees will still participate in politics. In the case of Italy, Chubb argues that tenured employees will continue participating because even though they already received a benefit, they seek to secure future benefits for their friends and family. In "a city where politics is widely perceived as the only road to obtaining secure employment" (1981: 112), voters continue to participate not because they want to secure their own employment but because they want to make sure they do not threaten the employment opportunities of their family and friends.

Using a survey experiment, Oliveros (2012) finds that in Argentina, 44 percent of public employees help voters with errands or tasks at city hall, 12 percent monitor elections, 22 percent help in electoral campaigns, and 21 percent participate in rallies. Her argument is that public employees provide the mayor with political services because they fear getting laid off or experiencing worsening working conditions if the mayor loses the election.

In the case of tenured employees, mayors implement "encouraging mechanisms" (Oliveros 2012: 21) to remind employees that although mayors cannot take their jobs away, they can significantly worsen their working conditions – for instance, by transferring them in order to make their commute longer, by refusing to promote them, or by transferring them to a hostile office. In the words of one public employee:

> The fear is not about losing the job, it is about changing it, changing the place of work; it is about being sent somewhere else, somewhere where he does not know how to do the job, or somewhere with a different schedule, or without the extra monetary benefits that his current job allows him to earn ... a lot of things can be changed.
>
> (qtd. in Oliveros 2012: 21)

Further evidence of brokers' use of lists to distribute benefits and to mobilize and monitor voters is found in the work of Levitsky (2003). In his study of neighborhood-level organizations of the Peronist Party in a lower-class public housing complex in La Matanza, a municipality in the province of Buenos Aires, Levitsky describes how he observed first-hand the use of lists to distribute goods in exchange for participation in intraparty elections:

> A local *puntero* distributed 400 bags of food a month among local residents, in exchange for which he demanded party membership and a vote in the internal election ... While distributing bags of food two weeks before intraparty elections, the *puntero* told recipients, "Remember you have to vote on June 29. If not, you are automatically crossed off the list!"
>
> (204)

In this case, we observe how a broker distributes small goods to voters who are on the list in exchange for their support. Moreover, the *puntero* explicitly states that the consequence of not participating in the election will be the withholding of benefits. During her fieldwork in Argentina, Oliveros found a similar use of lists to coordinate participation and clientelistic exchanges: "Employees were asked to vote and lists with their names were handed by their bosses to party leaders. The day of the election those lists were used to control turnout" (2012: 24).

While conducting fieldwork during the legislative elections of 2005 and 2008, I constantly experienced voters' disdain at having to participate at party rallies that took place in their municipalities and beyond. It was a well-known secret that everyone who was waiting to receive or was already receiving a state benefit had to attend these events to keep his or her benefits. Still, a legal document that I obtained through a key informant in José C. Paz is even more persuasive than my qualitative observations and the secondary literature. The document presents indisputable evidence of how party bosses control attendance at party rallies. In this case, the mayor of José C. Paz, Mario Ishii, requested the attendance of all untenured public employees at a party rally "without exception." The document, signed by the now-deceased secretary of the president, also "invite[s] all tenured public employees at the municipality."[16]

Without information about voters' participation, candidates would be unable to distribute goods and reward or punish voters based on their political participation. If voters were able to get their problems solved without having to participate in politics, clientelism would not be an effective strategy of political mobilization. Clientelism works because brokers succeed in linking problem solving with political participation by monitoring voters' attendance at rallies and elections and distributing rewards and punishments accordingly.

Monitoring Voters: Taking Attendance at Party Rallies and Elections

Monitoring includes the activities through which brokers gather information about voters' participation in politics. To monitor voters' participation at party rallies, brokers simply use the party list with the names of voters who are waiting to receive and are already receiving benefits to take attendance. Everyone who has come to ask for help or who has been offered assistance is on these lists.

Mabel, the private secretary of a Peronist councilor in the city of Córdoba, explained to me that candidates use rosters "made in Excel and organized alphabetically" with the names of beneficiaries of welfare programs, public employees, and voters who have asked for favors. She said this while showing me the rosters that she makes and updates "at least once a week, and during elections almost daily."[17]

At all of the weekly meetings that I attended during a national election in Buenos Aires and a primary election in Córdoba, someone was always taking attendance of voter participation. Voters talked with attendance takers if they needed to leave early or if they had scheduling conflicts for future rallies. Voters confirming their attendance (*dar el presente*) to ensure that the party activist had seen them (*nos haya visto*) repeatedly interrupted my informal conversations with activists at party rallies. Even though party activists decide autonomously what to do with voters who fail to participate, the action of taking attendance at rallies seems to have a disciplinary effect of its own among voters. By simply taking attendance or by letting voters know that attendance will or might be taken, parties effectively guarantee voter turnout.

Rational choice explanations predict that brokers will take attendance randomly at rallies. Unsure whether or not attendance will be taken, voters will participate in all rallies so that brokers will not have to take attendance at every rally. The activity of taking attendance is, nevertheless, a low-cost one, as it only entails using a list and checking the presence or absence of voters registered on the list. Despite being a low-cost activity, it is an important one that provides attendance takers with power over those whose attendance is taken. In a context in which most activists are unemployed, employed only in politics, or work in low-skilled jobs for which they have to fill strict hours, they are rarely in a position of being in charge of taking attendance of others. The combination of a network of activists happy to engage in taking attendance and the low cost of the activity encourages councilors that use clientelistic strategies to take attendance of voters' participation at rallies and elections.

At many of the rallies that I attended, the guarded jealousy toward the attendance takers over their duties greatly surprised me. As an attendant accurately told me while pointing me to one of the attendance takers, "They are more Papist than the Pope." Indeed, there is significance behind the position. Assigning the task of taking attendance – an easy, but vital activity for the organization – provides candidates with an opportunity to give visible recognition to party activists at virtually no cost.

Beyond taking attendance at party rallies, activists and candidates also monitor voters' participation at elections. Party monitors are key players in elections by making sure that there is a full supply of ballots inside every voting booth, controlling who turned out to vote, and helping count the votes at the end of the election. The absence of monitors often leads to a lack of ballots, presumably stolen by monitors from opposition parties and to the purposeful miscounting of votes. Consequently, the presence of monitors can be integral to the electoral success of a political organization.

The need to have territorial representation in more districts as well as to count with a network of party monitors led the former minister of economy Roberto Lavagna to make an alliance with the UCR in 2007. Also, after recognizing her defeat in running for president in 2007, Elisa Carrió, the candidate of the Support for an Egalitarian Republic Party (ARI), mentioned that the absence of party monitors in some key districts caused her numbers to fall.

In Argentina, monitors are assigned to screen elections at a booth located in either a private or public school during election day. Besides allocating individual booth monitors, parties also allocate a principal monitor to every school. Principal party monitors are in charge of controlling the election procedures at their particular voting site by helping individual monitors in case they need assistance, and more generally by gathering information about turnout and vote choice for the party boss.

By assigning brokers to monitor schools, bosses are able to further test and compare the ability of their agents to organize and mobilize party activists. Brokers who succeed in mobilizing voters to rallies are appointed to monitor a school, where they can show the party boss their ability to provide monitors for every booth and to ensure that the election occurs in the most favorable manner possible for the party. Brokers are not evaluated in terms of the electoral result of the school, as they are not necessarily assigned to schools in neighborhoods that they control, but rather on their ability to produce information about turnout and vote choice for the party.

Most councilors have participated in elections as booth monitors; once they have acquired experience by participating in several election days and have shown their potential to mobilize voters, they are given the opportunity to monitor the election at a school: "To be in charge of monitoring a school is an unavoidable step in your political education [*la escuelita*]. It signals that you are on the right path, that if you keep on turning out voters you might get promoted."[18] In contrast, brokers who have never been in charge of monitoring a school or who were principal monitors in the past but failed to be reappointed are not likely to run on the ticket.

Monitoring voter turnout during election day is easy and precise. Mayors assign councilors to monitor polling stations to secure and steal votes for the party and evaluate them based on their performance. In 2005, I was in José C. Paz on the day of the national election. Domingo, a Peronist councilor, had been appointed to monitor the election at a polling station located in his neighborhood. He had been "taking care" of this station for five years and thus knew "the face of almost everyone that comes to vote in this station."[18] Domingo had obtained a list with the names and identity card numbers of the voters assigned to "his polling station" from the electoral authorities months before the election. He also had lists of brokers and activists working for him with the names of the voters they were going to mobilize during election day. After the election, Domingo simply corroborated which activists and brokers had fulfilled their quotas and distributed rewards and punishments accordingly.

Candidates can be effective at taking attendance at rallies and screening turnout at elections, but monitoring works only if voters believe that failing to participate jeopardizes the receiving of benefits. To create and enforce this belief, candidates punish voters who fail to turn out to rallies and elections. During the 2005 electoral campaign in Buenos Aires, Enrique, a Peronist candidate in José C. Paz, had rented four buses to transport voters to attend a rally that was going to take place in a neighboring municipality. The day of the rally, voter turnout was much lower than Enrique had expected, and voters who participated at the rally traveled comfortably in only two buses.

José, an unemployed voter who was enrolled in a welfare program thanks to Enrique, was one of the candidate's followers who failed to attend the rally. The rally was on a Sunday, the same day as José's grandson's birthday, and he chose to remain at the party instead of attending yet another rally. The following month, José found out that he had been removed (*dar de baja*) from his welfare program:

> When I went to talk to Enrique, he explained to me that I couldn't get the welfare program anymore because this was a program for only four months. I told him that I had been receiving the program for almost a year, and if it was only for four months I should not have received it for the last couple of months. Also, I knew my neighbor was still getting it and it had been more than four months. He smiled and told me, "but Pedro [the neighbor] is a good fellow, he always comes when I ask him." I didn't know what to say, I felt so humiliated. I was there begging for 350 pesos [100 dollars per month] and promising anything. He just used me to set an example, and you know what the worst thing is? That it really worked. Since they took the program away from me, and people found out, no one else ever failed to attend a rally. And I mean no one.[20]

After Enrique showed that failing to attend rallies had consequences, his followers were more likely to participate in rallies and elections. Candidates are not as interested in punishing voters as in inducing turnout and deterring their defection to opposition parties. Observing that attendance is taken at every party rally, and that failing to turn out could imply being stripped from promised or existing benefits, voters participate.

Studying how brokers use the information collected on these lists, I found that instead of punishing every voter who failed to turn out, brokers choose to punish only a few, so as to set an example. Even though candidates decide autonomously what to do with voters who fail to participate, the threat of taking attendance at party meetings and rallies seems to have a disciplinary effect among voters. This logic unravels a modern mechanism of discipline and punishment whereby constant visibility contributes to the maintenance of the subjection of disciplined individuals (Foucault 1977: 187).

Conclusion

This chapter has shown how brokers regularly use clientelism and monitoring to mobilize poor voters to participate at party meetings, rallies, and elections. Voters are promised and often receive benefits in exchange for their participation. Candidates promise and deliver goods to voters, while monitoring and punishing those who fail to participate. Voters, on the other hand, learn that if they are patient and participate in political activities, they will be rewarded with goods. Voters also learn which political *agrupaciones* are most likely to reward them; thus, in deciding with whom to participate, they take into account both an organization's reputation and their own partisanship preferences.

Building a network, an *agrupación*, based only on the delivery of benefits has five important consequences. First, it implies that candidates who do not have access to resources but compete for the vote of poor voters are unlikely to succeed. Second, the fact that candidates who have access to resources and prefer using clientelism get promoted teaches activists and candidates about the efficacy of clientelistic strategies. Third, this creates a logic of perverse incentives through which candidates who are able and willing to use clientelism succeed. Fourth, this implies that office-seeking party activists who are beginning their political careers and have the capacity to use clientelism are more likely to turn to these strategies. Fifth, once activists begin using clientelism to mobilize voters, they are less likely or able to stop using these strategies while sustaining their party network.

Studying the Peronist Party, Levistky (2003) shows how loosely structured party organizations are often better equipped to adapt and survive in times of crises than are well-institutionalized party structures. The author explains how the Peronist Party's combination of organizational strength and flexibility has enabled it to adapt to the opportunities and constraints posed by a changing socioeconomic environment. Yet, while Levitsky focuses on the advantages of institutional flexibility, this book shows how flexibility also serves to enforce a logic of perverse incentives that encourages candidates to use clientelism to mobilize voters. The three factors that Levitsky recognizes as fundamental to explaining party adaptation and survival also serve to strengthen incentives that reward candidates based only on the number of voters they mobilized. These factors are weakly institutionalized linkages between different sectors of the party, the absence of stable career paths and secure tenure, and the absence of stable norms of accountability or routinized decision rules.

As organizations that seek to win elections, political parties are not likely to punish candidates capable of turning out a large number of voters. Moreover, even if parties were interested in inducing candidates not to use clientelism, they would be unable to achieve their goal because the same flexibility that enables parties to adapt prevents them from disciplining their members. Interestingly, flexibility is what explains why, under the same conditions, candidates make different decisions.

In "Transforming Labor-Based Parties in Latin America: Argentine Peronism in Comparative Perspective," Levitsky (2003) documents the Peronist Party's change from a union-based party to a patronage-based territorial organization that created and sustained linkages with voters during neoliberal policy changes. It was the combination of state resources and local autonomy that allowed activists who were critical of Peronist President Carlos Menem (1989–1999) to continue to engage in traditional Peronist practices even as the national party abandoned them.

Brokers made strategic decisions based on their understanding of the changes and their individual preferences of how to adapt to the new political environment. Activists constantly referred to the changes experienced in *agrupaciones*, as documented in various academic works (Auyero 2000; Levitsky 2003; Szwarcberg 2009). Asked about the state of Peronist *agrupaciones* in the Conurbano, one Peronist councilor in José C. Paz described the changes he experienced in the party's organization:

> What the old Peronist organization really was – the *unidades básicas* – no longer exists. That organization, which was very good, no longer exists. Because the UBs were service organizations where they provided services to *compañeros* [companions]: From school tutoring, to getting medicine, to teaching courses, being at the service of *compañeros* without playing politics [*para la rosca*], and they were there to share barbecues [*asados*], and especially for the day of the election. Today the *unidades básicas* are closed all year long and only open for the day of the election. They say, "We're going to open a *unidad básica*," as if it was a store in a shopping mall. No, an *unidad básica* has to be open all year long. Mine was open all of last year. Then, all of my resources stopped coming in and I couldn't keep it up, but that's

how it should work. Today, they just work to give out welfare programs. Today, the *agrupaciones* are created and sustain themselves only based on their access to benefits.

During the 2005 election, there were more than 20 *unidades básicas* in downtown José C. Paz. The most important *agrupaciones* in the municipality rented some small spaces available in the area a couple of months before the election. Most of these *unidades básicas*, however, were temporary and existed to better their respective *agrupación*:

> When the electoral season comes up, activities in the neighborhoods have to be organized, they have to mobilize, to plan different types of activities . . . Then, well, there are also moments in which the *agrupación* plays a really important role. What's more, even *unidades básicas* flourish: *agrupaciones* encourage the opening of new *unidades básicas* because it's a way to recruit *punteros*, giving them their own political space to mobilize voters.[21]

Most of these rental spaces were returned to the proprietors right after the election. While they were occupied by *unidades básicas*, they served mostly to publicize the *agrupación* and to recruit new voters who were then included on the party lists.

Agrupaciones that succeed in mobilizing voters using clientelism are unlikely to stop using the strategies that have proven successful in terms of turning out voters and winning electoral support. Furthermore, the more effective an *agrupación* is at providing votes for a party, the more likely it is that its members will be rewarded with political promotions and resources that cyclically strengthen the machine's organization by increasing its access to material goods and nonmaterial services with which to solve voters' problems. As a result, we observe the consolidation of political machines in democracies. In turn, this consolidation explains why voters may participate in politics without receiving anything but promises in exchange for political support. By participating with consolidated machines, voters are making an investment in their future by seeking benefits for themselves and their families.

Consolidated machines make the coordination and organization of opposition parties more difficult because voters learn how to elicit promises and come to trust that they will receive benefits from a particular organization; switching to a different political party or machine that is seen as unlikely to fulfill promises increases the risk on their investment in the future. To eliminate consolidated political machines, voters need to believe that others will also support and vote for the opposition. The outcome is that most voters choose to avoid the risks of losing their good standing with the machine, and, accordingly, opposition leaders remain unsuccessful.

In places where machines have been in power for more than two decades, as in the provinces of Santiago del Estero, San Luis, and Catamarca, voters have grown fearful and machines have remained in power. These political scenarios lead to one of two possible and opposite outcomes: either voters engage in politically and physically destructive collective protest (Auyero 2003; Svampa and Pereyra 2003; Szwarcberg 2004b) or the machine remains in power by using clientelistic strategies.

4

Moral Hazard and Asymmetric Information Networks

In 2005, Juan Carlos and Domingo were Argentine Peronist councilors in charge of similarly poor neighborhoods in the municipality of José C. Paz in Buenos Aires. Four days before a party rally with President Kirchner and his wife, Cristina Fernández de Kirchner, who was the candidate for a senate seat in the province of Buenos Aires, the party leader provided Juan Carlos and Domingo with the same number of mattresses, construction materials, and food boxes to distribute among voters. Juan Carlos distributed the goods to voters who were likely to turn out if they received something in exchange. Domingo, however, sent some of his activists to distribute food boxes but sold the construction materials and mattresses to make some extra cash. Although Juan Carlos had mobilized more voters than he would have had he not distributed the goods, on the day of the election, it was Domingo who had managed to turn out more voters than Juan Carlos. Clearly, Domingo's larger voter turnout was not the result of his distributing goods; rather, it was attributed to the fact that his neighborhood exhibited a tendency toward widespread voter participation.

This case illustrates that when voters turn out and vote for the party regardless of receiving benefits in exchange for their participation, candidates' actions are open to moral hazard. Candidates know voters' preferences and likelihood to turn out and thus can manipulate that information to obtain more resources from the party boss. Indeed, it is logical to assume that councilors such as Domingo who are able to mobilize voters will charge mayors a commission for delivering goods and mobilizing voters. The challenge mayors face is how to keep from paying candidates too high a commission that their investments in buying support become inefficient.

Assuming that candidates are independent agents who will take whatever course of action leads to their personal benefit, the literature expects them either to use the goods to generate cash for themselves or to build up their own local power (see, e.g., Kitschelt and Wilkinson 2007; Schaffer 2007; Stokes et al. 2013). Why is it that some candidates actually deliver goods to voters?

This chapter studies *candidates* as local elected officials, *councilors,* who represent a party in the neighborhoods where they live. It is a candidate's social proximity to voters that enables him or her to learn about an individual voter's political preferences and propensity to turn out to vote, as much as to monitor a voter's political behavior. In contrast to party activists and volunteers, candidates are all interested in pursuing a career in politics and getting reelected. A party leader is the mayor who commands candidates by distributing political promotions. The political career of a mayor depends on his or her ability to get votes for the party; thus, the mayor will always seek to maximize the party's vote share.

Although councilors can be reliable candidates who will distribute inducements to maximize the party's vote share because they believe in the party's program, mayors may not be able to determine a councilor's reliability without monitoring his or her ability to turn out voters. Councilors' opportunities to redirect party goods for self-enrichment will vary depending on mayors' expectations of voter turnout and the voters' propensity to participate in the neighborhood the councilor represents. Councilors in high-support neighborhoods, where voters are likely to support the party whether or not they receive clientelistic inducements, have more chances to increase their wealth by selling the goods than do candidates in low-support neighborhoods, where voters' support is conditional on receiving handouts.

Even though mayors have information about voters' participation and choices from past elections, such data do not enable them to determine whether voters would have behaved differently had they not received a clientelistic inducement. Unless mayors experiment by giving and taking away goods from councilors to test the responses of their constituencies, mayors are unable to determine if turnout is the result of the distribution of party goods or voters' propensity to participate.

In an in-depth analysis of party-voter linkages, Herbert Kitschelt and Steven Wilkinson (2007) accurately point out that politicians prefer to use clientelism when they can predict voters' electoral conduct and elasticity. Still, the authors do not explain how politicians make these predictions. Candidates are the party agents who possess the information that could help mayors make accurate predictions. Thus, while Kitschelt and Wilkinson effectively recognize the existence of principal-agent problems and the need for "finely balanced systems of incentives" for patronage-based party-voter linkages to work, they do not explain either the mechanisms politicians use to predict voter behavior or the incentives they employ to force candidates to distribute goods (8).

The argument presented in this chapter focuses on the strategies mayors use to distinguish between reliable and unreliable candidates. This chapter proposes a fully fledged theory of the incentives and mechanisms party leaders employ to overcome the principal-agent problem between mayors and candidates by comparing a candidate's performance at rallies and elections over time and the distribution of rewards and punishments accordingly.

Incentives and Voter Turnout at Rallies and Elections

A party mayor will collect as much information as possible to hold candidates accountable for their distribution of goods to voters. Information about neighborhood-level turnout in previous elections provides mayors with a baseline from which to evaluate councilors' abilities, even though the data do not necessarily reflect councilors' efforts, but rather voter preferences. Surveys are unlikely to provide accurate information because voters may falsify their preferences in order to avoid being punished or to receive more goods if they believe that pretending to be swing voters will enable them to obtain more benefits.

To diminish the risk of moral hazard, mayors will motivate councilors to reveal their ability to mobilize voters at rallies, where voters' willingness to participate and councilors' abilities to mobilize them explain turnout. Voters who choose to participate at rallies independently are easily distinguishable from mobilized voters because the former do not wear any identification such as councilor-provided hats and T-shirts to signal them as mobilized party supporters.

Rallies also induce mobilized voters to choose a councilor with whom to attend, and these decisions are made public, enabling mayors to avoid miscalculations. In other words, rallies enable mayors to act preemptively by avoiding the distribution of goods to councilors who are unlikely to turn out the expected number of votes on election day, given their performance at rallies. In reallocating goods from unreliable to reliable councilors before elections, mayors manage to enhance their vote share. More importantly, rallies enable mayors to adjust the distribution of goods before an election, thus avoiding a suboptimal allocation of goods, and possibly helping them gain additional votes by redistributing resources to reliable candidates in neighborhoods where voter turnout is historically low.

To induce councilors to mobilize as many voters as possible to participate in rallies, mayors promise to distribute party goods and political promotions according to councilors' turnout numbers. Mayors shape the political future of councilors by deciding their positions on the closed-list ballots, thus determining the likelihood of their getting elected and reelected.

Assumptions and Hypotheses

Classic works on distributive politics assume that parties use outcome-contingent transfers to allocate resources among districts (e.g., Cox and McCubbins 1986; Lindbeck and Weibull 1987; Dixit and Londregan 1996). The logic implies that machines will gather neighborhood-level data about voter turnout and choose to target goods to core or swing neighborhoods based on the number of votes the party received in a previous election. The problem with outcome-contingent transfers is that they do not enable party leaders to distinguish if the outcome is the result of the clientelistic transfers or voters' propensity to turn out and vote for the party. Party mayors, for instance, can effectively gather information about voter turnout at the neighborhood level and thus evaluate a candidate's performance based on the number of voters who participate in neighborhood rallies and elections. In using only neighborhood-level data to reward or punish councilors, mayors are likely to reward councilors in high-support neighborhoods who pocket clientelistic inducements rather than distribute them, and punish councilors who use goods to solve voters' problems but represent low-support neighborhoods where the results could be potentially worse without clientelistic inducements.

I argue that mayors will compare voter turnout at elections and rallies to infer a councilor's reliability and decide whether to reward or punish the party agent. Cases in which turnout at rallies differs from turnout at elections provide mayors with more information than cases with similar levels of voter participation at rallies and elections. Councilors who succeed in mobilizing voters to participate at rallies and elections can be either reliable party agents who distribute goods or unreliable councilors who represent the party in core neighborhoods.

With regard to voter turnout at elections, candidates can either succeed or fail in meeting their party mayor's expectations. In the case of party rallies, candidates can also fail or succeed in mobilizing voters, but they can also surprise mayors by turning out more voters than expected. Table 4.1 illustrates the implications of my theory and highlights how it differs from existing explanations.

In the upper-right corner are councilors who succeed in turning out voters in elections but not in stimulating rally turnout. The literature predicts that councilors who turn out as many or even more voters in elections than in the past will be rewarded. In contrast, I hypothesize that the difference between low turnout at rallies and high turnout at elections enables mayors to label councilors as unreliable and punish them accordingly. In the lower-left corner are councilors who only succeed in turning out voters at rallies. Again, the literature assumes that these councilors

Table 4.1. *Hypotheses and Expected Findings*

		Voter turnout at rallies		
		Above expectations	Expected	Below expectations
Voter turnout at elections	Expected	Reward	Reward	**Punish**
	Below expectations	**Reward**	**Reward**	Punish

Note: Bold type represents cases for which the author's expectations differ from those in the literature.

will be punished given their failure to sustain or boost the party's vote share. By contrast, I hypothesize that mayors will reward councilors who are clearly identified as reliable and who turn out the expected number of voters at rallies.

Methods

To test the effects of voter turnout in candidates' careers, I trace the political trajectories of party candidates. To measure whether voter turnout at rallies and elections matches party mayors' expectations, I conducted in-depth and semi-structured interviews with party leaders in the selected municipalities after the national election of October 2005. To test the effects of voter turnout on candidates' political careers, I traced their political trajectories after the election of 2005.

By combining information from printed party ballots at the municipal, provincial, and national level with electoral data from the Ministry of the Interior, the Electoral Provincial Judiciary, and the Electoral Municipal Judiciary, I was able to establish whether candidates ran in the next election, which office they ran for, their position on the ballot, and if they were elected or reelected. Still, factual information did not provide sufficient insights about the decision-making rationale of candidates and party mayors at the time of establishing the party ballot.

To understand how party leaders evaluate their agents, I conducted in-depth interviews with the mayors of Río Cuarto, Villa María, Colonia Caroya, José C. Paz, and Bahía Blanca, as well as with party leaders of the opposition parties in each selected case. During these interviews, I asked mayors if candidates had met their expectations in turning out voters during the 2005 election.[1] When I was unable to interview party mayors, I conducted semi-structured interviews with main advisors and/or private secretaries to gather information about mayors' assessments of candidates' electoral performances. Descriptive statistics provide information about general patterns that, when combined with qualitative information, establish plausibility for the hypotheses proposed in this chapter. In 2005, half of the candidates in Buenos Aires were running to get elected or reelected because the city council in the province is renewed by halves every two years. Candidates in Córdoba, by contrast, were competing to show their ability to turn out voters for the party so that they might be considered for reelection in the upcoming election of 2009. In contrast to Buenos Aires, voters in Córdoba elect their mayors and councilors together every four years.[2]

Voter Turnout at Rallies

In using voter turnout at rallies to test a councilor's reliability, mayors encourage candidates to turn out as many voters as possible and make every mobilized voter visible to the party mayor. Incentives to maximize voter participation induce candidates to buy turnout by distributing clientelistic inducements to individuals and groups of voters. The following vivid description of rally participants illustrates how candidates buy the support of individual voters with boxes of food and the support of gangs with free cocaine and alcohol:

> The majority were very young people, teens [*pibes*] of sixteen, seventeen, or eighteen years old. They didn't seem to be party activists. To tell you the truth, they look like a terrible mafia [*tenían una pinta de mafia terrible*]. The atmosphere was strange, very crazy. I saw people sitting in the grass with infant babies surrounded by gang members [*los clásicos grupos de la esquina del barrio*]: black t-shirt, or shirtless and a lot of tattoos. There were people with guns [*calzados*]. They were on the floor [*tumbados*] for the alcohol and out of control for the coke [*merca*] and next to them was a family that I believe was there for the box of food.[3]

While waiting for a rally to begin in San Miguel, I met a group of young voters drinking and smoking marijuana. Asking them why they were there, one of them said: "We come here to get drunk [*a escaviar*]."[4] Describing a rally from the voter's point of view, Auyero quotes the testimony of a voter referring to Matilde, a party broker: "She calls people whenever there is a rally; she uses those guys, who are idling around . . . she uses them for the rallies . . ., and, when the day is over, she gives them a packet of food or a joint" (2000: 6).

In Argentina, studies have shown the role unions play in mobilizing voters to attend political events such as rallies (e.g., Collier and Collier 1991; Levitsky 2003). More novel and less studied is the support provided by evangelist groups (Semán 2004). The Catholic Church has a policy of not explicitly endorsing political candidates, but evangelical churches do not have such a constraint and negotiate accordingly with politicians who secure for them more benefits (Gutiérrez 2000). Indeed, this was the case of the successful Party in Communion (*Partido en Comunión*) in José C. Paz which had two councilors elected in 1999.

Soccer hooligans (*barras bravas*) are also employed by all parties to organize the security and entertainment (mostly to play the drums) and to provide attendance for party rallies (Alabarces and Rodríguez 1996; Veiga 1998; Grabia 2009). In an interview, a famous hooligan leader declared that the most important party leaders frequently came to buy his support: "Everyone [politicians] comes to ask us favors ... Do you want me to give you a list with all the politicians that gave us tons of money to play drums and bring soccer fans to their rallies?"[5]

Argentine hooligans became so skillful at mobilizing people that they began selling their tactics to soccer clubs elsewhere in Latin America. In a report published by *Olé*, an Argentine daily newspaper devoted to soccer, Rafael Di Zeo, former leader of Boca Juniors' (one of the most important Argentine soccer teams) hooligans, said that groups such as his are considered "the Harvard" of hooligans worldwide.[6]

These testimonies highlight the paradoxical effects of the incentives mayors produce to determine their agents' reliability. In using turnout to establish reliability, mayors induce councilors to mobilize any voter, regardless of his or her partisan preferences, and spend scarce resources in hiring the support of groups such as the hooligans. Councilors interested in getting reelected are thus induced to buy turnout.

Councilors who invest in buying turnout also seek to make their investment visible and will distribute free T-shirts and hats for participants to wear at rallies. Councilors also make strategic use of space, concentrating the voters they have mobilized together near banners that allow mayors to easily count them. The fact that every party symbol contributes to the visibility of a councilor's party network supports my contention that rallies serve to signal to mayors a councilor's ability to turn out voters, and to enable mayors to count votes.

At the time of evaluating candidates' performances, party mayors, regardless of location or partisanship, highlight the same factors. Using the words of the former mayor of Colonia Caroya: "[A]t rallies, I expect a certain number of voters based on how competitive the election is, how well (or not) the economy is doing, how good the leading candidate is, and how many goods I gave the candidate."[7] Thus, expectations vary based on a combination of political, economic, and social circumstances at the national and local levels and with the amount of goods individual party candidates receive to distribute to voters before the election.

In conducting fieldwork before the elections in José C. Paz and San Miguel and a couple of months after them for the remaining cases, I was able to listen to party mayors' recent memories of their evaluations of candidates' performances at both rallies and elections. While it is plausible that some mayors adjusted their evaluations to the electoral results, the time they took to consider their responses and the testimony I gathered from other key informants and party candidates makes me confident regarding the accuracy of their evaluations.

During the Argentine national election of 2009, I spent two weeks carrying out interviews with candidates in San Luis, a center-west province of more than 447,000 inhabitants that has been governed by the brothers Adolfo and Alberto Rodríguez Saá since the return of democracy in 1983. Throughout my stay in the municipalities of Villa Mercedes and San Luis Capital, I observed numerous daily political events, almost too many for any one person to attend. This is yet another indicator of Peronists' incessant and intense campaigning to diffuse their image of invincibility. However, the story behind these high levels of mobilization in San Luis is more complex.

Invited to a rally by Nélida Perez, a party candidate who lives and works in a neighborhood built by the government in Villa Mercedes, I asked her why the governor would spend time campaigning in a neighborhood he knew he would carry. Why not visit a swing neighborhood where his presence could contribute to changing voters' minds? On our way to the rally, Nélida explained to me that the governor was not concerned about getting votes but with monitoring candidates' reliability: "Here everyone votes for the Rodríguez Saá. Alberto [Rodríguez Saá] knows this. He is not here to get the votes but to monitor us. They use rallies to see who is working in the neighborhoods, who is solving people's problems."[8]

Candidates can either meet or fail to meet the party mayors' expectations with regard to mobilizing voter turnout at party rallies. Candidates can also exceed expectations by mobilizing more voters than expected. As Table 4.2 illustrates, the number of agents in the sample who mobilized

Table 4.2. *Party Mayors' Evaluations of Candidates' Abilities to Turn Out Voters at Rallies*

		Voter turnout at rallies	
		Number of candidates	Percentage
Did the candidate turn out the expected number of voters at party rallies?	Yes (*Above* expectations)	13	9.49
	Yes (Expected)	53	38.69
	No (*Below* expectations)	71	51.82
	Total	137	100

more voters than expected is less than 10 percent. More than a third of the candidates (38.69 percent) managed to mobilize as many voters as expected, while the majority (51.82 percent) failed to meet the mayors' expectations.

Voter Turnout at Elections

The fact that voting is compulsory in Argentina means that party mayors are unable to determine if voters turn out because they are mobilized, because they have strong partisan preferences, or some combination of both. Whereas mayors and councilors can monitor voter turnout, they are still unable to monitor voter choice. Studies in political science (e.g., Stokes 2005; Diaz-Cayeros et al. 2007; Nichter 2008, Cox 2010; Stokes et al. 2013; Gans-Morse et al. 2014) are combining formal models and empirical evidence to test what type of voters a political party under budgetary constraints will target with clientelistic inducements.[9]

Voters are defined as (a) core supporters when they will vote for the party regardless of receiving material rewards in exchange for their vote, (b) swing voters when they will only vote for the party if they receive a material reward, and (c) opposition voters when they will never support the party regardless of whether they receive clientelistic inducements. Building on the classic studies of Cox and McCubbins (1986) and Dixit and Londregan (1996), current works focus on how clientelistic parties combine multiple strategies of mobilization to win votes (see, e.g., Cox 2010; Stokes et al. 2013; Gans-Morse et al. 2014). Here, however, I focus on the relationship between mayors and candidates and proceed from the assumption that candidates target either core or swing voters and combine strategies of mobilization to turn out voters. Asymmetries of information are the result of party mayors' ignorance about the type of voters who live in candidates' neighborhoods.

In evaluating the ability of a party candidate to mobilize voters on election day, mayors take into account how many voters the agent mobilized in the past adjusted by the popularity of the party's nominee, the economic situation, and certain contextual events such as media scandals that can affect the popularity of a party or candidate before an election. In contrast to rallies, where candidates sometimes surpass mayors' expectations, in elections candidates either succeed or fail in obtaining the expected electoral outcome. Table 4.3 provides descriptive statistics for party mayors' evaluations, showing that, as was the case with party rallies, the majority of party candidates (62.77 percent) fail to fulfill the mayors' expectations. More than a third of councilors (37.23 percent) succeed in turning out as many voters as expected in their neighborhoods.

Table 4.3. *Party Mayors' Evaluations of Candidates' Abilities to Turn Out Voters at Elections*

		Voter turnout at elections	
		Number of candidates	Percentage
Did the candidate turn out the expected number of voters and votes in the neighborhood he or she represents?	Yes	51	37.23
	No	86	62.77
	Total	137	100

Causality and Measurement

In Argentina, mayors distribute rewards to reliable candidates and punishments to unreliable ones by assigning candidates' positions on the party's closed ballot. As a result, we expect to observe that candidates who succeed in turning out voters are rewarded with higher-ranked positions, while those who fail are punished with lower-ranked positions. Positions on the party ticket provide information about the mayor's assessment of candidates' reliability; by tracing changes in a candidate's position on the ticket, we can measure his or her reliability for the party mayor.

The distribution of electable positions that are high in demand and scarce in supply inevitably leads to conflicts between candidates and the mayor. In interviews I conducted in Buenos Aires and Córdoba, I constantly heard former and current councilors complaining about the positions they had been assigned on the ballots after their hard work in legislating for the mayor because of their failure to build a political base and display it at the rallies. Those in charge of creating the party ballot were also acutely aware of the consequences of their decisions, as the mayor of Río Cuarto explained to me when talking about councilors' responses to their positions on the ticket:

> One has to distribute positions based on the number of votes each candidate can give to the party. I understand that this upsets councilors who work hard, but are unable to mobilize voters; however, in the end, we all want to win the election, and you win elections with votes, not with good intentions.[10]

In comparing candidates' positions, I established the cutoff points in the previous elections in which the candidate got elected in 2003 (all candidates in Córdoba and half the candidates in Buenos Aires) and in 2005 and compared that with the position they were assigned in 2007 (all candidates in Córdoba and half the candidates in Buenos Aires) and 2009 (candidates elected in 2005 in Buenos Aires). Based on this information, I established whether a candidate received a better, equal, or worse position in the following election by comparing information from printed party ballots at the municipal, provincial, and national level.

Another indicator I used was reelection. In contrast to ballot position, where the outcome depends only on party mayors' evaluations, the possibility that reliable candidates will get reelected varies based on a combination of factors that are not under the party mayors' control, such as the charisma of the opposition party nominee, the economic situation, the performance of other parties, the social context, and so on. Thus, a candidate can succeed in getting reelected with a small turnout or lose with a high turnout depending on the turnout of the opposition and other factors. Still, reelection serves to provide another, admittedly imperfect, metric for the effects of reliability on a candidate's political career.

Results: Voter Turnout and Reliability

To test the argument advanced in this chapter, I recorded the performance of party candidates at rallies and in the 2005 election and observed whether the party mayor either punished or rewarded party candidates in the upcoming election. Table 4.4 shows how many candidates ran in the following election given their abilities to turn out voters at rallies and in the 2005 election. Of the sixty-three candidates who ran in the following

Table 4.4. *Party Candidates' Positions on the Party Ticket and Reelection Based on Voter Turnout at Rallies and Elections*

		Voter turnout at rallies		
		Above expectations	Expected	Below expectations
Voter turnout at elections	Expected	N = 5 *Positions:* 5 better positions *All reelected*	N = 25 *Positions:* 10 did not run 1 worse position 10 same positions 4 better positions *13 reelected*	N = 21 *Positions:* 13 did not run 5 worse positions 3 same positions *None reelected*
	Below	N = 8 *Positions:* 2 did not run 1 same position 5 better positions *6 reelected*	N = 28 *Positions:* 17 did not run 11 same positions *7 reelected*	N = 50 *Positions:* 32 did not run 14 worse positions 4 same positions *None reelected*

election, fourteen ran in higher positions than those they held in the past election, twenty-nine ran in similar positions as those in the past, and twenty ran in worse positions. Only thirty-one candidates succeeded in getting reelected.

The results support this chapter's thesis that party mayors compare information from voter turnout at rallies and elections to infer a candidate's reliability and distribute rewards and punishments accordingly. For instance, all candidates who turned out more voters than expected at rallies were reelected regardless of whether or not they fulfilled the mayors' expectations on voter turnout at the election. It is important to note that five candidates were even rewarded with higher positions in spite of failing to generate voter turnout at the election. On the other hand, candidates who failed to turn out voters at rallies were not reelected, and only three of them ran in similar positions. In tracing these cases, I found that these candidates were local celebrities – two athletes and one actress – and were likely to be reelected regardless of their inability to mobilize voters to participate in rallies. The case of Héctor "Pichi" Campana, a famous basketball player who was able to get elected as councilor and vice governor of the Argentine province of Córdoba, having neither political experience nor a territorial base of supporters, illustrates this point. Councilors who do not enjoy the same name recognition as celebrity candidates understand that actresses and athletes belong to a different category and are thus not evaluated by turning out voters at rallies.

Quantitative data enables me to demonstrate the relationship between and effects of voter turnout at rallies and elections in a candidate's political career. In addition, I trace candidates' trajectories across the selected municipalities to explain the causes of the observed outcomes. I found that party candidates get promoted only after proving to the party mayor that they are reliable agents. Once reliable agents succeed in getting elected, they have access to material and nonmaterial resources that enable them to gain more followers. Yet, candidates have to systematically demonstrate their reliability to continue having access to this flow of resources. To illustrate the importance of continuously proving a candidate's reliability, I compare the political careers of two candidates who represent similar neighborhoods in José C. Paz.

Matilde and Alicia began their political careers as community organizers in their neighborhoods.[11] They were both Peronist Party activists in charge of a welfare program targeted at pregnant women and infants. Based on their community work and their daily interaction with voters when delivering the welfare program goods, Matilde and Alicia succeeded in building a party network that they mobilized for rallies and elections.

After observing the ability of these women to turn out voters, the party mayor decided to give them a similar amount of party goods to sustain and build a larger party network. For more than three years, Matilde and Alicia showed similar turnout numbers at rallies and elections, and both were selected to participate on the party ticket in consecutive positions. Although neither of them was elected the first time they competed, both continued distributing goods and solving problems through a network of contacts in the municipality. After participating in four elections, both were elected as councilwomen in 1999.

After the election, Matilde and Alicia had more access to party goods and contacts that enabled them to solve more voter problems. Both candidates distributed goods and favors to voters in exchange for their participation. But whereas Alicia chose to concentrate her efforts in solving the problems of her community, Matilde chose to build an alliance with a union representative in José C. Paz. The union leader had a known reputation as a mafia mayor and was accused of drug trafficking on several occasions, though none of the accusations could be proved.

At the time of the rallies, the union mobilized voters from the poorest and most dangerous neighborhoods in the municipality to support Matilde's candidacy. Most of the voters who held Matilde's signs at party rallies had no idea who Matilde was, or even which party she represented, as a series of articles written by local journalist Fabián Domínguez in *La Hoja* demonstrated.[12]

Matilde's followers at rallies and elections easily doubled those of Alicia. When, after four years in office, the mayor assembled the party ballot, Matilde received a much higher-ranked position than Alicia. After the election, Matilde and Alicia remained politically active, but Alicia received fewer goods than Matilde, making it harder for her to sustain her party network. Slowly, Alicia's not-so-loyal followers began to participate in rallies and elections with an emerging Peronist activist who ran a soup kitchen and supervised another welfare program. By the time I left José C. Paz, Alicia was still interested in a political career, but she was aware of not having enough followers to make it to the party nomination. Matilde, in contrast, was a reelected councilor with a party network three times larger than the one she had when she began her political career.

The political careers of Matilde and Alicia illustrate a pattern I observed across municipalities: candidates have to continuously demonstrate their reliability to get promoted. In this case, if Alicia had followed Matilde's path by building alliances with organized groups to mobilize more voters to rallies and elections, she would have also been rewarded. Matilde's union connection provided her candidacy with more resources than she would have otherwise had as a councilor. By using these resources to mobilize voters for rallies and elections, Matilde showed the mayor her ability to build effective and reliable alliances that provided the party with electoral support. Reliability is, therefore, a necessary and in some cases sufficient condition to succeed in a political career and is not related to the quality of political participation, but simply to the quantity of voters who turn out at rallies and elections.

By measuring a candidate's reliability in every election, the party mayor succeeds in selecting and rewarding candidates who contribute the most votes to the party. In understanding political parties as organizations that seek to maximize votes, this chapter focuses on the strategies party leaders employ to achieve this goal. In promoting candidates based only on their ability to turn out voters, party leaders implicitly foster the use of clientelistic strategies of political mobilization.

Conclusion

Party mayors make comparisons between a candidate's performance at rallies and elections over time to identify reliable party agents and distribute rewards and punishments accordingly. In studying the mechanisms party mayors employ to monitor candidates, this chapter highlighted the importance of incorporating candidates' agency to understand how party mayors solve the principal-agent problem.

Reliable agents are important for party leaders to secure the distribution of scarce party goods to voters. Using reliable candidates, however, does not guarantee winning elections. Even when every mobilized voter does not change his or her vote inside the voting booth, mobilized voters alone do not define electoral outcomes. Although reliable candidates may not be able to secure electoral victories, they nevertheless provide parties with a solid base of votes that could turn out to be key in defining highly contested elections. Moreover, in addition to mobilizing voters, reliable candidates provide party leaders with several needed services such as organized squadrons of party activists who paint walls with the name of the party nominees, display the party's signs, distribute party literature, and provide security at rallies.

Political parties need these services in order to conduct campaigns and get votes. In cases where sustaining networks of party candidates who are likely to charge commissions for delivering goods and mobilizing voters become more expensive than engaging in programmatic politics, political leaders will consider abandoning spending to sustain candidates and monitoring structures. Moreover, it is not unlikely that the impossibility of perfectly distinguishing between reliable and unreliable candidates could eventually lead party mayors to look for alternative strategies that do not require intermediaries.

While programmatic politics has always been the only possibility for campaigning and gaining votes for parties that lack access to particularistic inducements and networks of party activists and candidates, it can also become an option for incumbent parties that seek to get rid of unreliable candidates. A research agenda that seeks to explain transitions from clientelistic to programmatic politics will benefit from incorporating the strategies and incentives party candidates and mayors use to mobilize voters.

This chapter focused on the strategies party leaders employ to determine the reliability of their candidates by monitoring their ability to turn out voters at rallies and elections. When voter turnout decreases together with mayors' abilities to monitor candidates, party leaders might consider alternative strategies to mobilize voters. The transition away from clientelistic strategies is a response to mayors' inability to monitor candidates' reliability. If candidates continue turning out voters, party mayors have no incentive to change strategies. On the other hand, if candidates fail to turn out voters and mayors are unable to monitor candidates' distribution of party goods, mayors are likely to consider abandoning clientelistic politics.

Instead of spending scarce party resources on sustaining a network of candidates who fail to turn out the expected number of votes, mayors will invest in media campaigns that contribute to the spread of the party message. But for the transition to be effective and permanent, mayors will have to find that programmatic politics deliver similar or greater returns than clientelistic politics.

5

The Logic of Perverse Incentives

The logic of perverse incentives in which political leaders promote candidates based solely on the number of voters they mobilize leads to the emergence and consolidation of *mercenary candidates*. Like other candidates already discussed in the preceding chapters, mercenary candidates are rewarded based on the number of voters they mobilize, but mercenaries are concerned *only* with getting material rewards in exchange for their political work rather than with any other consequences of their actions. As a result, mercenaries will distribute small goods, welfare benefits, public jobs, and even money, alcohol, and drugs to voters in exchange for political participation.

The emergence of mercenary candidates induces other candidates who are capable of using clientelism to employ that strategy; they know that poor voters will follow whoever provides them with benefits. Thus, office-seeking party activists who cannot afford to lose followers are perversely encouraged to use clientelism. I refer to the logic of perverse incentives as having unintended consequences because mercenary candidates can pose several unexpected challenges to party leaders. For example, mercenary candidates can prefer to use their capacity to mobilize political support for the opposition or for themselves, thus challenging the authority of party leaders in their territories. In addition, the consolidation of mercenary candidates helps to explain current crises of political legitimacy and representation that have considerably handicapped governments' capacity to effectively administer public policies. In short, the consolidation of mercenary candidates illustrates the effects of the logic of perverse incentives in Argentina.

Choosing Clientelism

The first time a party candidate makes the decision to use clientelism, he or she is making a choice that will define the candidate's political future.

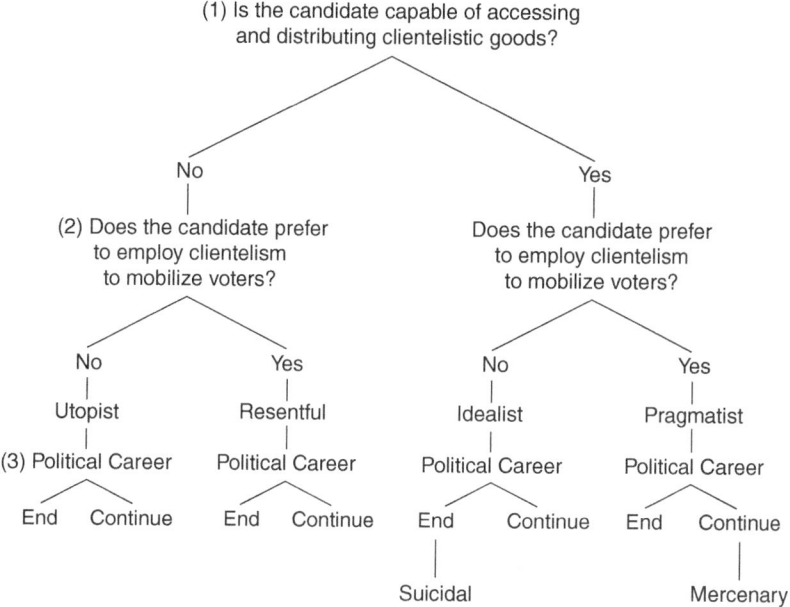

Figure 5.1. Candidates' decision making

I propose a sequential theory of strategic decision making in which candidates' decisions about whether or not to use clientelism to mobilize poor voters affect the possibilities available to them. I examine the situation from the candidate's point of view that first time he or she has to choose how to mobilize poor voters to participate at rallies and elections. Candidates are divided between those who have the capacity to use clientelism and those who do not. Candidates' capacities vary based on their positions in partisan networks that provide them with access to material and nonmaterial goods and to party activists who are capable of distributing goods to voters and monitoring their participation at rallies and elections. Figure 5.1 illustrates candidates' political trajectories based on their ability or inability to access and distribute clientelistic goods.

The left side of the decision tree belongs to opposition candidates who are deeply familiar with the limitations of not having access to resources and their effects on their ability to turn out voters. Even if voters are interested in their proposals and would prefer to support them, voters may not be able to express their true preferences because they need to secure the flow of benefits. As this candidate explained:

> I'm very familiar with voters because I go to them; I talk to them; I walk with them. But I don't have a reliable party network

because I don't have money [*la caja*] to mobilize them. Voters listen to you, they're interested in what you have to say, but unfortunately, they aren't interested in participating in politics. They prefer to go to work, to spend time with their families; and unfortunately those who are in politics are in it to make money, so if you don't have money, they are not with you. They are with those who have money.[1]

Candidates talk openly about the relationship between money and politics. Indeed, most politicians working in poor neighborhoods are aware of – and some of them actively participate in – the distribution of money, whether directly through small amounts of cash or indirectly through social welfare programs and employment at city hall, in exchange for political participation.

The theory advanced in this chapter examines my finding that candidates unable to use clientelism are incapable of building a party network, not because voters do not trust or believe in them, but because voters need solutions to their problems. Hence, candidates who are unable to solve problems are also unable to build a party network; as a result, they fail to mobilize voters and advance their political careers. *Resentful* candidates prefer to use clientelism but are unable to do so simply because they do not have the capacity; *utopist* candidates, however, would not use clientelistic strategies even if they had the opportunity.

In contrast, candidates on the right side of the decision tree are capable of using clientelism and are more likely to build a party network and succeed in mobilizing voters. Not all candidates who are capable of using clientelism to mobilize voters will choose to do so. Among candidates who are capable of using clientelism, I distinguish between *idealist* candidates – those who prefer not to use clientelism – and *pragmatist* candidates – those who turn to these strategies to mobilize voters.

> You see ... he [referring to another candidate] doesn't have paid party activists [*punteros*]. He has friends who know other friends to whom he can say: "*Che*, there will be a rally this week, why don't we go with Juan [the name of the candidate]?" On the other hand, if I hired *punteros*, I just take out my wallet and say: "Here, I'll give you 100 pesos [10 dollars] and I want you to bring me a bus full of people." And then what happens? With 500 pesos [50 dollars], I secure six or seven buses ... you buy alcohol and drugs [*frula*], and people turn out.[2]

This testimony from a party candidate in José C. Paz illustrates the difference between the pragmatist and idealist candidates described in Figure 5.1. Whereas both types of candidates are capable of distributing goods in exchange for political participation, only pragmatist candidates turn to these strategies. In this case, the candidate uses money, alcohol, and even drugs to buy voters' participation at a party rally. Idealist candidates, however, seek to persuade voters to participate through their daily work in the neighborhood and by pursuing the party's program. Still, they recognize that it is impossible to mobilize voters without distributing goods:

> I went to the neighborhoods of really poor people, people who have worked with me in politics before, people who knew me and respected me, and nevertheless, one of the guys [*muchachos*] whom I had helped in the past asked me for 200 pesos [20 dollars] because he wanted to buy some construction materials [*chapas*] for his house. "It's not that we ask you just because you want us to vote for you. It's okay if you can't give us the money, but you know … we are in need." Today you can't turn out 20 people unless you buy them.[3]

I collected several testimonies like this one from a party councilor in San Miguel that show how the grassroots work of one candidate can be easily ignored if another candidate simply distributes money to voters. Thus, getting to know voters personally and helping them is not as effective as simply giving them money:

> Our *agrupación* characterizes itself by hard work in very difficult places without many resources. We are always on the side of the people. But now what has happened? In the moment of truth, they've turned on us for cash: people to whom I had come to help at eleven at night, people for whom I had gone to the middle of nowhere to drive a baby girl to a hospital. I could speak of a thousand things: building a house for a family in a settlement … and collecting cash [*la guita*] by selling empanadas. … I have done everything you can think of. So if you ask me today, strictly from a point of view of efficacy, what do you need to mobilize people? You need to have money. Money is the only thing that you need to win elections and be effective in politics.[4]

Finally, the sequence shown in Figure 5.1 examines the effects of candidates' decisions on their political careers. Focusing on candidates who have the capacity to use clientelism (the right side of the decision tree), it is clear that differences in candidates' preferences have significant consequences with regard to their political careers. While preferring not to use clientelism leads to political suicide, turning to and utilizing these strategies transforms pragmatist candidates into mercenaries. Mercenaries mobilize voters only by using clientelism and are capable and willing to use money, small goods, alcohol, and drugs to do so. Suicidal and mercenary candidates are the unintended consequences of the logic of perverse incentives. Even when party leaders do not seek to reward mercenary candidates, the logic by which they distribute rewards and punishments leads to this unintended outcome.

The systematic promotion of pragmatic candidates and the defeat of idealist, utopist, and resentful candidates teaches activists interested in a political career that in order to succeed, they need to be capable and willing to use clientelistic strategies of mobilization. The logic of perverse incentives is built on three necessary conditions: (1) a system of rewards and punishments that is blind to the strategies candidates use to mobilize voters, (2) the dynamics of intra- and interparty competition, and (3) the absence of informal and formal punishment from party leaders and the courts.

First, by distributing career promotions based only on the number of voters candidates mobilize regardless of the strategies they employ, party leaders encourage candidates competing for the support of poor voters to use clientelism. Second, candidates are always competing with other candidates from their own party (intraparty competition) and from opposition parties (interparty competition) to mobilize voters; hence, the candidates who are capable and willing to use clientelism are more likely to succeed in solving voter problems than the candidates who are either unable or unwilling to exchange benefits for political support. Third, if formal and/ or informal institutions effectively punished the use of these strategies, we would not observe as many candidates employing them. Yet, neither party leaders nor the courts prosecute the use of clientelism, allowing pragmatic candidates to continue using these strategies.

The causal argument advanced here maintains that the result of the logic of perverse incentives explains the emergence and consolidation of mercenary candidates. Signaling to party candidates that their value hinges only on their capacity to mobilize voters empowers mercenary candidates vis-à-vis candidates who reject the use of clientelism and explains why voters expect goods in exchange for their political participation. The unexpected consequence of the logic of perverse incentives is the consolidation of mercenary candidates who end up building their own armies of poor voters to trade them to whoever provides more resources for themselves and their followers. Voters are held perversely accountable to mercenary candidates, who are able to negotiate with politicians for rewards and benefits as long as they are capable of mobilizing a large network of party voters.

Measuring the Logic of Perverse Incentives

To test the theory advanced in this chapter, I combine quantitative and qualitative data gathered more than twenty-four months of fieldwork in

Argentina. First, I describe and analyze the strategies party candidates use to mobilize voters to participate at party rallies. Studying political participation at rallies enables me to observe and compare different strategies that party candidates employ to turn out poor voters. Building on in-depth interviews with party leaders, candidates, and voters, as well as direct observation and archival information, I examine some of the consequences of the logic of perverse incentives.

Then I trace the political decisions of party leaders and candidates during and after the national election of 2005 in the municipalities studied in this book. Focusing on the political decisions of 137 councilors provides suggestive findings about the logic of perverse incentives and its unintended consequences. Finally, I complement these quantitative findings by tracing and studying the political decisions of 144 candidates more than fourteen years in one municipality. To establish the mechanisms through which perverse incentives shape candidates' individual choices, I provide an account of candidates' decision making by examining the political careers of every candidate elected in one municipality, José C. Paz, from its creation in 1995 until 2007.

By studying a single case, I can use thorough and contextualized ethnographic data to represent the whole universe of cases. Despite the questionable use of a single case to test a general theory (King 1994), José C. Paz is a municipality that reproduces the relevant causal features of the general domain of urban municipalities in the developing world; thus, it fulfills the requirement of representativeness while providing variation along the dimensions of theoretical interest (Gerring 2007: 88). This research strategy echoes a broader trend of empirical work that relies on micro-level data to develop new theories and enhance our empirical knowledge (e.g., Wantchekon 2003; Wilkinson 2004; Posner 2005; Kalyvas 2006).

Visibility, Party Rallies, and Perverse Incentives

The outcome of the system of perverse incentives is visible at party rallies where candidates threaten voters who are receiving benefits to ensure their participation; advise voters who are seeking benefits to show their commitment; and distribute small goods such as cleaning products, food, alcohol, and drugs to every voter in exchange for participation:

> Do you know why everyone comes here? People come because they are getting paid [*porque les garpan*]. People are here for the *chupi* [alcohol]. Most of us are here for the *escabio* [alcohol].
>
> I'm here for the plan [social welfare program]. You have to come to all the rallies. You have to attend the rally because if you don't, they will come and take away the plan from you.[5]

On Argentine television, there are a constant stream of images of voters being bussed to rallies and interviews with participants in which they systematically express having no idea what the rally is for, and that they are participating to continue receiving social welfare programs as the testimonies just quoted (and also videotaped) illustrate.

The combination of goods that party candidates distribute in exchange for attendance and the groups they hire to mobilize voters explain the heterogeneity of the audience at these events, where drunk and high young adults stand near young mothers and senior citizens.[6]

Being evaluated only by the number of turned-out voters motivates candidates to lump together a mother who attends to preserve a social program and a drug addict who attends to get high for free. I observed this mixture in rally attendants during my fieldwork across Argentine municipalities and found support for my impressions in ethnographies (Auyero 2000; Frederic 2004) and works of investigative journalism (Otero 1997; Vaca Narvaja 2001; Carreras 2004).

Candidates recognize the existence of perverse incentives that motivate them to do whatever they can to mobilize voters. In asking the president of San Miguel's city council how they get voters to turn out in primary elections, he smilingly responded: "We do whatever we can to mobilize voters. And I mean whatever."[7] Fabián Domínguez, a local journalist who has covered every political event in the municipality, shared with me how common these responses were:

> When candidates begin talking, they put you in a very awkward situation; and if it is off the record [it] is even worse, and if they trust you, you just want them to stop talking because it is scandalous. It is at that moment when you ask them to stop talking that it stops being about politics and becomes sheer delinquency.[8]

As indicated in Chapter 3 in the discussion of partisan networks, candidates who are involved in illegal activities such as gambling, prostitution, and drug trafficking may employ the resources obtained through these activities in political mobilizations. Perverse incentives motivate candidates to accept resources and favors from illegal activities to increase the possibility of being elected or reelected. Yet, candidates continuously point out that there are unwritten rules (*códigos*) about which strategies are considered acceptable. For example, although it is acceptable to offer voters food and merchandise in exchange for turning out at party rallies, marijuana and alcohol are considered to be unacceptable gifts: "I am against getting the vote of someone who is drunk and high all day. I am against turning out those voters because they enable any wretch [*infeliz*] to win."[9] This was the response from the city council president of José C. Paz when I was talking with several candidates about the strategies of mobilization they used to turn out voters at rallies. Interestingly, the majority of candidates who use clientelism talk about how they distribute social programs, food, and small goods to mobilize voters, but they also quickly differentiate themselves from those who use alcohol and drugs and in some cases cash to buy voter turnout. They refer to these candidates as mercenaries because they work for whoever gives them money.

The emergence and consolidation of mercenary candidates who use clientelism to mobilize voters constitute a relatively new phenomenon. Voters who attended political rallies during the first and second Peronist governments (1946–1952 and 1952–1955) and during the return of democracy in 1983 were not given particularistic goods to participate. Although union leaders and territorial party brokers used to provide free transportation, meals, and small goods to poor voters who participated at rallies, it is safe to argue that voters were not there just to get a free meal. That is not the case anymore. At present, it is hard for any politician, regardless of his or her party, to mobilize voters without distributing something in exchange for turnout. Young people who in the past were politically involved and motivated to the extent of risking their lives to change social reality (Ollier 1998) now prefer to attend a rock or *cumbia* concert instead of turning out at political rallies (Svampa 2000).

Another interesting, if contested, expression of the logic of perverse incentives is the use of controversial groups and organizations in political mobilizations. For instance, several party candidates employ soccer hooligans, not just as additional attendees at rallies but also as security and entertainment, mostly to play drums (Alabarces and Rodríguez 1996; Veiga 1998; Grabia 2009).

Party leaders are well aware of the logic of perverse incentives that encourages candidates to mobilize any voter who will turn out in exchange for benefits. Here is the assessment of one elected councilman:

> At a rally, you can easily distinguish the voters who are there because they agree with the politician who's going to be on stage, from the voters who couldn't tell you why they go if you asked them. The politician notices immediately the types of people, but if he wants votes, he doesn't care. That is the big problem.[10]

This testimony points to the complicity of party leaders as well as their reasons for continuing to rely on perverse incentives. Party leaders assume that voter turnout at rallies will translate into voter turnout at the polls; thus, they are agnostic about the strategies candidates employ to mobilize them. Chapter 4 showed that candidates who succeed in turning out voters at rallies but fail in turning out voters at elections are identified as unreliable party agents and punished. Hence, only candidates who succeed in turning out voters at rallies and elections are rewarded with political promotions.

Three reasons explain why party leaders do not mind the mobilization of voters who have no interest in politics. First, crowded rallies send a signal to the opposition about the strength of the incumbent, making the organization of the opposition more difficult. Second, the same display of muscle gives those who might be thinking about leaving the incumbent clientelistic party to start a new party reason to reconsider their exit strategy. Third, the fact that party candidates can pay voters for turning out and even use resources from the municipality without punishment shows not only the connections between political and partisan networks – the use of public resources for political purposes – but also, and more important, the existence of judicial impunity as no one has ever been charged for using public money to finance political mobilizations.

Comparative Evidence: Perverse Incentives and Visibility at Party Rallies

Assuming that candidates' capacities to use clientelistic strategies of mobilization vary based on their positions in partisan networks, I distinguish between candidates who were capable of using clientelism and those who were not. Capable candidates must meet two necessary conditions. First, they must be affiliated with a party that held one or more executive offices in 2005. Second, candidates must be affiliated with a party that has access to party networks capable of distributing goods to voters and monitoring their political behavior.

In Argentina, only the Peronist and Radical parties have had systematic access to public office and large networks of party activists capable of effectively trading favors for votes. More than 80 percent of the candidates (81.01 percent) who met the two necessary conditions had the capacity to use clientelistic strategies of mobilization. As shown in line 1 of Figure 5.2, only 26 candidates out of 137 were unable to use clientelism to mobilize voters.

After distinguishing candidates who are capable of using clientelism from those who are not, I focus on candidates' preferences to use clientelism. My criterion for measuring a candidate's preference is whether or not the candidate, or a designated party activist, took attendance of voter participation at rallies. Candidates who prefer to use clientelism will monitor voters' participation so as to avoid the risk that voters will follow the political advice of opposition candidates and "take the goods with one hand and vote with the other" (Szwarcberg 2004a: 4). To monitor voter participation at rallies, candidates simply screen voters by taking attendance. Among the 111 candidates capable of turning to clientelistic strategies, the division between those who prefer to use clientelism – pragmatist candidates – and

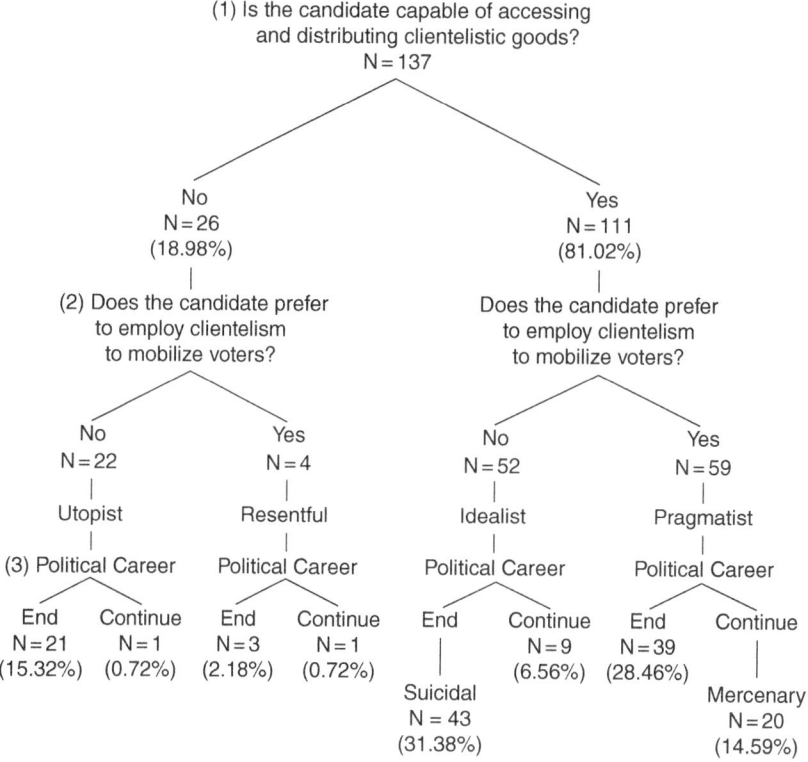

Figure 5.2. Results of candidates' decision making

those who reject the use of these strategies – idealist candidates – was almost even, as line 2 in Figure 5.2 illustrates.

By focusing on the extended political careers of elected candidates (line 3 in Figure 5.2), we find (a) that the number of reelected candidates is low, and (b) that pragmatist candidates are more than twice as likely as idealist candidates to get reelected. In contrast, only one resentful and one utopist candidate succeeded in getting reelected. These findings illustrate the two lessons candidates learn when mobilizing poor voters: first, regardless of the strategy they employ, the chances of getting reelected are low, and second, clientelistic strategies are more effective than non-clientelistic strategies.

Mobilizing Poor Voters in José C. Paz: Poverty, Unpaved Streets, and Peronism

"José C. Paz is a giant slum." This is how a Peronist councilor described the municipality.[11] In 2001, the Argentine National Institute of Statistics and Censuses found that almost half of the population was unemployed, and 63.2 percent of the residents did not have health insurance. More than half of the residents of José C. Paz had not finished high school, and less than 10 percent attended college.

The poverty of the district is visible to anyone visiting José C. Paz. The absence of public spaces and shops is striking. As soon as one moves away from the main square and meeting point in the municipality (which is the food court of a mega-supermarket similar to a U.S. Walmart), one finds unpaved streets and extremely poor housing conditions. There are between 6,000 and 7,000 unpaved streets "where politicians come to look for votes."[12]

My fieldwork observations, statistical data from censuses, surveys, and testimonies from social workers and politicians from different parties document the extent of structural poverty. José Mondovi, president of the city council, provided this description of the social situation of the municipality:

> There isn't anyone here who isn't aware that people in this district have to walk in mud up to their knees. And I'll tell you, it's inhuman to live like this. There are people who have to walk fifteen blocks without sidewalks or asphalt to take the bus. We are aware of all of this.[13]

Although everyone is aware of the extent of physical, economic, social, and cultural poverty of José C. Paz, no political changes have occurred in the municipality since its creation in 1995; until the present day, only Peronist mayors have governed the municipality.

Figure 5.3 describes the composition of the city council from the creation of the municipality until 2011. The distinction between the Peronist Party and the opposition presented in Figure 5.3 denotes the strength of the PJ in José C. Paz. Only in 1999, when the Peronists lost the presidency, was the opposition able to elect five out of twelve councilors. Still, on the whole, the pattern of evidence is consistent with the notion that the Conurbano is a stronghold of the Peronist Party.

Perverse Incentives, Visibility, and Party Rallies

José C. Paz gained national visibility when President Néstor Kirchner (2003–2007) chose it as the location from which he would launch his political campaign for the national elections of October 2005. It was the first time that a president had decided to host a rally in José C. Paz, and it attracted national media attention. José C. Paz's mayor, Mario Ishii, knew from political experience and survey data that the majority of voters in his municipality supported the candidacy of the president's wife for the senate seat for the province of Buenos Aires and were likely to attend the event.

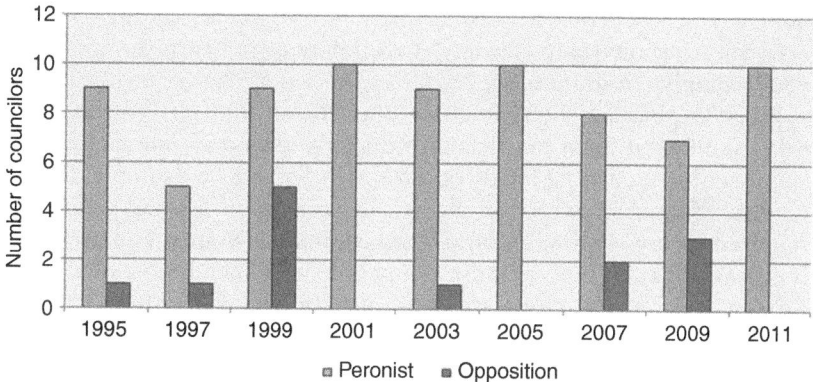

Figure 5.3. Party affiliation of elected councilors in José C. Paz

Note: Adding the Peronist and opposition candidates in each year yields the number of councilors elected in that year's election. The total number of councilors was twelve until 1999, when the city council expanded to twenty members. Councilors elected in the province of Buenos Aires have a term of four years with no limits on reelection. One-half of the city council is renewed every two years. Variation in the number of councilors elected each year is a result of José C. Paz's formation: in 1995, the city council had a total of twelve seats, two of which were not elected in 2005 but inherited from the old municipality of General Sarmiento, of which José C. Paz was a part. In 1997, six new candidates were elected. In 1999, the expansion to twenty members required the election of fourteen councilors that year. Since 2001, ten seats have been elected every two years.

Yet, he could not afford to run any risk. The stakes were too high to risk failing to display to the president the mayor's capacity to deliver votes.

The rally was an absolute success because it enabled Ishii to display the impressive size of his party network and also enabled President Kirchner to differentiate his government from previous administrations that had not done anything to alleviate the poverty of the poorest voters in the province of Buenos Aires. By visiting the poorest municipality in the province to distribute housing subsidies, the president signaled his commitment to show up and deliver goods to those who had been previously ignored.

During the political campaign, Cristina Fernández de Kirchner went to the municipality three times, thereby providing local politicians with several opportunities to demonstrate their political value. The local government required municipal workers to participate at the rally, and local businessmen were pressured to participate as well.[14] Raúl, the owner of a local *remisería* (taxi service), told me at a rally in José C. Paz in 2005 that he and "his boys [*los muchachos*]" had to attend rallies "to guarantee our job": "These people [local politicians in charge of organizing the rally] need you to show some courtesy. If you dare to not turn out, next day you're simply out of business."[15]

When explaining this system of punishment and retribution, Raúl told me that "if local politicians want to punish a businessman, they simply enforce existing local regulations." To give an example, in José C. Paz, *remiserías,* which in most cases consist of a small office, are required by law to have separate bathrooms for women and men. For businesses that employ at most five people who spend most of the day driving cars on the streets and who are almost entirely men, the law functions simply as an opportunity to collect bribes: "They know that you cannot afford a place with two bathrooms, and for whom? We can all use one bathroom." Still, Raúl knew that his *remisería* did not comply with the law and that he must return favors to avoid possible sanctions.

I heard of similar testimonies at rallies that took place in the municipality before Kirchner's arrival. When journalists asked a group of small business owners who were at a political rally in 1999 about the reason for their participation, one businessman responded:

> They [candidates] invited me and I can't say no. I came here so they could see me [*hacer acto de presencia*] because they are the ones who can choose to stop me any day for hours on the road on my way to work. I need to go back and forth to the general market, and if they decide to inspect my truck daily, I cannot work.[16]

The level of participation and organization of every rally was impressive. Local representatives had an assigned space closer or farther away from the stage based on their capacity to mobilize voters. To make the number of mobilized voters visible, activists and candidates distributed T-shirts and hats that displayed the names of and slogans associated with the candidate. Voters were also asked to remain close together near banners that repeated the slogans imprinted on the hats and T-shirts to give a visual measure of the size of the party network of the candidate who had mobilized them.

Candidates with the capacity and the preference to engage in clientelism distributed favors in exchange for voter turnout at rallies. From the mayor, who distributed benefits and small goods before every rally, to opposition candidates who made sure that those who were receiving benefits were present at their events, all potentially successful candidates engaged in clientelism. Still, asymmetries in candidates' capacities to deliver goods implied that Peronist incumbent candidates were in a much better position to mobilize voters than candidates from opposition parties. Not only did most voters want to support a popular candidate regardless of receiving benefits, but these candidates also had more resources with which to secure that support.

Unintended Consequences: Clientelism Consolidated

The argument advanced in this chapter claims that candidates who have the capacity to use clientelism but prefer not to use such strategies commit political suicide. As such, the finding that candidates who succeeded in getting reelected used clientelism would support this argument. Still, to substantiate my theory, I must find that candidates who do not use clientelism are less likely to get reelected than candidates who do rely on clientelism. Based on the political careers of candidates in José C. Paz, I find that only candidates who use clientelism get reelected.

From the creation of the municipality until 2007, voters in José C. Paz elected fifty-six candidates. Out of the fifty-six candidates, only twelve succeeded in getting reelected. The fact that only 21.43 percent of candidates got reelected provides further support for a well-known and documented fact of Argentine politics: "While most Argentine legislators are 'Amateur Legislators,' they are nonetheless 'Professional Politicians'" (Jones et al. 2002: 358). Studying the Argentine congress, Mark Jones and his collaborators (2002) find that the design of Argentine political institutions encourages legislators to focus on their careers as politicians rather than on the production of public policy or on checking executive powers. Given that reelection decisions for legislators are in the hands of party leaders, and not voters, legislators have an incentive to please the party more than voters in order to advance their political careers.

Focusing on the municipal level, I observe the same dynamic that Jones and his collaborators (2002) find at the provincial level. I also find at the local level a similar percentage of reelected officials as Jones et al. found when studying reelection rates in the Chamber of Deputies at the national level.[17] Argentina employs a system of proportional representation with closed-list ballots, making mayors' decisions about a candidate's position on the ballot key in determining his or her likelihood of getting elected and reelected. As candidates are rewarded – in this case with reelection – based only on the number of voters they mobilize, we expect to observe that all reelected candidates employ clientelistic strategies.

Table 5.1 lists the number of times candidates were reelected (column 1), the total number of candidates (column 2), and whether or not candidates used clientelistic strategies to mobilize voters (column 3). The table reveals that only candidates who use clientelism succeeded in getting reelected, as predicted; and it is worth mentioning that all candidates were affiliated with the Peronist Party.

Peronist candidates have been very effective in convincing opposition candidates of the value of having access to resources through their

Table 5.1. *Reelected Candidates, 1995–2007*

Number of times candidates got reelected	Total number of candidates	Did candidates use clientelism to mobilize voter?
1	8	Yes: 6
		No: 2
2	1	No
3	2	Yes
4	1	Yes
Total: 10	*Total: 12*	*Total: Yes: 9*
		No: 3

Note: All candidates are Peronists.

connections at city hall. Once elected, opposition candidates are offered opportunities that would remain unavailable if they did not begin to support the incumbent. As one councilor said, the convincing discourse that incumbent candidates employ is "always the same ... that without money you can't mobilize anyone, you can't support your people, etc."[18]

Opposition candidates can always choose not to support the incumbent, but some simply decide to compromise their ideals in order to secure their own political promotion. Thus, the logic of perverse incentives explains not only the pressure that candidates face to use clientelism but also why they are likely to alter their original rejection of clientelism once elected. Learning that their probabilities of getting reelected or even rewarded after their tenure with a position in city hall hinge on their ability to continue mobilizing voters, candidates are endlessly pressured to employ clientelistic strategies of mobilization.

The use of this pressure is the Peronist Party's traditional strategy of co-opting opposition candidates. For instance, the party bought the support of two candidates of the Party for Bonaerense Unity (PUB) after they were elected in 1999. The leading figure and candidate of the PUB, Sergio, knew that he was not going to win the election as a non-Peronist candidate, but he decided to run out of conviction. Unlike the majority of mayoral candidates in the province, Sergio chose not to also run for the position of city councilor. Most candidates run for both positions simultaneously, enabling them to become a councilor in case they do not obtain enough votes to become the mayor. This practice implies that the first two candidates on the ballot become mayor and vice mayor, and voters end up electing as councilors the third and fourth candidates on closed lists who are generally unknown to them. In conversations I had with the president of the city council in Villa María in Córdoba, the city council president explicitly addressed how his party purposely took into account this institutional design when planning their electoral strategy:

> I ended up on the city council through a political strategy. It was already known that whoever was first on the list was going to be the mayor, so I ran on the ballot as a substitute [*suplente*], even though we knew that I was going to be elected. Personally, I don't like these strategies too much. I recognize that they're effective and useful in certain instances in politics, but if I could choose, I don't think I'd do them myself. They're more for cheaters. All the same, in almost every case there is a cheater, and if you ask me if such practices are wrong I'd say no. But in reality, I end up being president of the city council and voters did not even directly elect me.[19]

Sergio saw this type of electoral strategy as cheating and thus decided to run for mayor only, and he chose his closest collaborators to be candidates for the city council. The PUB had an extraordinary election leading to the selection of two candidates: Guillermo and Daniel. Yet, both candidates decided to abandon the party shortly after getting elected, leaving Sergio without representation – and without power – on the city council.

To buy the support of Guillermo and Daniel, Peronist candidates offered them resources to distribute to their voters that would allow them to build and sustain a party network and move forward in local politics.

> Thus is politics: you have to realize that people are all good until you give them a bit of power. When you give someone a bit of power, you realize what kind of person he or she really is. I put two councilmen in positions of power in '99 and they f***** me over: Daniel, who is now director of transportation, and Guillermo, who is now the director of the news agency. After betraying me, Guillermo was politically dead, but he decided to bring Kirchner to José C. Paz before Kirchner became Duhalde's chosen candidate for the presidency. Today he [Guillermo] is running as the fourth candidate for provincial senator on Kirchner's ticket.[20]

Observing such outcomes, candidates interested in pursuing long-term political careers learn about the constrained means by which they can advance those careers, whether they align themselves with the opposition or the incumbent party. Office-seeking candidates also observe what happens to those who reject working with the incumbent; in the words of one of these candidates, they "stayed at the bottom of the sea":

> The election of '99: it was then that I borrowed a freezer and an oven, and I started making pizzas. Since I always had business, I went to see some people who sold industrial machinery for businesses. I asked them for a freezer and an oven on credit.

And I asked for a space to rent out for the future, to start up. And I got myself a pizzeria and delivered pizzas on a small motorcycle, while these guys [the incumbent candidates] gave themselves the good life. It's painful. I was a mayoral candidate in 1999, a rookie, but a candidate. After that, going out for a ride to deliver pizzas to houses, people look at you and you know that they're sh**** their pants from laughing at you. You have to have pretty big balls. After the campaign, you're left broke. You put in the time – and cash that you don't have. You don't dedicate yourself to your things. If things go badly, you're broke. So in '99 I stayed at the bottom of the sea.[21]

The fact that candidates who decide to work with the incumbent party end up being rewarded while those who decide to follow their idealism end up delivering pizzas encourages office-seeking candidates to become pragmatic and work with those who are able to secure them the stream of resources they need to continue delivering votes.

One of the hypotheses advanced in this chapter is that candidates are unable to mobilize poor voters without access to resources and the ability to solve voter problems. However, there are multiple channels through which to gain access to resources, as the case of the previously mentioned Peronist councilor Pino demonstrates. Pino successfully sustained a party network without the support of the Peronist machine through his contacts with multiple nonpolitical funding sources. After losing a primary election in 1999, a key informant told me that "Pino was in the desert; you know, when the Peronists decide not to give you water, you are in the desert."[22] How did Pino manage to survive without water in the desert?

Although Pino had contacts and access to resources from the church and some nongovernmental organizations, those relationships would not have allowed him to solve voter problems to the extent that he could before he lost the election. Moreover, while it is true that his charisma contributed to his ability to sustain voters' support, charisma alone could not have supplied Pino with medicine, jobs, and money. I speculate that Pino resorted to illegal sources of financing for a period of his career, which enabled him to successfully sustain independence from the mayor. Pino grew such a large party network that the mayor could no longer ignore him and chose to integrate him back into the Peronist network. He continued to build a party network by combining his unquestionable charismatic personality with a renewed access to legitimate resources for problem solving.

The suicidal political careers of Elida and José illustrate cases in which candidates who decide not to use clientelism are unable to continue building a party network and fail to get reelected. José was an important politician and a skillful legislator in the old municipality of General

Sarmiento. Because he was able to mobilize his union in favor of the mayor, he succeeded in getting reelected in the new municipality of José C. Paz. Yet, after his tenure in General Sarmiento, he was unable to build a party network in the new municipality of José C. Paz as a result of his unwillingness to use clientelistic strategies. Consequently, the size of his party network faded in comparison to that of other candidates who built large party networks by employing clientelistic strategies.

Elida was an apprentice of José; she was elected in the municipality when José was backed by the unions because the party leader needed a female candidate to fulfill the closed-ticket gender quota requirement. In following her advisor's preference of not using clientelism, Elida also followed his luck. Neither José nor Elida was invited to run for reelection.

Conclusion

During the electoral campaign of October 2005 in the province of Buenos Aires, I observed how party leaders chose to overlook the illegal methods used by a mercenary candidate who had a party network with a sizeable number of voters. In addition to threatening, monitoring, and punishing poor voters, this candidate built a reputation for distributing welfare programs to young females in exchange for sexual favors, regardless of whether or not the women met the prescribed requirements for such programs.[23] Party leaders' decisions to build alliances with mercenary candidates were publicly acknowledged and discussed by the minister of the interior and de facto speaker for the president, Aníbal Fernández:

JOURNALIST: Is it not strange that the president campaigns to build a new politics and then has as one of his allies a representative of the old politics [candidates who employ clientelistic strategies of mobilization] to be the mayor of José C. Paz, Mario Ishii?

A. FERNÁNDEZ: Look, one does politics with those who do politics, not with those whom one would like to do politics.[24]

Fernández's reasoning reflects the consequences of the mechanisms described in this chapter. The minister noted that although he would like to build alliances with candidates who do not employ clientelistic strategies, the absence of such candidates forces him to negotiate with those who do use clientelism. Still, the minister does not recognize that this outcome is the result of the logic of perverse incentives that systematically punishes those with whom he would like to do politics:

> What I see as perverse is that today Buenos Aires is run by a checkbook. So, when you have that pressure it's really difficult.

It's like the woman with three kids who gets hit by her husband, and so she goes to the social worker. I've seen it. She goes and says, "He beat the sh** out of me." And the social worker says, "And why don't you leave him?" "Because I don't have anyplace to go. . . . Where do you want me to go?"[25]

Rewarding mercenary candidates reinforces a circle of poverty, power, and domination in which poor voters' participation in party rallies and elections empowers candidates who exploit voters' needs. Living, as they do, in a context of material deprivation, voters who can only get their needs met through mercenary candidates have no option but to support those who have the resources to solve their problems.

Paradoxically, democracy provides voters with a Pyrrhic victory: by supporting mercenary candidates, voters contribute to their election as local representatives. Over time, this cycle contributes to the consolidation of political representatives who employ clientelistic strategies to mobilize voters.

6

Scaling Up: The Logic of Perverse Incentives at the Subnational Level

> When the government is faced with institutional obstacles that do not allow it to operate that is not a Peronist libretto, but a script by Francis Ford Coppola, and the result is not a manual for political conduct, but *The Godfather*.
>
> Cristina Fernández de Kirchner

When at the start of her political campaign for a senate seat in Buenos Aires, Cristina Fernández de Kirchner compared Eduardo Duhalde, president and former governor of the province of Buenos Aires, with the Godfather, she decided to publicly burn the ships. After her husband, Néstor Kirchner, won the presidency in 2003, in large part because of Duhalde's support, the 2005 midterm elections presented the Kirchners with an important choice: they could either run with Duhalde, which would hand the reins of real power back to the former president and governor, or they could run against him, fracturing the close alliance that had propelled Néstor Kirchner to the presidency in 2003.

Although it was a midterm election, the national election of October 2005 was the turning point that defined the electoral results for the presidential election two years later. President Néstor Kirchner needed an electoral victory in the province of Buenos Aires to secure his place against Duhalde as the leader of the Peronist Party. Kirchner had won the 2003 election with only 22 percent of the vote after former President Carlos Menem decided to abandon the runoff election, and Duhalde had supplied him with the key electoral support of the voters of the province of Buenos Aires. Kirchner needed to use the midterms to show that he was a real president – not someone just occupying the office until the Peronist Party resolved its internal disputes.

Néstor Kirchner knew that as long as Duhalde was the boss in the province of Buenos Aires, his presidency was tied to Duhalde's policies. Hence, Kirchner's only chance for independence was to challenge

Duhalde, his Godfather, in his own political territory. Using the race for a seat in the senate from the province of Buenos Aires as an opportunity, Kirchner placed his wife, Cristina Fernández, at the top of the FPV senatorial ballot for Buenos Aires. Duhalde responded by replicating Kirchner's strategy and placing his wife, Chiche Duhalde, at the top of the PJ ballot. As a result, voters in the province of Buenos Aires participated in what opposition candidate Elisa Carrio accurately described as an open primary of the Peronist Party.

The electoral victory in the province of Buenos Aires in 2005 marked the beginning of a decade of Kirchner administrations, one government under Néstor (2003–2007), and two governments under Cristina (2007–2011, 2011–2015). The mayors of the Conurbano, a group of several municipalities that surround the city of Buenos Aires and provide 73 percent of the votes in the most important electoral municipality in the country, mobilized the voters who defined the electoral outcome.[1] The argument advanced in this chapter focuses on the key, and often overlooked, role that these mayors play in mobilizing poor voters in their municipalities.

A rich literature on subnational politics (see, e.g., Fox 1994; Cornelius et al. 1999; Snyder 2001; Eaton 2004; Montero and Samuels 2004; Falleti 2005, 2010; Gibson 2005, 2012; Gervasoni 2010) has focused on pointing out the need to attend to actors below the national level to understand the dynamics of national politics. But because the term *subnational* is often used to describe provincial governments only, scholars have largely ignored the importance of municipal officials in implementing clientelistic electoral strategies.[2] The role of governors dominates the literature on subnational politics in Latin America, even though mayors are also central in determining electoral outcomes. This is problematic for three reasons.

First, many mayors in the Cornubano have a constituency as large as or even larger than that of several governors, and they can use their capacity to mobilize voters to bargain with provincial and national officials for influence, resources, and reelection. In Argentina, mayors are not bound by term limits; as a result, we observe nearly indefinite reelection among those who are capable of mobilizing large networks of voters in the Conurbano.

Second, if mayors are rewarded based on the number of votes they are able to deliver to provincial and national candidates, then mayors in poor and working-class municipalities have an incentive to turn to clientelism. Consequently, I expect to observe the same logic of perverse incentives that explains councilors' use of clientelism at the municipal level to be used at the provincial and national levels.

Third, in distributing political promotions in the form of indefinite reelection to mayors who succeed in delivering votes, regardless of the strategies they employ to mobilize voters, provincial and national leaders contribute to the consolidation of local political machines. Mayors who are effective in delivering voters by encouraging candidates to use clientelism are likely to remain in power as long as they are able to deliver votes.

Focusing on the role of mayors, I test whether the theory of perverse incentives posed in this book can be scaled up to explain the relationship between mayors and governors and between mayors and presidents. Does the logic of perverse incentives that encourages local candidates to use clientelism to mobilize voters apply in the strategic political decisions of mayors? Are mayors, like councilors, encouraged to use clientelistic strategies to mobilize voters at the local level as a means of gaining the political support of provincial- and national-level politicians?

To answer these questions, I examine the relationship between mayors and governors and between mayors and presidents to identify how mayors are rewarded or punished based on their capacity to mobilize voters. I also address the conditions under which mayors are able to remain in office without mobilizing voters via clientelism and without the support of governors and the president.

I find that by distributing political promotions in the form of indefinite reelection to mayors who succeed in delivering votes, regardless of the strategies they employ to mobilize voters, provincial and national leaders contribute to the consolidation of local political machines.

Subnational Politics and the Logic of Perverse Incentives

Studying why existing explanations of electoral outcomes in Latin America have focused on the provincial instead of the municipal level, Edward Gibson highlights the combination of three factors: (1) the subordination of municipalities to provinces in the Argentine constitution, (2) fiscal federalism that puts economic resources in governors' hands, and (3) asymmetrical provincial representation in national politics. These three structural factors imply that "the hegemony of governors over mayors in provincial life has thus been a regular feature of Argentine federalism to this day" (2004: 78). In his study of the design of subnational political institutions in Argentina, Kent Eaton arrived at a similar conclusion: "provinces have trumped municipalities as the key subnational level of government" (2004: 38).

The literature on subnational politics has focused on explaining the persistence of authoritarian governments at the local level in national democratic countries. To explain "the existence of democratic national government alongside an authoritarian subnational government" (5), Gibson (2004) builds the idea of "boundary control." As long as the conflicts do not cross the boundaries and intervene in national politics, subnational leaders are allowed complete control over the territories. Agustina Giraudy (2009: 30) argues that democratization occurs when "the costs of promoting the democratization of undemocratic enclaves outweigh the cost of dismantling them" and focuses on explaining the same outcome. Still, in exchange for their political autonomy, subnational leaders have to mobilize voters for the national government. National democratic majorities are thus obtained with the electoral contributions of authoritarian provincial governments.

Focusing on municipal politics, I argue that mayors employ the same tactics as governors in dealing with the national executive. Yet, given that mayors' access to large financial resources tends to be considerably more limited than that of higher-level officials, a positive relationship with governors and presidents is indispensable to their ability to secure material benefits. Even when mayors already have access to material resources, they still require support from provincial and national authorities to solve problems related to public transportation, crime, and security, which directly affect their administrations. To build partnerships with governors and presidents, mayors provide them with their most valuable resource: votes.

Tracy Beck Fenwick claims that "municipalities are creatures of the provinces, and as such, have little agency to behave without either, the approval or, the involvement, of the provincial government to which they are institutionally subordinate" (2010: 174). Still, she recognizes that "a position of mayor in and of itself does not offer many inducements to ambitious career politicians, unless it is a key electoral district like in much of the *Bonaerense*" (168). This chapter shows that the mayors of the Conurbano that Fenwick refers to as the Bonaerense are not an exception to the rule of provincial power over municipalities but an illustration of cases in which mayors have what most governors in the country do not: the capacity to mobilize a large party network of voters.

This chapter argues that when mayors are able to mobilize larger networks of party voters than governors, mayors are capable of negotiating their political future with national authorities and ignoring their provincial leaders. Giraudy claims that fiscal federalism constrains municipal politicians in their relationships with their provincial and national counterparts (2009: 94), but I show how mayors' capacities to mobilize voters are just as important as revenue-sharing arrangements in shaping subnational political relationships within political parties. Indeed, there are good reasons to think that the number of voters mayors are able to mobilize provides them with bargaining power in provincial and national negotiations.

From a broader perspective, the theory advanced in this chapter implies that the capacities of local candidates to mobilize voters for national and/or provincial authorities should be taken into account in explaining the relationships between the different levels of government. More specifically, this chapter claims that mayors who have the capacity to mobilize large party networks, such as the mayors of the municipalities of the Conurbano, are able to negotiate directly with presidents and governors to secure their own reelection in exchange for mobilizing their party networks for the president and/or governor. By rewarding mayors with reelection in exchange for delivering votes, governors and presidents reinforce the logic of perverse incentives, while also encouraging the persistence and consolidation of machine politics at the municipal level.

Extending the Logic of Perverse Incentives: Delivering Votes for Reelection

When governors and presidents reward mayors based only on the number of voters they are able to mobilize, mayors are incentivized to reward councilors who mobilize large party networks contributing to governors' and presidents' electoral success. Mayors are likely to remain in power as long as they can expand and sustain their network of voters and deliver those votes to the president and/or governor.

The same logic that encourages candidates to turn to clientelism to mobilize voters also encourages mayors to reward candidates who use these strategies. As a result, I expect national and provincial candidates to build electoral alliances and work together with municipal clientelistic candidates. The rationale of the foregoing hypothesis implies that national and provincial politicians will reward local politicians with reelection when they succeed in delivering votes regardless of the strategies they employ to turn out those voters.

This chapter uses the reelection of mayors as an indicator of their success in mobilizing voters for presidents and governors. Mayors who are effective in delivering votes for their party will be rewarded with reelection, whereas those who fail to deliver votes will be punished by means of removal from power. The continued reelection of mayors is thus a visible indicator of the success of local executives. Still, not all successful mayors rely on clientelistic electoral strategies. Mayors could be rewarded with reelection given their administrations' achievements independent from delivering votes to provincial and national authorities and the use of clientelism.

To account for mayors' reelection, Rebecca Weitz-Shapiro (2012) and Matthew Cleary (2007) point to several independent variables: the capacity of local executives to provide public and private goods to voters, the strength of civil society, and the strength of the political opposition. Using evidence from Argentine municipalities, Weitz-Shapiro finds that clientelism decreases support from non-poor constituencies, indicating a relationship between economic conditions and electoral competition that contributes to explain variation in mayors' use of political clientelism.[3] Still, her results demonstrate that as long as poverty is high, clientelism remains largely effective: "Only when high competition is coupled with low rates of poverty does clientelism decline" (2012: 568). In the case of the municipalities studied here, only a few are rich in resources and poor on votes; thus, we can assume that non-poor constituencies are insufficient to shape the decisions of local mayors as they choose how to mobilize voters. Hence, whereas Weitz-Shapiro's theory provides some insights about the conditions under which politicians opt out of clientelism, she focuses mostly on the electoral costs of clientelism without paying any attention to the strategies political parties and incumbent and opposition candidates pursue as well as the reasons for their decision making.

In contrast to Weitz-Shapiro, Cleary finds in a study of Mexico's 2,400 municipalities that electoral competition has no effect on the performance of local governments. Instead, Cleary shows that the quality of local government "depends on an engaged citizenry and cooperation between political leaders and their constituents, rather than the threat of electoral punishment" (2007: 283). With contradictory findings, both works implicitly assume the demise of political machines – through electoral competition for Weitz-Shapiro or through an engaged citizenry for Cleary.

Building on these explanations, I argue that mayors have three alternative or complementary paths to reelection. First, they can exchange the support of their party network with provincial and/or national authorities for their reelection. Second, they can carry out an effective local administration that voters would likely support at the polls. Candidates are able to get reelected – even if they fail to deliver votes to national and provincial authorities – when they succeed in winning the support of voters given the success of their local administrations or if they do not face an organized opposition. Yet, it is only under exceptional circumstances, which I examine in detail in Chapter 8, that mayors could succeed in getting elected at the municipal level without mobilizing voters for the governor or the president. Third, they can compromise the viability of the opposition to ensure that they run essentially unopposed.

This chapter focuses on the first path because I am interested in testing whether or not the logic of perverse incentives holds when extended to the subnational level. In order to predict accurately if the mayor is going to be rewarded, we need to assess the influence that governors and presidents have upon the mayor's territory. Table 6.1 presents the predictions of the theory developed in this chapter, using reelection as an indicator of a

Table 6.1. *Hypotheses, Votes, Rewards, and Reelection*

Mayor delivers votes for the		Mayor is likely to be rewarded with reelection
Governor	President	
Yes	Yes	Yes
Yes	No	Indeterminate
No	Yes	Indeterminate
No	No	No

Note: Indeterminate implies that when the mayor delivers votes for the governor, but not for the president, and vice versa, we are unable to establish if he or she is going to be rewarded with reelection.

mayor's capacity to deliver votes to national and/or provincial leaders. In cases where mayors deliver votes for both the president and the governor, I expect those mayors to get reelected. In contrast, when mayors fail to deliver votes for both the president and the governor, they are unlikely to get reelected. Cases in which mayors deliver votes for either the governor or the president are indeterminate because their reelection hinges upon the relative power that the governor has over the president and vice versa in each case.

Research Design

To study the relationships among mayors and governors and presidents, I focus on the largest electoral district in the country: the province of Buenos Aires. The forty-four municipalities that surround the city of Buenos Aires are collectively known as the Conurbano Bonaerense, and they provide 73 percent of the votes in the province. Almost 70 percent of the province's voters live in 25 of the 134 municipalities in the province; among these twenty-five municipalities, all but one, Bahía Blanca, which is also studied in this book, are located in the Conurbano.

The province is divided into eight electoral sections as shown in Table 6.2, which also includes the number of voters in each section, the percentage of voters in the province in each section, the number of municipalities, and whether or not they belong to the Conurbano. Overall, the table shows the significant differences in the number of municipalities and voters between municipalities located in the Conurbano and those that are not.[4]

It is the combination of poverty, number of votes, and proximity between those living in the Conurbano and those living in the city of Buenos Aires that makes the Conurbano the center of every political campaign. In 2005, one out of three residents of the Conurbano was

Table 6.2. *Province of Buenos Aires and the Conurbano*

Electoral section	Number of voters	Percentage	Number of municipalities	Conurbano
1	3,351,353	34.3	24	Yes
2	481,967	4.9	15	No
3	3,394,219	34.7	19	Yes
4	441,272	4.5	19	No
5	946,945	9.5	26	No
6	539,707	5.7	22	No
7	228,219	2.3	8	No
8	427,601	4.1	1	Yes
Conurbano	7,173,173	73.1	44	
Province	2,638,110	26.9	90	
Total	9,811,283	100	134	

either unemployed or underemployed, and these twenty-five municipalities had an unemployment rate of 15 percent, the highest in the country. Savvy political operators know that it is in the Conurbano where electoral differences are made.

Within the Conurbano, I study the municipalities of Malvinas Argentinas, San Miguel, and José C. Paz. I chose these cases because they allow me to focus on understudied cases with a unique methodological advantage. Studying municipalities located in the first and eighth electoral sections expands on the findings of the seminal works from Auyero (2000) and Levistky (2003), which focused on Peronism and clientelism in municipalities in the third electoral section.

The three selected municipalities were created in 1995 as a result of Governor Eduardo Duhalde's political decision to split the municipality of General Sarmiento. Before the creation of the three municipalities, General Sarmiento was the second-largest electoral municipality in the province behind La Matanza. Any candidate who had the capacity to win both electoral municipalities would have a chance to become president. In fact, it was the potential to provide presidential candidates with a large number of votes that led the governor of the province to divide the territory. Given that the brother of the governor of Tucumán Province, Ramón "Palito" Ortega, was the mayor of General Sarmiento, Duhalde understood the municipality's potential to provide a presidential candidate at a time when he had not yet lost his aspirations to the highest office. In this context, the decision to divide the area into three new municipalities in 1995 seemed logical. After proponents argued about the difficulty of efficiently administrating a municipality of that size, and aligned with politicians who saw much more opportunities in the division than in the union, the project was approved. La Matanza, the largest electoral municipality in the country was never divided.

By selecting these municipalities, I am able to control for a common social, historical, and economic history given that until 1994, all these voters lived in the same territory under the same political administration. Cultural explanations cannot account for variation in mayors' decisions to work for or against governors and presidents or for their capacity to deliver votes. Thus, I can focus on providing an analytical narrative (Bates 1998) of politicians' strategic decisions.

To test the hypotheses advanced in this chapter, I study the relationships among mayors, governors, and presidents since the beginning of democracy in the country in 1983 until the last democratic election of 2011. Combining a large-N dataset with comparisons from small-N research, I carried out a nested analysis (Lieberman 2005) to test the predictions of my theory. The large-N dataset contains information from all elected mayors since the return of democracy until the present. The small-N dataset contains in-depth, qualitative, and ethnographic data from four selected cases: the three municipalities created in 1995 and located in the Conurbano, and a municipality of similar size, Bahía Blanca, also located in the province of Buenos Aires but outside the Conurbano (see Map 2.1 in Chapter 1). Bahía Blanca's population is similar to that of the municipalities of the Conurbano studied in this book, but it is nevertheless very distant geographically as well as politically. The municipality has had a bipartisan city council and was governed by Radicals from the beginning of democracy in 1983 until 1999, and by Peronists since 2003.

Using ethnographic methods, I was able to collect high-quality data for the four selected cases. I conducted fieldwork that included direct observations and in-depth interviews with more than 50 political actors: mayors, councilors, activists, and voters before, during, and after the election of 2005 in each selected municipality. I also conducted archival research and collected socio-demographic and economic data. In addition, I conducted follow-up trips in 2007 and 2009 and conducted a survey with councilors in 2012.

The research design developed in this chapter shows the advantages of combining quantitative and qualitative research in measuring and understanding the relationships among different levels of government. Studying alternative explanations contributes to defining the scope of the theory presented in this chapter and the logic of perverse incentives in general. After presenting evidence based on the large-N dataset and a close study of the cases selected in this chapter, I summarize the findings and their implications in the conclusion.

Table 6.3. *Reelection of Mayors in the Province of Buenos Aires,*
1983–2011

Reelection	Frequency	Percentage
Not reelected	239	22.87
Still in first term*	49	4.69
Reelected 1x	4	0.38
Reelected 2x	260	24.88
Reelected 3x	258	24.69
Reelected 4x	127	12.15
Reelected 5x	60	4.59
Reelected 6x	48	4.59
Total	1,045	100

* Mayors elected in 2011 will be up for reelection in 2015.

Results

Descriptive statistics on elected mayors in the province of Buenos Aires are based on 1,045 observations of all elected mayors in every municipality between 1983 and 2011.[5] More than half of the mayors are Peronist, and only 2.2 percent of the mayors are female.[6] On the whole, the evidence is consistent with the literature that focuses on the predominance of the Peronist Party in the province of Buenos Aires. Almost 71 percent of municipal executives get reelected. Table 6.3 describes the number of times municipal mayors were reelected. Column 1 distinguishes among mayors who fail in getting reelected, mayors who have been elected but are not up for reelection yet (their terms will end in 2015), and mayors who have been reelected. Among reelected mayors, the number of times they succeeded in getting reelected also varies. Approximately 50 percent of the mayors succeed in getting reelected two or three times.

Observing general patterns of reelection in the province serves to demonstrate the frequency of reelection at the municipal level, as well as the predominance of the Peronist Party. Still, to test the relationship between mayors and governors and between mayors and presidents, we need more specific information about the linkages between local and provincial and local and national politicians. To examine these relationships, I gathered detailed information from the selected cases. Focusing on four cases enabled me to trace the political careers of every elected mayor in the selected municipalities and their evolving relationships with presidents and governors since the return of democracy in 1983.

Between 1983 and 2011, there were three elections (1983, 1987, and 1991) in the old municipality of General Sarmiento and five elections

(1995, 1999, 2003, 2007, and 2011) in each of the three created municipalities. Reelection data are available for all the cases of General Sarmiento and for all the elections until 2011 in the new municipalities. Hence, I have information for a total of fifteen cases.

Assuming that mayors are likely to mobilize voters for governors and/or presidents who share their partisanship affiliation, I use partisanship as an indicator of support, access to resources, and thus the possibility of using clientelistic strategies of mobilization. Yet, it is not correct to assume that partisanship translates into political and economic support for local executives. Even within the same party, governors can have negative relationships with mayors as a result of past history or a wide variety of other factors. Furthermore, several factions within the same party can form and oppose one another in elections, as was seen at the national level in the 2003 and 2005 elections with the rivalry between the Duhaldes and the Kirchners.

I focus on the cases in which candidates have the support of both presidents and governors, as well as cases in which candidates run without the support of provincial and national leaders. Cases in which candidates run with the support of either the governor or the president, but not both, are more difficult to predict because they depend on different combinations of support and context. Table 6.4 shows the years, names, and partisan affiliation of every Argentine president, governor of the province of Buenos Aires, and mayor of the selected municipalities between 1983 and 2011.

Table 6.5 presents findings from the selected cases using partisanship as an indicator of a mayor's likelihood to deliver votes to presidents and governors in exchange for reelection. I assume that mayors will deliver votes for presidents and governors of their own party. The first three columns describe whether the mayor delivers votes for the governor (column 1) and the president (column 2) and whether the mayor is likely to be rewarded with reelection (column 3). The two columns that follow include the mayors' names and year(s) of election(s); each mayor is identified as either confirming the hypothesis advanced in this chapter (column 4) or denying it (column 5). Twelve out of the fifteen cases confirm the hypotheses advanced in this chapter. The last column addresses the cases that the theory fails to explain accurately.

To contribute to theory building and testing, I trace the political careers of candidates who confirm and reject the proposed theory. I study the cases of mayors in José C. Paz who reject (Rubén Glaría) and confirm (Mario Ishii) the theory by using different combinations of support for governors and presidents. I also study the case of Jesús Cariglino in Malvinas Argentinas as he also confirms and disproves the theory, showing the effects of different combinations of national and provincial support on the same candidate. Moreover, from all the cases studied, Cariglino is the only mayor who has succeeded in remaining in power

Table 6.4. *Timeline: Presidents, Governors, and Mayors*

		1983	1984	1985	1986	1987	1988	1989	1990	1991	1992	1993	1994	1995	1996	1997	1998	1999	2000	2001	2002	2003	2004	2005	2006	2007	2008	2009	2010	2011
President		Ricardo Alfonsin						Carlos Menem										Fernando De la Rua		Ramon Puerta, et al. / Eduardo Duhalde		Nestor Kirchner				Cristina Fernandez de Kirchner				
Governor	Buenos Aires	Alejandro Armendariz				Antonio Cafiero				Eduardo Duhalde								Carlos Ruckauf			Felipe Sola					Daniel Scioli				
Mayor	General Sarmiento	Remigio Lopez				Eduardo Lopez				Luis Ortega																				
	San Miguel												Jose de Luca			Aldo Rico		Oscar Zilocchi						Joaquin De la Torre		Carlos Urquiaga			
	Jose C. Paz												Ruben Glaria			Mario Ishii													
	Malvinas Argentinas												Jesus Cariglino																
	Bahia Blanca	Juan Carlos Cabiron								Jaime Linares												Rodolfo Lopes				Cristian Breitenstein				

UCR
PJ
Alianza
Modin
FPV

Table 6.5. *Testing the Theory: From the Municipality of General Sarmiento to San Miguel, José C. Paz, and Malvinas Argentinas in the Province of Buenos Aires, 1983–2007*

Theoretical expectations			Empirical results		
Mayor delivers votes for the		Expected outcome	Was the mayor reelected?		Mispredictions (Causes)
Governor	President		Yes (Confirms the hypothesis)	No (Disproves the hypothesis)	
Yes	Yes	Mayor is rewarded with reelection	Joaquin De La Torre (2007) Mario Ishii (2003, 2007) Jesus Cariglino (2003)	José De Luca (1995) Rubén Glaria (1995)	Corruption scandal Refused to use clientelism
Yes	No	Indeterminate	Eduardo López (1987) Aldo Rico (1999) Oscar Zilocchi (2003) Mario Ishii (1999)		
No	Yes	Indeterminate	Jesus Cariglino (1995, 1999) Luis Ortega		
No	No	No	Remigio López	Jesus Cariglino (2007)	A combination between an effective local administration and the absence of political alternatives

Note: Indeterminate implies that when the mayor delivers votes for the governor, but not for the president, and vice versa, we are unable to establish if he or she is going to be rewarded with reelection.

since the creation of the municipality. Finally, I study the case of the first mayor of San Miguel, José De Luca, who was impeached only two years after being reelected.

Mayors in José C. Paz

Beyond sharing the same partisan network, President Menem did not have a relationship with Rubén Glaría, the first mayor of José C. Paz. The governor of the province, Eduardo Duhalde, on the other hand, had a very close, almost familial relationship with the mayor, whom he saw every Sunday in his weekend home when Glaría organized weekly soccer matches. A former successful soccer player himself, Glaría had been the province's director of the Institute of Provincial Sport in the province before becoming mayor.

In 1997, Mario Ishii, a candidate from Glaría's party and then-president of the city council, challenged the mayor's authority in a primary election. Running without the support of the president, the governor, or the mayor, Ishii succeeded in building a party network by distributing construction materials, specifically wooden tables, to build precarious homes (*casillas*). Every weekend, Ishii went to different poor neighborhoods to distribute materials so people could build their homes. Glaría, on the other hand, did not work every day to build trust and loyalty among voters beyond distributing and administering existing resources at the municipality. One of Glaría's party candidates remembered trying to persuade the mayor to use clientelism without success:

> To me it [not using clientelism] seemed like a mistake because everyone went one way and we went the other, and for that you have to pay the political consequences. It was a political failure: we had control of the municipality [*el aparato*], we had the possibility of using state resources from the municipality for the campaign, and we didn't. The mayor did not use many of these resources. Why? Because he was a sane guy [*un tipo sano*]. So the *agrupaciones* that were not with that mayor went against him, along with the independents and those who were receiving things from other candidates.[7]

It was not until Glaría realized that it was possible to lose the primary election that he decided to begin distributing goods to voters in exchange for political participation. A large number of voters who were targeted by the mayor's paid activists with particularistic goods weeks before the election still preferred and supported Ishii, who had been there throughout the years and not just in the weeks before the election, but Glaría won the election. The disparity of resources available and the number of voters who were still in need of problem solving provided the mayor with a razor thin margin of victory: fifty votes. Ishii claimed fraud and decided not to recognize the authority of Glaría as mayor until every single vote was counted.

Glaría claimed to have won the primary election, but recognizing that his margin of victory was minimal, he sought to do away with Ishii, who was still the city council's president. The situation led to a stalemate that included a shootout between activists from both Peronist factions on the doorsteps of city hall to define who was the legitimate authority of the municipality (see O'Donnell 2005, and daily reports from *La Hoja*). It was not until after the municipality's violent clashes between Peronist factions reached the pages of national newspapers that Governor Eduardo Duhalde decided to intervene to achieve a favorable electoral verdict for his personal friend Glaría. The governor's decision to favor Glaría over Ishii in the primary election was not forgotten, and Ishii has remained a political enemy of Duhalde.

Even though he secured the support of the president and the governor, Glaría failed to get reelected because he did not mobilize enough voters. In 1999, Mario Ishii became mayor, and while he could not count on the support of the Radical administration of President De la Rua, he did have a good relationship with Peronist governor Carlos Ruckauf. Ishii was reelected and continued on as the municipality's mayor in the following term. Ishii had a very positive relationship with President Néstor Kirchner. Kirchner was the first presidential candidate that the mayor decided to support openly. Ishii offered his support even before Kirchner became a popular and successful candidate. The mayor also had a positive relationship with Governor Felipe Solá.

In 2007, Ishii was reelected for his third consecutive term. Although he could have easily continued as mayor in 2011, he decided to run for governor against his friend Daniel Scioli. Ishii's decision to run against Scioli was in response to Scioli's need to face a primary election that would garner his candidacy with some legitimacy. In short, Ishii did Scioli a favor by running for and losing an election.

Given that all candidates in his municipality, José C. Paz, supported Ishii's candidacy for governor, he promised that the candidate who mobilized more voters for his candidacy in the primary would become the next mayor of the municipality. Carlos Urquiaga won that race and became José C. Paz's mayor with Ishii's support.

Malvinas Argentinas: Jesús Cariglino

Jesús Cataldo Cariglino has been the mayor of Malvinas Argentinas since the creation of the municipality. Before becoming mayor in 1995,

Cariglino did not have any political experience, but he did have the money needed to run for mayor. A former union leader and councilor of the municipality remembered the challenge of being in charge of Cariglino's first political campaign:

> Cariglino had three problems to advance his candidature: nobody knew him, he did not know how to speak in public, and his last name was very hard to remember. We could not invent anything, so we came up with the idea that he was just a *regular* neighbor [*simple vecino*].[8]

The campaign brochures showed Cariglino wearing a suit with the slogan: "Cariglino: Peronist and a good neighbor."

In his first election, Cariglino ran against Raúl Ortega, councilor of the old municipality of General Sarmiento and brother of the mayor of the municipality and of the governor of the Tucumán Province, Palito Ortega, who had a close relationship with President Carlos Menem.

The Ortega family's closeness with President Menem led Cariglino to ask Governor Eduardo Duhalde for political support. Although Cariglino was a rookie political candidate, Duhalde was eager to help him get elected in Malvinas Argentinas, which would prevent the potential empowerment of the Ortegas in the province. Duhalde's political ambition to become president in 1999 could have been challenged if the Ortegas succeeded in mobilizing voters in the province of Buenos Aires. Cariglino also succeeded in getting the support of the military, which constitutes a solid voting bloc in the municipality where Campo de Mayo, a military base, is located. He also secured the support of church groups, which together with Raúl Ortega's corrupt administration, contributed to his electoral victory.

During his first term in office, Cariglino focused on paving streets, improving hospitals, and building health clinics. Although his administration suffered strong accusations – some of them leading to convictions – of corruption in the assignment of public construction projects and over budgeting (*sobre-facturación*), the mayor nevertheless enjoyed a positive image among voters who recognized the improvements. He succeeded in winning the 1999 election, even though Duhalde, the Peronist's candidate for the presidency and a close friend, was defeated.

Cariglino also succeeded in getting elected in 2003, 2007, and 2011. The combination of a corrupt but efficient administration of the municipality and the mayor's control over social programs, public contracts, and public employment explains the mayor's success. Cariglino's capacity to deliver votes also made him a good ally for Peronist governors and presidents until the Kirchners came to power. The mayor's enduring loyalty to Duhalde made him one of the few successful Peronist politicians opposed to the president.

The mayor of Malvinas Argentinas relied on different combinations of support at the national and provincial levels, as shown in Table 6.5. Regardless of the support of the president or the governor, both, or neither, Cariglino succeeded in getting reelected. It is his reelection in 2007 that challenges the theory advanced in this chapter, which does not predict that mayors will be reelected when they do not have the support of either the president or the governor. The answer to this apparent contradiction is found in the mayor's capacity to independently build a solid political machine. As the theory advanced in this book predicts, it is the mayor's capacity to mobilize voters that enables him to succeed.

José De Luca's Impeachment

The case of the first mayor of San Miguel, José De Luca, does not fulfill the predictions advanced in this chapter. Even with the support of the president and governor, the Peronist mayor failed to get reelected. Less than a year after being elected in October 1995, De Luca was involved in a corruption scandal that ended in his detention and destitution. Key informants and archival information – including several hidden cameras that showed the corruption of local officials – suggest that the level of corruption was too high to be able to save a mayor.

In 1997, two years earlier than expected, Aldo Rico, a former military official who led a group of army mutineers, the *caparintada* movement, against a recently elected democratic government, became the mayor of San Miguel.[9] Although not a Peronist, Rico had a good relationship with the province's governor, Eduardo Duhalde, after Rico instructed his representatives to support the governor's changes to the provincial constitution to enable his reelection. Before the constitutional changes that took place in 1995, neither the presidents nor the governors of the province of Buenos Aires were able to stand for reelection.

When De Luca lost voter support because of his corruption scandals, provincial and national politicians did not do anything to save him, as he would not have been able to provide them with votes. Hence, it is not corruption per se that led to the mayor's dismissal, but his inability to gather support from provincial and national authorities despite the corruption scandals.

Lessons from Mispredictions

In comparing the cases of De Luca in San Miguel and Cariglino in Malvinas, we observe that corruption in itself does not explain a mayor's ability or inability to get reelected. Like De Luca, Cariglino was convicted in corruption cases. But Cariglino was still able to mobilize voters and thus was valuable to provincial and national politicians. As long as politicians are able to deliver votes, it is likely that they will be valuable to governors and presidents who in turn would be willing to support their reelection campaigns in spite of corruption scandals.

Overall, these cases provide rich insights regarding the complex relationship between presidents and mayors and between mayors and governors. Of the fifteen cases examined here, the theory predicts twelve with accuracy. In reviewing the theory's mispredictions, we can identify the importance of mayors' ability to deliver votes as a key factor in explaining their successes and failures in getting reelected. Thus, Mayors Ruben Glaría and José De Luca failed to get reelected because they were unable to mobilize voters; however, the reelection bids of Mario Ishii and Jesus Cariglino were successful because of their ability to deliver votes.

Alternative Explanations: Bahía Blanca

In contrast to citizens in the Conurbano who live in the province but commute daily to the city of Buenos Aires, those living in Bahía Blanca do not commute daily to the city. Bahía Blanca is a municipality where everyone knows everyone, a fact that is known as *pueblo chico, infierno grande* (small town, big hell). In discussing the differences between Bahía Blanca and the municipalities studied in this chapter, Councilman Marcelo Feliú said that Bahía Blanca "combines the situation of a city with 300,000 residents that nevertheless has the mentality of a much smaller city. As a result, we end up saying that *'nos conocemos todos'* [we all know each other]."[10]

The combination of geographic distance and close community ties means that voters are likely to be familiar with the program of the mayor and to know the mayor personally. It is not the case that voters in Bahía Blanca are not mobilized through clientelistic strategies, but the use of these strategies is not as prominent as in the Conurbano.

Moreover, given the geographical distance and the dynamics of the municipality, provincial and national politicians are unlikely to invest resources and attention in a remote municipality on the periphery of Buenos Aires. As a result, local administrations are likely to have less access to resources than are municipalities in the Conurbano, and they are also less likely to be asked to contribute voters to mobilizations that are taking place in the city and in the Conurbano.

Table 6.6 provides information about the eight administrations of Bahía Blanca between 1983 until 2011. Only two administrations of

Table 6.6. *Testing the Theory beyond the Conurbano: The Municipality of Bahía Blanca in the Province of Buenos Aires, 1983–2007*

Mayor delivers votes for		Mayor is likely to be rewarded with reelection	Is the mayor reelected? (confirm the hypothesis)		Mispredictions (Causes)
Governor	President		Yes	No	
Yes	Yes	Yes	Juan Carlos Cabirón (1983) Rodolfo Lopes (2003) Cristian Breitenstein (2007, 2011)		
No	Yes	Indeterminate	Juan Carlos Cabirón (1987) Jaime Linares (1999)		
No	No	No		Jaime Linares (1991, 1995)	Time in power (twelve consecutive years)

Note: Indeterminate implies that when the mayor delivers votes for the governor, but not for the president, and vice versa, we are unable to establish if he or she is going to be rewarded with reelection.

Jaime Linares did not support the theory advanced in this chapter. Radical administrations governed the municipality for sixteen years, from the return of democracy until 2003. Jaime Linares was elected in 1991 after two Radical administrations of Juan Carlos Cabirón, and it was not until Linares lost his fourth consecutive reelection that the municipality began electing Peronist administrations, which it has continued to do up to the present.

Linares succeeded in getting reelected in 1991 and 1995 without the support of the national and provincial governments because voters were satisfied with his good Radical administrations. Peronist and Radical local politicians and voters said that the change which led to the election of a Peronist mayor in 2003 had to do with Linares' attempt to continue in power. Indeed, in a personal interview with a former mayor of the municipality, Cristian Breitenstein, I learned that the problem was Linares' decision to run for his re-re-re-reelection. For Breitenstein, if "Linares had given someone else from his party the opportunity to run for office, Radicals would remain in power for forty years. There was no rejection, only exhaustion: 'Enough of Linares' [*Basta de Linares*]. It wasn't even enough of the UCR; the discussion was about Linares. If the candidate had been Frankenstein, then Frankenstein would have won that election."[11]

To conclude, studying a municipality with a similar number of voters but remote location enabled me to further test the theory advanced in this chapter. The case of Bahía Blanca shows the importance that local administration can have when provincial and national politics are not relevant. Bahía Blanca's geographical location and smaller party network of voters make it less interesting for national and provincial politicians who prefer to focus their energy in municipalities of similar size that are closer geographically and politically to the city of Buenos Aires.

In addition, the case of Bahía Blanca provides interesting insights with regard to the limits of reelection for local candidates. Whereas reelection is not legally limited for municipal executives, time in power in itself does not seem to benefit authorities who remain in the same position for extensive periods of time.

Conclusion

Studying the empirical evidence from four municipalities of similar size in the province of Buenos Aires, I find support for the theory advanced in this chapter. The majority of the mayors who delivered votes to either the president or the governor, or even both, succeeded in getting reelected in their municipalities. Over time, this led to the consolidation of Peronist administrations in the Conurbano, as well as to the consolidation of mayors in different municipalities. In this regard, the logic of perverse incentives developed in this book explains the persistent support that the Peronist Party receives from poor voters in Buenos Aires. In rewarding mayors with reelection based only on the number of voters they mobilize, governors and presidents perpetuate a status quo that reinforces the power of the Peronist Party in the Conurbano.

The persistence and electoral strength of the Peronist Party in the Conurbano is also reflected in the higher reelection rates of its mayors. It is the mayors' capacity to mobilize large networks of voters that enables them to secure their local political monopoly, leading to the consolidation of political machines at the local level. Building on Gibson's theory of boundary control to explain the persistence of authoritarian enclaves in national polities, this chapter finds that mayors' capacities to mobilize their party networks to support provincial and national politicians enable mayors to control their bounded territory, which in this case is not as in Gibson the subnational, provincial level, but the local municipal level.

Findings presented in this chapter strongly suggest that the logic of perverse incentives could be scaled up to explain the relationships between and among mayors and governors and presidents. The chapter also provides some insights about the causes that can lead to the demise of local political monopolies in which clientelism is consolidated. In the cases under study in this chapter, we observe that mayors fail to get reelected when they reject using clientelism or when they remain in power for too long. Both cases are predicted in the theory advanced in this book as the outcome of the unintended consequences of the logic of perverse incentives.

Appendix

Table A.1. *Municipalities and Voters in the Province of Buenos Aires*

Municipality	Number of Voters	Percentage
La Matanza	755,300	7.7
General Pueyrredon	452,222	4.6
La Plata	427,601	4.4
Lomas de Zamora	419,688	4.3
Quilmes	387,605	4
Lanus	360,640	3.7
Almirante Brown	325,206	3.3
General San Martin	304,205	3.1
Merlo	296,990	3
Avellaneda	261,377	2.7
Moron	251,953	2.6
San Isidro	252,942	2.6
Tres de Febrero	255,797	2.6
Vicente Lopez	230,906	2.4
Moreno	220,793	2.3
Bahia Blanca	**210,960**	**2.2**
Florencio Varela	205,469	2.1
Tigre	201,074	2
Berazategui	190,615	1.9
Malvinas Argentinas	**178,140**	**1.8**
San Miguel	**165,603**	**1.7**
Esteban Echeverria	152,436	1.6
José C. Paz	**143,308**	**1.5**
Hurlingham	126,736	1.3
Pilar	122,343	1.2
San Fernando	113,231	1.2
Escobar	107,835	1.1
Ituzaingo	110,966	1.1

(Continued)

Table A.1.

Municipality	Number of Voters	Percentage
San Nicolas	102,303	1
Tandil	83,918	0.9
Pergamino	76,442	0.8
Zarate	74,265	0.8
Olavarria	80,066	0.8
Lujan	66,554	0.7
Ezeiza	71,089	0.7
Junin	68,913	0.7
Necochea	72,186	0.7
Campana	57,672	0.6
Berisso	62,233	0.6
Mercedes	44,985	0.5
Chivilcoy	47,768	0.5
Coronel Rosales	44,285	0.5
Tres Arroyos	45,967	0.5
Azul	49,247	0.5
General Rodriguez	43,542	0.4
San Pedro	39,086	0.4
Ensenasa	43,313	0.4
Pte. Peron	38,928	0.4
Chacabuco	36,261	0.4
Nueve de Julio	36,351	0.4
La Costa	42,628	0.4
Marcos Paz	27,827	0.3
Cañuelas	28,962	0.3
Lobos	24,674	0.3
San Vicente	30,846	0.3
Bragado	32,126	0.3
Lincoln	32,210	0.3
Pehuajo	30,079	0.3
Trenque Lauquen	29,776	0.3
Balcarce	33,347	0.3
Chascomus	29,543	0.3
General Alvarado	28,346	0.3
Coronel Suarez	29,305	0.3
Bolivar	26,622	0.3
Veinticinco de Mayo	27,422	0.3
Arrecifes	20,628	0.2
Baradero	22,756	0.2
Colon	17,129	0.2
Exaltac de la Cruz	15,932	0.2
Ramallo	21,331	0.2
Rojas	18,427	0.2
Salto	23,248	0.2

(Continued)

Table A.1.

Municipality	Number of Voters	Percentage
San Antonio de Areco	15,718	0.2
Brandsen	16,477	0.2
Carlos Casares	16,677	0.2
Genereal Villegas	20,150	0.2
Ayacucho	15,398	0.2
Dolores	20,094	0.2
Las Flores	18,637	0.2
Mar Chiquita	16,440	0.2
Villa Gesell	17,750	0.2
Benito Juarez	15,519	0.2
Coronel Pringles	18,771	0.2
Patagones	20,117	0.2
Saavedra	16,279	0.2
Villarino	19,735	0.2
Saladillo	22,802	0.2
General Las Heras	9,390	0.1
Navarro	11,472	0.1
Suipacha	7,089	0.1
Capitan Sarmiento	9,546	0.1
Carmen de Areco	10,526	0.1
San Andres de Giles	14,630	0.1
Magdalena	11,793	0.1
Punta Indio	7,568	0.1
Alberti	8,384	0.1
Carlos Tejedor	9,188	0.1
F. Ameghino	6,346	0.1
General Arenales	12,549	0.1
General Pinto	8,226	0.1
General Viamonte	14,416	0.1
Hipolito Yrigoyen	7,225	0.1
Leandro N. Alem	13,183	0.1
Rivadavia	11,444	0.1
Castelli	6,083	0.1
General Belgrano	12,690	0.1
General Madariaga	14,349	0.1
General Paz	8,471	0.1
Loberia	13,197	0.1
Maipu	8,874	0.1
Monte	12,888	0.1
Pinamar	13,002	0.1
Rauch	11,664	0.1
San Cayetano	6,622	0.1
Adolfo Alsina	13,334	0.1
Coronel Dorrego	13,539	0.1

(Continued)

Table A.1.

Municipality	Number of Voters	Percentage
Daireaux	11,981	0.1
General La Madrid	7,989	0.1
Gonzalez Chavez	9,782	0.1
Guamini	9,075	0.1
Laprida	7,631	0.1
Puan	14,392	0.1
Salliquelo	7,174	0.1
Tornquist	9,286	0.1
Tres Lomas	5,814	0.1
General Alvear	7,126	0.1
Roque Perez	8,211	0.1
Tapalque	6,723	0.1
Pellegrini	4,577	0.05
Monte Hermoso	4,195	0.04
General Guido	2,316	0.02
General Lavalle	2,266	0.02
Pila	2,362	0.02
Tordillo	1,652	0.02
Total	**9,811,283**	**100**

Note: Selected cases are bolded.

7

Mobilizing Poor Voters: A Comparative Perspective

More than forty years ago, James Scott identified poverty as "perhaps the most fundamental quality shared by the mass clientele of machines" (1969: 1150). As poverty persists in many developed and developing countries, clientelistic candidates who can solve poor voters' problems are likely to succeed in gaining their political support. Hence, most of the descriptive and analytical findings presented in this book should apply to many developing and developed countries that experience poverty. Specifically, I expect to find similar unintended consequences from the logic of perverse incentives in countries, regions, provinces, states, and neighborhoods where candidates have the capacities and preferences to use clientelistic strategies to mobilize poor voters, and where using these strategies enables – or at least does not inhibit – the candidates' political promotions.

The practice of paying poor voters to show support at party rallies is not unique to the Argentine case. In both Mexico and Peru, clientelistic strategies are so commonplace that unique vocabulary has emerged to describe its participants. In Peru, voters who are paid in exchange for turning out at rallies receive the creative and descriptive name of the portable people (*portátiles*), and in Mexico they are referred as the hauled people (*acarreados*). This chapter studies strategies of political mobilization in Peru and Mexico to examine the scope conditions of the theory advanced in this book. Additionally, this chapter seeks to illustrate how the logic of perverse incentives could be effectively used to explain the consolidation of clientelism and its unintended consequences in other new democracies.

In contrast to Argentina, Peru is a democracy without parties (Levitsky and Cameron 2003; Tanaka 2005) and a "party non-system" (Sánchez 2009). Partisan networks that can target and deliver particularistic goods to voters in exchange for their support and that can monitor their political behavior do not exist in Peru. As such, studying the case of Peru enables me to provide further support for the logic of perverse incentives in a context that lacks the institutionalized political parties and partisan networks found in Argentina.

I did field research in Lima spanning six months before, during, and after the presidential election of 2006. I conducted more than 40 in-depth interviews with party candidates, operatives, mayors, councilors, and political brokers. I also interviewed several key informants and attended more than a dozen rallies in poor neighborhoods in Villa María del Triunfo, Villa El Salvador, San Juan de Lurigancho, El Agustino, and Comas. I selected these districts based on differences in population and housing quality which quantitative studies of vote buying and clientelism have used to explain variation in strategies of mobilization.

Using empirical evidence from Peru, I show how political and social networks enable brokers to solve voters' problems without using partisan networks. I focus on the role of female social brokers in soup kitchens in Lima and the methods by which they exchange the support of their group of followers for benefits for themselves and/or their community. This case demonstrates that even in the absence of political parties and partisan networks, we can still expect brokers to opt for employing clientelistic strategies to mobilize poor voters over non-clientelistic strategies, provided that political leaders reward them based only on the number of voters they mobilize. Moreover, I expect to observe the emergence and consolidation of mercenary brokers more than idealist ones over time.

Mexico, on the other hand, saw a single party, the Mexican Institutional Revolutionary Party (PRI), maintain power for seventy-one years (1929–2000). Building on a vast and solid literature that focuses on explaining the persistence and decline of the PRI (see, e.g., Langston 2001; Magaloni 2006; Greene 2007; Simpser 2013), I found further support for the logic of perverse incentives developed in this book. I also used secondary sources from interviews with Mexican candidates (Bruhn 1997; Greene 2007; Hilgers 2008; Holzner 2010) to illustrate how the distinctions among pragmatists, idealist, utopist, and resentful candidates advanced in this book can be applied beyond the Argentine case.

While further work is needed to test the theory more rigorously, the significant similarities between these cases and the ones studied in-depth in this book provide suggestive evidence about the unintended consequences of the logic of perverse incentives in the consolidation of clientelism in new democracies.

Clientelism without Parties: The Case of Peru

Clientelism works when party candidates know and solve voters' problems in exchange for their political support. The absence of political parties in Peru does not imply the absence of problem-solving networks, as *dirigentes sociales* – the local brokers in Peru – are key actors in charge of solving voters' problems (Tanaka 1999; Ansión et al. 2000). *Dirigentes* are community leaders and organizers who hold central positions in nonpolitical problem-solving networks, which involve relationships that enable voters to solve everyday problems unrelated to politics, such as the need to borrow money and access to child care and counseling (Szwarcberg 2012b). By solving voters' problems, Peruvian *dirigentes* build a network of followers that they mobilize during elections.

In contrast to Argentina, it is not uncommon to observe *dirigentes* switching their support for parties and candidates from election to election, and even within the same election. The lack of overlap between political and partisan networks in Peru enables *dirigentes* to switch their support from rally to rally and election to election. Luciano Andrenacci, the Capacity Development Program coordinator for the Inter-American Development Bank in 2006, acknowledged this dynamic in a comparison of brokers in Peru and Argentina:

> Here you don't have a network of paid party activists [*punteros*] as well assembled as the one you have in Argentina. Here you have intermediaries, agents that secure you votes, who are able to mobilize a small number of voters surrounding some visible leader. It looks much more fluid, the loyalties are much more fragile, and it's less professional, inclusive in the case of the APRA.[1]

The American Popular Revolutionary Alliance (APRA) is the oldest surviving party in Peru. The absence of partisan networks, even in the case of the APRA, explains why voters do not cultivate loyalties with political parties, but instead with *dirigentes* who solve their everyday problems. As a result, while partisan networks are not developed in Peru, social networks constitute the core of civil and political life in the country. The absence of party machines, nevertheless, intensifies the logic of perverse incentives and its unintended consequences, leading to a political market in which *dirigentes* sell their support to whoever is willing to pay more for their services, and candidates buy the support of whoever can mobilize a larger number of voters for a lower price. In the same interview, Andrenacci described this electoral market as a "festival of clientelism":

> For the same reason that loyalties aren't fixed, vote buying is a festival. My impression is that political machines are not effective; it's not even serious, it's a festival because it's not as well organized as in the case of Buenos Aires where not anyone could

be a paid party activist. Second, there is not as much money to be distributed as in Argentina given that the state is weaker and it doesn't have much money to invest in clientelism. At the same time, people's needs are more intense. Put everything in a dice cup, shake it, and you get clientelism.[2]

I conducted fieldwork at party rallies that took place at soup kitchens (*comedores escolares*) during the presidential election of 2006. These organizations are of widespread importance in Peru: Julio Cotler and Romeo Grompone (2000) estimate that 42 percent of Peruvian households receive food (*ayuda alimentaria*) through the National Program of Food Assistance (PRONAA). Another food assistance program for pregnant and lactating mothers and children up to age six, Glass of Milk (*Vaso de Leche*), is also available to poor families mostly through the soup kitchens.[3] Poor families visit soup kitchens daily, enabling *dirigentes* to listen to and understand their problems. The *dirigentes* are able to build trust with these families by helping to solve their problems whenever possible.

The concentration of poor families in soup kitchens makes them a preferred electoral stage for party rallies at the local level. Female *dirigentes* in charge of distributing the PRONAA and the Glass of Milk programs through soup kitchens undoubtedly constitute one of the largest social and political networks in the country. As a result, all party candidates seek their endorsement and political support during elections.

While conducting my fieldwork in Lima, I participated in more than a dozen of the party rallies that took place at soup kitchens in poor neighborhoods. After walking the streets of the neighborhoods, candidates ended up at soup kitchens where poor voters were waiting to receive food after listening to political speeches. In-depth interviews and anecdotal evidence strongly suggest that candidates' political discourses were secondary to food distribution. That is, voters participated in rallies to get food, not to listen to politicians' promises.

I attended a rally at a soup kitchen in Comas for a candidate who had been accused of sexual harassment. The candidate was clearly trying, without much success, to repair his political image in light of these charges. Most of the voters, while aware of the charges, were more interested in the opportunity the rally offered them to have *guiso con yuca* (local food) and a glass of Inca Cola than in listening to the candidate.

At another party rally at the *Club de Madres* in Lima, I observed that participants were required to present a ticket with the following information in order to receive food: first and last name, address, phone number, document number, *dirigente* who invited them, and the name of the soup kitchen. While parties do not have the networks needed to monitor individual or groups of voters in Peru, social networks such as those of the Mothers' Club (*Club de Madres*) and Glass of Milk do have enough leaders and activists to mobilize and monitor the participation of their beneficiaries. Indeed, Cotler and Grompone (2000: 137) claim that soup kitchens were either rewarded or punished based on their explicit support to the PRONAA. Candidates buy the support of these social networks because they signal their likely electoral support and viability. Studying electoral clientelism in Peru, Paula Muñoz argues that "politicians may engage in clientelism not once they have a viable political machine but because they lack one" (2013: 5).

I have argued elsewhere that rallies provide (a) party leaders with information that enables them to monitor brokers' capacity to mobilize voters, (b) party brokers with an opportunity to display their ability to turn out voters while monitoring voters' responses, and (c) voters with an opportunity to display their gratitude or fear toward brokers. In addition, rallies provide the opposition with an opportunity to gather information about the electoral strength or weakness of the clientelistic party (Szwarcberg 2013). Studying this dynamic in the case of Peru, Muñoz (2013) claims that candidates use clientelism to signal their electoral prospects while gaining name recognition.

During the 2006 presidential campaign in Peru, I participated in more than thirty rallies of the three main contenders: Alan García (Peruvian Aprista Party, APRA), Ollanta Humala (Union for Peru, UP), and Lourdes Flores (National Unity, UN). In each rally, I observed Peruvian candidates from different parties using the same strategies to turn out voters as Peronist and Radical candidates in Argentina.

In his memoir about the presidential campaign of 1990, the acclaimed writer and front-runner presidential candidate, Mario Vargas Llosa (2005 [1993]), describes the problems, challenges, and continuous headaches he experienced when having to organize party rallies and distribute candidacies. In his narrative about the organization of the rally to celebrate the coalition of his party, *Libertad* (Freedom), with *Acción Popular* (Popular Action) and the *Partido Popular Cristiano* (Popular Christian Party), Vargas Llosa recalls his awareness of the rally's signaling utility. The rally would provide to parties the opportunity to display the number of voters they could mobilize. Vargas Llosa remembers having explicitly asked party leaders of the coalition to advise candidates not to divide voters by making them easily identifiable to a specific party.

> Contrary to what was agreed to unify the groups of supporters to show the fraternal spirit of our political alliance each group of voters only applauded and cheered his political leader to prove how many voters they had mobilized.
>
> (Vargas Llosa 1993: 104)

The Peruvian newspapers *El Comercio* and *La República* covered the rally describing how voters were purposely seated in different sectors of the stadium to identify the number of voters each party had mobilized to the rally.

Examining changes in the linkages between the society and the state in Peru, Aldo Panfichi and Omar Coronel (2012) find the construction of neo-clientelist and anti-political linkages through independent political brokers during the 1990s. For instance, Panfichi and Coronel (2012) show how President Alberto Fujimori distributed public housing to sectors of the population that had been more disconnected from the state; a fact that Schady (2000) demonstrates by studying the distribution of the Peruvian Social Fund (FONCODES).

As the theory of perverse incentives predicts, these networks of authoritarian clientelism translate politics on the ground into a feast of clientelism. The feast is observed in the constant distribution of goods at political rallies. As Washington Román – a union leader, journalist, and former candidate for Cusco's regional presidency – said: "Today people ask you 'What have you brought us?' If you haven't brought anything, they do not listen to you" (Muñoz 2013: 92). The construction of these authoritarian political networks without parties strengthens the role of *dirigentes* who are able to turn out voters to participate at rallies. Without partisan networks, distributing goods is the only method available to party candidates of mobilizing poor voters to participate in their political events.

Furthermore, as this theory predicts, the emergence and, over time, consolidation of pragmatic candidates who use clientelistic strategies to mobilize poor voters encourages office-seeking candidates to turn to clientelistic strategies of mobilization regardless of their individual preferences. For instance, I observed how the majority of APRA candidates used clientelistic strategies to mobilize poor voters to a party rally in Lima. When asking them why they were using these strategies, a party activist told me: "If I don't distribute food in exchange for attendance people will go to someone's rally to get the food I am not giving. I am not saying this is right, but it's just as simple as no food, no people."[4] Observing the political mobilizations used by the APRA in Piura, Muñoz found that APRA's local brokers distributed goods to voters.

The combination of a sizeable number of poor voters, a state without the capacity to solve their problems, and the absence of consolidated parties that could constitute viable alternatives to the status quo leads to the unintended consequences of the logic of perverse incentives: the consolidation of mercenary brokers. In describing the political behavior of *dirigentes sociales*, a former councilman in Cusco said: "*Dirigentes* sell themselves to the highest bidder. They rent themselves. They are mercenaries."[5] The persistence of clientelism and the consolidation of mercenary brokers in a country without parties provide further support to the logic of perverse incentives advanced in this book.

Clientelism and Political Machines in Mexico

Focusing on arguably the most effective political machine in Latin America, the PRI, several groundbreaking works (e.g., Magaloni 2006; Greene 2007; Simpser 2013) recognize the importance of the party's capacity to mobilize poor voters in shaping its image of invincibility, and disrupting the organization of the opposition.

The logic of perverse incentives advanced in this book is consistent with the PRI's need for crowded rallies and inflated turnout numbers, which serve to enhance the perception of the invincibility of the incumbent party (Bruhn 1997; Simpser 2013) and weaken the organization of the opposition (Greene 2007). Beatriz Magaloni even argues that "autocratic regimes reward with office those politicians who prove most capable in mobilizing citizens to the party's rallies, getting voters to the polls, and preventing social turmoil in their districts" (2006: 8).

The dynamic use of clientelistic strategies to turn out poor voters in Mexico is also similar to the one described in this book for the Argentine case.

> "In March 1999 I attended a rally in Oaxaca's main square organized by the PRI's *Movimiento Territorial* (Territorial Movement), a loose federation of neighborhood associations linked to the PRI. José Murat, the governor of the state of Oaxaca, was scheduled to speak, so it was important for leaders of squatter organizations to demonstrate to the local PRI leadership that they were capable of mobilizing large numbers of residents for political events. Each neighborhood base committee prominently displayed a sign with the group's name so that the governor and his entourage could see it. As the rally got underway, the moderator called out the name of each neighborhood group over the loudspeaker, and when each group was called the members of that group enthusiastically waved a small banner with the word "*Presente*," signaling to the leadership that they were present in great numbers. The PRI was in effect taking roll, and no doubt someone was writing down which groups had mobilized the largest number of followers."
>
> (Holzner 2010: 49–50)

Claudio Holzner's fieldwork observations echo those presented in this book. Indeed, if we replace the name of the governor and the party, we can think about these actions taking place in other new democracies in which party leaders use rallies to distribute rewards and punishments among party candidates. Field observations also show how party leaders use lists to monitor voter attendance at party rallies. Attendance is taken frequently: members of PRI groups describe hourly roll calls at all-day events as a method of making sure they "do not leave in the middle of the demonstration to do [their] shopping or take care of other errands." (Holzner 2010: footnote 38).

In addition, these observations demonstrate that party brokers do monitor voter participation at rallies, so failing to attend these rallies could have a significant impact on voters who did not participate. In some cases, attendance might exempt participants from work requirements (Holzner 2010: 50); in others, failure to attend may put a person's paycheck at risk:

> "People participated in PRI campaign rallies mostly because attending might have a specific material payoff, or because failure to do so could have personal economic costs. For example, union members who failed to attend such rallies could expect to lose a day's pay."
>
> (Cornelius 1996: 96)

This system rooted in the logic of perverse incentives, which systematically rewards pragmatic candidates over idealist candidates, helped to maintain the PRI's electoral monopoly. By securing the support of many poor voters and sending signals of invincibility at rallies, the PRI's use of clientelism left opposition parties with little opportunity for success. Nonetheless, opposition parties did persist – and eventually succeed – and the logic of perverse incentives can now be observed within these parties as well.

The use of clientelistic strategies to mobilize poor voters is not unique to incumbent parties; the opposition also uses clientelism to turn out poor voters to participate at rallies. Using the case of the *Frente Popular Francisco Villa*, one of the PRD's (Party of the Democratic Revolution) base organizations in Mexico City, Mexico, Hilgers (2005) describes some of the strategies used to ensure the loyalty and discipline of its followers:

> "Until the moment the new owners take possession of their apartment, they are a captive resource of the Front. They must attend the organization's meetings every Sunday, do community work during the week, pay weekly quotas to the leaders, and participate in political events. Leaders record attendance at all of these activities and those who are absent pay a fine. In addition, points are given for participation, so that when a building is finally constructed, those with the most points are the first to

choose their apartment. Leaving the Front, if one tires of the system, is also difficult. Saving for the down payment is not done in individual accounts, but on a group basis. People who give up may lose the money they have already put aside because the leaders will simply ignore their requests for repayment . . . In a PRD affiliation campaign leading up to the March 2005 elections to the party's national and executive committees, all Front members were required to join the party. Photocopies were taken of everyone's electoral credential and these were then used to fill out party membership forms."

(qtd. in Holzner 2010: 50, footnote 39)

Beyond the mobilization of poor voters to participate at rallies and elections, the case of Mexico also provides further support for understanding candidates' decisions to use clientelism in terms of the logic of perverse incentives. Kenneth Greene, "[i]mpressed with their [activists' and candidates'] level of commitment – intellectual, ethical, and physical – to political change," provides further support to the microfoundations of political clientelism and the logic of perverse incentives advanced in this book (2007: xiii). Highlighting the importance of differential resource endowments between the incumbent and opposition parties, Greene observes that "resource-poor parties face particular problems of political recruitment. They have such a low chance of winning that they cannot provide potential joiners with instrumental benefits for their participation over the short term. As a result, resource-poor parties typically rely on volunteers to serve as both candidates and activists rather than the paid professional party personnel found in most parties with resources. But these volunteers still need reasons to participate in a high-cost activity that is unlikely to succeed" (304).

Explaining why some activists would join a disadvantaged party, Greene argues that "ideologically charged citizens act on their principles over their interests" (12). Analogous to the pragmatic and idealist candidates discussed in Argentina, Greene observes two different attitudes toward clientelistic strategies within opposition parties. Most of his interviews with party activists and candidates from opposition parties highlight the same tension that I observed in the decision making of pragmatists and idealist candidates. Greene differentiates between two types of candidates: office seekers "interested in affecting political change from the top-down through the use of the bully pulpit" and message seekers "committed to political change from the bottom-up" (124). The quotes that follow from Greene's work came from Mexican activists and candidates, but they could just as easily have come from Argentine activists and candidates interviewed for this book:

Office seekers' quotes:

> You can't really influence policy unless you first win the election. I want to change a lot of things in Mexico, but we can't do any of that unless we win.

> From the very beginning, the idea was to win office. We didn't have the resources to get anyone elected, and we had to convince friends and family to run as candidates, but we always wanted to get our people elected.

Message seekers' quotes:

> I want our party to win, but not at the risk of becoming just like the PRI.

> If we win without changing people's minds, then what have we won? First, we need to be a party of civic education.
>
> (qtd. in Greene 2007: 124)

Office seekers resemble pragmatist candidates; message seekers' testimonies are similar to those of suicidal candidates. Greene explains the suicidal political action of message seekers by arguing that activists and candidates "thought about their participation in terms of both expressive and instrumental benefits" (124). Borrowing from Dennis Chong's "narrowly rational expressive benefits" (1991: 73), Greene claims that participating in opposition parties provides activists and candidates with an option to "effectively express their anger or disapproval over a policy or existing state of affairs" (Chong 1991: 88, qtd. in Greene 2007: 123). Based on in-depth interviews with candidates and activists affiliated with Mexico's opposition parties (National Action Party, PAN, and the PRD), Greene finds that "one has to be a true believer to join a losing and potentially dangerous cause" (120).

Katherine Bruhn's (1997) earlier study of the PRD provides further support to Greene's findings. Studying the reasons that led activists to join opposition parties such as the PRD during the 1980s, Bruhn describes a level of commitment and dedication that led activists to spend significant time and resources in their political lives. "In '88 people were completely mobilized, and some spent all their savings, everything they had ... to follow Cárdenas [the PRD leading figure] ... then in '89, in the July elections, they participated again in the same way. And in those [elections] of December of the same year. Well, then, no pocket can bear all that ... This campaign would have been easier for me if I hadn't spent so much in 1988 also ... People are spent economically, emotionally too" (confidential interview, p. 200).

As described in these testimonies, it is activists' commitment to political change that leads them to spend considerable economic resources and emotional energy. Interviews with activists in Argentina and my field notes point toward similar actions in cases in which activists express their commitment to change the status quo.

By systematically rewarding pragmatic rather than idealist candidates, the unintended consequences of the logic of perverse incentives help to explain how the PRI was able to build an electoral monopoly. It took an economic crisis and the willingness of suicidal candidates to build opposition parties to end the PRI rule.[6]

Conclusion

Original fieldwork data from Lima, Peru, and secondary literature from Mexico document the persistence of clientelism. Building on the empirical evidence presented in these rich works, I found further evidence for the logic of perverse incentives and its unintended consequences. From the motivations that lead office-seeking activists to turn to clientelism to mobilize poor voters to the use of party rallies to signal candidates' and parties' capacity to deliver votes, this chapter presents significant evidence to support the arguments advanced in this book.

Whereas more research is needed to establish the specific mechanisms through which the logic of perverse incentives is translated in different countries and across regions, states, cities, and neighborhoods, this chapter provides evidence that the argument advanced in this book could be extended to explain the persistence and decline of clientelism in democracies in Latin America and beyond. As Jonathan Fox recognized in the case of Mexico, "the main point here is that if political action can create (or revive) clientelism, it can also undermine it" (1994: 155). Change is so difficult to achieve in poor neighborhoods simply because parties need votes to win elections and clientelism is still effective in getting those votes inexpensively. As José Woldenberg, President of Mexico's Electoral Federal Institute (IFE), said over a decade ago: "Mexico is a very poor country with enormous disparities. For a lot of people, one kilo of sugar or beans is more important than a vote. There are unscrupulous political operatives who know these needs and will find ways to capitalize on them" (Cornelius 2004: 47).

8

Conclusions: Winners Lose

"Like so many sadnesses you get used to live with" are the words written on the wall of a small drugstore a few blocks away from Laura's home.[1] The graffiti captures the everyday experience of poor voters like Laura who participate in party rallies and elections to receive benefits in exchange for their political support. Laura lives today with a disabled son as a result of her attending a rally to continue receiving a welfare benefit. She continues participating in rallies and elections and voting for candidates that Mario, now an elected local representative, supports. Laura still struggles every day to make ends meet regardless of the benefits she receives from a social welfare program and a scholarship from the government for her disabled son. Mario still uses clientelism to mobilize voters; he has even succeeded in building and sustaining a party network of poor voters like Laura that enabled him to get elected as a local representative. Their relationship, from its origins until the present, illustrates the findings presented in this book.

It is the logic of perverse incentives, which rewards party candidates based only on the number of voters they mobilize, that hindered Mario from being compassionate toward Laura. If Mario had not forced Laura to attend the rally, other voters could have assumed that they could receive or seek to receive – benefits without having to participate in rallies and elections. Mario could not run the risk of excusing Laura and strongly encouraged her to attend the rally. The tragic outcome was the result of the logic of perverse incentives that led Mario to force Laura to attend a party rally, and its unintended consequences – that Laura's son, a healthy baby boy, suffered an irreparable injury as a result of negligence that could have been avoided if Laura had not been forced to attend the rally.

This book finds that office-seeking candidates competing to mobilize poor voters are encouraged to use clientelism to succeed. In rewarding candidates based only on the number of voters they mobilize, party

140

leaders motivate candidates to turn to clientelism. The combination of the electoral success of candidates who employ clientelism, the dynamics of political competition, and the absence of effective punishment encourages candidates to use clientelistic strategies to mobilize poor voters.

First, candidates learn through experience that those who employ these strategies succeed in their political careers. Hence, while candidates can get elected for reasons that are unrelated to the strategies they employ, the fact that candidates who use clientelism get elected teaches them that the use of clientelism does not hurt their chances of getting elected and reelected.

Second, the dynamics of political competition induce candidates to turn to these strategies. Even when a candidate prefers not to use clientelism to turn out voters, another candidate from his or her party (intraparty competition) or from the opposition (interparty competition) will employ these tactics and receive the reward of a political promotion for his or her success in turning out voters.

Third, candidates also learn that neither the political parties nor the justice system punishes the use of clientelistic strategies to mobilize voters. The absence of effective punishment teaches candidates that there are no negative consequences for choosing to use clientelism.

However, this book also finds that, while candidates face perverse incentives to turn to clientelistic strategies, not all candidates are capable of employing them, and not all who are capable choose to pursue these strategies. Existing explanations simply assume that candidates capable of using clientelism will always turn to these strategies in neighborhoods where they compete to mobilize poor voters, but this research demonstrates that candidates can choose not to employ these strategies.

By incorporating a candidate's agency in decision making, this book distinguishes candidates who are capable of using clientelism but choose otherwise, idealist candidates, from those who will choose to employ them, pragmatic candidates. Candidates who are capable of using clientelism but choose not to are committing political suicide by making a decision that will decrease – if not totally eliminate – their chances of getting reelected. The existence of suicidal candidates demonstrates that even in the face of incentives to turn to clientelistic strategies, not all candidates prefer using these strategies to mobilize poor voters.

Still, the logic of perverse incentives implies that when political leaders reward candidates based only on the number of voters they mobilize, party leaders contribute to the emergence and consolidation of mercenary candidates. As they are rewarded based on the size of their party network, mercenary candidates will distribute money, small goods, and even alcohol and drugs to voters in exchange for political participation. In contrast to other candidates, mercenaries are careless about the consequences of their actions; they are only interested in the material rewards they will receive in exchange for their political work. The emergence and consolidation of mercenary candidates is the result of this system of incentives that forces candidates to turn to clientelistic strategies.

This book examines the unintended consequences of the logic of perverse incentives that poses several unexpected challenges to party leaders and contributes to the deterioration of the quality of democracy. By empowering candidates who only care about material rewards, political leaders build their own Frankensteins. Once mercenary candidates consolidate a party network large enough to secure their election and reelection, they succeed in reinforcing a logic of perverse incentives that rewards candidates based only on the number of voters they mobilize. Over time, this leads to the consolidation of clientelism in democracy and, thus, to the translation of voter income inequalities into low-quality representation. After all, a direct consequence of clientelism is that, although poor voters can participate in electoral democracy, their preferences are not voiced.[2] Voters can attend rallies and even support candidates without providing much information, if any, about their policy preferences.

The unintended consequences of the logic of perverse incentives create the conditions that enable the emergence and persistence of mercenary candidates. Understanding the mechanisms through which political candidates who use clientelism succeed in getting elected and reelected is essential to improve the quality of democracy. Observing that candidates who use clientelism succeed in getting elected and reelected poses severe challenges to our understanding of democratic representation, especially when we think about the consequences that these actions have in the everyday life of poor voters like Laura.

A study of the persistence and consolidation of political clientelism in democracy is also a study about inertia. According to Barrington Moore:

> The assumption of inertia, that cultural and social continuity do not require explanation, obliterates the fact that both have to be recreated anew in each generation, often with great pain and suffering. To maintain and transmit a value system, human beings are punched, bullied, sent to jail, thrown into concentration camps, cajoled, bribed, made into heroes, encouraged to read newspapers, stood up against a wall and shot, and sometimes even taught sociology [or political science].
>
> (1966: 486)

Explaining the consolidation of clientelism implies not only studying the conditions under which these strategies are effective in mobilizing poor voters, but also studying the human costs these practices have upon poor voters. Thinking about Laura's pain and suffering should force us not to naturalize the status quo of a system that exploits the most vulnerable.

Perverse Incentives and Political Mobilization

Party activists and brokers are key political actors in machine organizations. Brokers have information about voter needs and political preferences and are able to deliver and target benefits to them in exchange for support while monitoring their political behavior. Thus, without brokers, political parties' attempts to use clientelism to mobilize voters are likely to fail either because they are unable to distribute benefits or because they deliver these benefits to the wrong supporters.

Still, brokers can use clientelistic inducements to pursue their own careers or to support an opposition candidate, even against their party leader's interest; they can also pursue personal enrichment, also (potentially) at the cost of lost votes for their party. To make brokers pursue the party's goals in addition to their individual preferences, party leaders reward and punish brokers based on their capacity to turn out voters at party rallies and elections.

Studying political, partisan, and social networks, I trace the political careers of party activists interested in pursuing a career in politics. The book focuses on the political decisions of party brokers or candidates, terms that I use interchangeably, and I define and study in their position as local elected officials, councilors who represent a party in the neighborhoods where they live. In contrast to party activists and volunteers, candidates succeed in building a party network large enough to enable them to get elected, and in some cases reelected once or multiple times. A party leader or boss is the mayor who commands candidates by distributing political promotions.

To test the mechanism through which party leaders distribute rewards and punishments to candidates, I focus on party rallies because, in contrast to elections, they enable party bosses, candidates, and voters to make their support visible. Party bosses use rallies to observe and measure how many voters each one of his or her candidates is capable of turning out. In mobilizing voters to participate in party rallies, candidates seek to be rewarded with political promotions. Voters attend rallies to support candidates for their help in solving their everyday problems, to continue receiving particularistic goods, and/or to be considered to receive future benefits.

I argue that party rallies have multiple meanings for those who organize and attend these events but choose to focus on the effects rallies have on the dynamics of intra- and interparty competition. Within the party, rallies enable candidates to observe the capacity of rival candidates to mobilize voters. In addition, rallies enable party bosses to curtail the distribution of rewards to their favorite candidates if they turn out fewer voters than other candidates. Rallies also enable opposition parties to assess a party's capacity to mobilize voters and thus to get a better sense of their likely support so that they can plan accordingly.

These demonstrations are held with the assumption that voters who support candidates at rallies will do the same in elections. Therefore, attendance at rallies highlights a candidate's suitability to run for office, deters internal and external opposition, builds possibilities for future alliances, and allows candidates to win spaces for future negotiations inside and outside their party. It also implies that candidates interested in getting promoted within the party have incentives to employ strategies that enable them to achieve their goal of increasing voter turnout.

Even though candidates can be reliable party agents who distribute party goods to maximize the party's vote share because they believe in the party's program, party leaders are nevertheless unable to determine the party agents' reliability without monitoring their ability to turn out voters. Candidates' opportunities to appropriate party goods for self-enrichment will vary depending on party leaders' expectations of voter turnout and the voters' propensity to participate in the neighborhoods the councilor represents. Candidates competing to mobilize voters in high-support neighborhoods, where voters are likely to support the party regardless of receiving clientelistic inducements, have more chances to increase their wealth by selling the goods than do candidates in low-support neighborhoods, where voters' support is conditional on receiving handouts.

Information about voter turnout at the level of the neighborhood provides party leaders with a baseline against which to evaluate a candidate's performance. Still, this information is insufficient to persuade candidates to maximize party votes. I argue that party leaders combine information from turnout at rallies and elections to diminish the risks of moral hazard. Comparing a candidate's capacity to mobilize voters at rallies and elections over time enables party leaders to identify reliable party candidates and distribute rewards and punishments accordingly. In cases where sustaining networks of party candidates who are likely to charge commissions become more expensive than engaging in programmatic politics, political leaders will consider abandoning clientelistic politics. If candidates continue turning out voters, party mayors have no incentives to change strategies.

Implications of the Logic of Perverse Incentives

Rewarding candidates with political promotions based only on the number of voters they mobilize leads to the consolidation of mercenary candidates. The persistence of political machines is a direct consequence of the logic of perverse incentives. This book examines this outcome by studying the emergence and persistence of political machines at the local level in Argentina. A consequence of the consolidation of local political machines is also its Achilles' heel: political stability. The longer a mayor remains in power at the local level, the more likely it is that he or she will be able to consolidate his or her power by placing political candidates in the city council and city hall. Over time, several mayors even extend their influence to the local police and justice system. In short, they have enough power at the local level to decide the political fate of any politically ambitious candidate. Candidates who seek a political career, therefore, need to follow the system in place; otherwise, they will not succeed in getting elected.

Voters and political agents who are dissatisfied with the existing political arrangement find it very difficult to change a well-established local monopoly. The combination of absence of resources and the use of local institutions from the municipality discourages the organization of the opposition. And the absence of an organized alternative through which to voice voters' concerns could only lead to quiet acceptance and resignation or to social outbursts and protests.

Scholarly studies about social protest in Argentina and elsewhere (Kuran 1991; Lohmann 1994; Auyero 2003; Svampa and Pereyra 2003) show how singular events such as the death of a teenager, a prevented fire accident, or a videotaped incident of police brutality can trigger a cascade of events that concludes with the demise of an enduring political monopoly. While existing theories are unable to explain why people decide to protest at a specific moment, they demonstrate that people do organize and go to the streets to shout "enough is enough" (*basta ya*).[3] If the repression is successful, things will remain the same; if it is unsuccessful, there will be an opportunity for change.

Massive protests could pave the way for critical junctures that "disrupt the existing balance of political or economic power" (Acemouglu and Robinson 2012: 106). Still, in the case of Argentina as in the case of many new democracies, it seems that major watersheds in political life fail to open certain paths for change while closing others "in a way that shapes politics for years to come" (Collier and Collier 1991: 27). Interestingly, the logic of perverse incentives explains why this is the case.

Referring back to Minister Fernández's comment that "he does politics with those who do politics," the logic of perverse incentives highlights that as long as politicians are rewarded based only on their capacities to mobilize voters, political renovation is a difficult, if not impossible, task. Without changes in the logic of incentives, we are unlikely to observe changes in politicians' actions and, therefore, in the strategies they employ to mobilize poor voters, as well as in the strategies they employ to build and sustain a party network.

Political parties as organizations that seek to win elections are not likely to punish candidates capable of turning out a large number of voters. Moreover, even if parties were interested in inducing candidates not to use clientelism, they would be unable to achieve their goal because the same flexibility that enables parties to adapt to the context dissuades them from disciplining their members. In contrast to Levitsky (2003), my book shows how institutional flexibility has also served to enforce a system of perverse incentives that encourages candidates to use clientelism to mobilize voters. The factors that Levitsky uses to explain party adaptation and survival also serve to strengthen the logic of perverse incentives that reward candidates based only on the number of voters they mobilize.[4] Political parties will not punish candidates capable of mobilizing a large network of party voters who will contribute to winning elections.

Whereas "clientelism does not always emerge or persist because of the wishes of political leaders alone, and when it dies, it often does so in part as a result of leaders moving against the machine" (Stokes et al. 2013: 199), focusing on individual candidates' preferences and capacities to use clientelism within social, political, and partisan networks is the only way to provide an adequate explanation of its emergence and persistence. The theory and empirical evidence examined in this book presents and tests a logic of perverse incentives that provides a full-fledged explanation of the consolidation of clientelism in a democracy.

Studying the consolidation of clientelism in a democracy is of ultimate importance in understanding its unintended consequences and the profound implication of its effects for the quality of political representation and, thus, for the dynamics of regime stability or breakdown in new democracies in the region and beyond.

Political Alternatives: Transitions away from Clientelism

Transitions from clientelistic to programmatic politics are complex processes that involve several changes at multiple institutional levels. My theory predicts that transitions will take place when voters cannot be mobilized in exchange for benefits and/or party agents are not rewarded based only on the amount of goods they distribute. The relationship between economic development and the disappearance of clientelism is consistent with theories of modernization (Lipset 1959). In their process-tracing analyses of England and the United States, Susan Stokes and her contributors (2013) find that clientelistic parties are likely to shift to programmatic strategies as the electorate gets larger and wealthier, making voters' electoral preferences less observable, and with the advancement of technology that reduces parties' cost to communicate their programs.

Studying clientelism as an electoral investment in Mexico, Magaloni and her collaborators find that clientelism is most prevalent at intermediate ranges of development: "as a country develops and the pivotal voter becomes wealthier, clientelism should erode as a dominant form of political exchange simply because it becomes too costly" (2007: 204). For Magaloni (2006), modernization is a strong predictor of voter support for the opposition, but it does not directly lead to the establishment of democracy. In her explanation, economic growth and development have conflicting effects on transitions to democracy; only when economic recession is perceived as systematic will voters defect from the ruling party en masse. In contrast, Greene (2007) focuses on the capacity of opposition parties to take advantage of voters' dissatisfaction with incumbents' mismanagement of the economy.

Building on the seminal works on transitions from authoritarian rule in Latin America (O'Donnell and Schmitter 1986), my work suggests the possibility that transitions away from clientelism could take place when candidates from clientelistic parties decide to break away from their party leaders to build their own party and take with them idealist candidates they know would not have a career in politics if they stayed within the clientelistic party. I argue that the mechanisms that explain transitions away from clientelism are similar to those that Guillermo O'Donnell and Philippe C. Schmitter identify in explaining transitions from authoritarianism to democracy: "there is no transition whose beginning is not the consequence – direct or indirect – of important divisions within the authoritarian regime itself, principally along the fluctuating cleavage between hard-liners and soft-liners" (1986: 19).

In the case of transitions from clientelism, I argue that the cleavage always takes place within the incumbent party between pragmatist and idealist candidates. When idealist candidates observe that it is possible for them to build a political opposition party, they will split from their original party. To explain this mechanism, I study the cases of two opposition parties that succeeded in winning local elections against entrenched Peronist and Radical administrations in Argentina: the Partido Nuevo (New Party, PN) in Córdoba Capital, and the Partido Nuevo Morón (New Morón, NM) in the municipality of Morón located in the Conurbano of the province of Buenos Aires. In these cases, transitions took place when candidates from within the clientelistic party made the most of a critical juncture that offered them a unique historical opportunity.

The *Partido Nuevo* won the government of Córdoba Capital in 2003 after the administration of Peronist mayor Germán Kammerath, who was considered the worst mayor in the municipality's history. Even the Peronist governor who chose Kammerath as his candidate asked voters to forgive him for contributing to the election of Córdoba's most corrupt and oligarchic mayor. Peronist Party leaders knew voters would not pardon the party's catastrophic administration in the capital; thus, the governor did not even campaign for the party in the most important district of the province. With the PJ out of the competition, the Radical Party, whose past administrations had been prized and remembered by voters, could have benefited, regardless of the party's national defeats.

Yet, the provincial and local party leadership was fractured. Eduardo Angeloz, who had governed the province between 1983 and 1995, had been charged with embezzlement; and although he was found not guilty in 1998, too much suspicion and discontent still remained to nominate him again. Ramón Mestre, his successor (1995–1999) and party rival, died in 2003. And finally, Rubén Martí, who led the third faction of the UCR in Córdoba and was a former mayor of the city, was ill. Unable to nominate any leader of the party's representative factions, the UCR nominated Luis Molinari Romero, a qualified but uncharismatic candidate who was remembered for being Angeloz's right hand. The party did not manage to fulfill the electorate's demand: a fresh face without ties to the past.

Luis Juez, a former Peronist and provincial anticorruption prosecutor, emerged as the favorite candidate in opinion polls. After being fired by the governor, Juez, a media figure, decided to establish a party to compete for office. The name of Juez's party, the Partido Nuevo (New Party), summarized his political campaign: Córdoba needed a change, something new, different from Peronism and Radicalism. In an election with the lowest voter turnout since the return of democracy, Luis Juez became mayor with the most hegemonic city council since 1983. The PN obtained twenty seats, and the remaining eleven were distributed among four parties, making a strong, homogeneous opposition unlikely.[5] After governing the capital for sixteen years, and serving as the primary source of political opposition, the UCR obtained only two seats in the city council, and the Peronist Party obtained eight out of the thirty-two council seats. It is very unlikely that Juez would have won if the Peronist administration was not a disaster and the Radical Party's leadership was either alive or unquestioned.

A similar critical juncture enabled the electoral victory of the youngest mayor in a municipality in the Conurbano of the province of Buenos Aires, Martín Sabatella. After being councilor and president of the commission that investigated Juan Carlos Rousellot, the former mayor of Morón, Sabatella was nominated by the Alliance (*Alianza*), a political coalition between the UCR and the Front for a Country in Solidarity (Frepaso), to run for mayor of the municipality.[6] In 1999, together with the national victory of this political alliance, Sabatella won the municipal election; although the government of the Alliance ended up with the political crisis that forced President Fernando De la Rua to resign in 2001, Sabatella managed to get reelected.

In 2002, the mayor funded the New Morón Party, which obtained a surprisingly high voter share – 58 percent of the votes – for a local party that did not present candidates for provincial and national offices. Indeed, the case of Morón shows that when voters approve of a local administration, they are willing to support different party candidates for different offices or only vote for local offices to support their municipal government. Thirty-four percent of the voters who supported Martín Sabatella's reelection voted for another party for other offices, and 19 percent voted only for Sabatella. Martín Sabatella's administration garnered international recognition when the mayor was profiled in the *Wall Street Journal* in an article entitled "Local Battle: One Tough Mayor Shows Argentina How to Clean House."[7]

The cases of Luis Juez in Córdoba and Martín Sabatella in Buenos Aires demonstrate the challenges faced in building political alternatives. Both parties were unable to use clientelism to build a party network, given that they did not have a network of party activists and resources. Moreover, it is highly unlikely that these parties would engage in these strategies even if they had goods and activists, given the origins of their candidates (mostly professional individuals who were working in politics for the first time), the party electorate, the support of middle-class and professional voters, and the party's program of eliminating clientelism. Still, once elected, these two parties had to prove that they were able to administer the municipalities in a more transparent and effective way than their predecessors to sustain and increase their vote share among the local population.

This places a substantial burden on new parties without any government experience. If their administrations prove unsatisfactory, these parties will disappear completely. Critical junctures provide political alternatives with an opportunity to win seats, even the local executive office, while making these parties' administrations crucial for the party's political future, or their survival.

The absence of a common history, core supporters, and even leadership (after all, the PN and NM were created by one individual; Luis Juez is the *Partido Nuevo* and vice versa) implies that an unsatisfactory administration will lead to the party's disappearance. In contrast to Radical and Peronist candidates, whose parties can survive disastrous administrations, voters affiliated with these new parties do not have anywhere to go if their parties' administrations turn out to be a disappointment. Still, this also implies that if these parties' administrations are successful, they will pave the way for a different way of doing politics, one that is neither Radical nor Peronist nor clientelistic.

At present, Luis Juez is a state senator and Martín Sabatella a national deputy from the province of Buenos Aires for their respective parties. Juez almost won the election for governor of Córdoba in 2007 in an election plagued with denunciations of electoral fraud; Sabatella joined the Kirchners' administration by working in the Federal Authority of Media Services (*Autoridad Federal de Servicios de Comunicación Audiovisual*). From his new political space, the party *Nuevo Encuentro* (New Encounter), Sabatella decided to support the president's project at the national level while providing his own candidates at the provincial and municipal levels.

Future Research Agenda

Studies about distributive politics in new democracies have produced significant and meaningful findings. My work contributes to this literature by building a theory about the logic of perverse incentives that explains why, how, and under what conditions political parties encourage candidates to employ clientelistic strategies to mobilize poor voters. Studying the effects of this system of perverse incentives, I explain the consolidation of clientelism in democracies and its pernicious effects in new democracies by using a novel research design that combines network analysis with qualitative and quantitative data. Still, even beyond the contributions made in this book, I envision five different areas for future research in the subject.

First, as I noted at the beginning of this book, an interesting and prolific research agenda exists on questions of *clientelism and commitment*. I believe that questions about visibility and commitment are a surprising omission from our own research agenda. Studying visibility entails theorizing differences in participation at party rallies and elections. In my work, for instance, I show how party leaders use rallies to gather information about voter turnout and party agents' reliability (Szwarcberg 2012a). Studying party rallies in Peru, Paula Muñoz (2013) builds an "informational theory" to explain why clientelism is effective in a "democracy without parties" (Levitsky and Cameron 2003; Tanaka 2005).

We need to build comparisons not only between the use of party rallies in democracies with strong parties as in Argentina and weak parties as in Peru, but also between democratic and non-democratic regimes. Many of the factors that I identify as explanatory of the continuity of rallies in Latin America (Szwarcberg 2014) are also present in non-democratic settings. As such, we need better and more refined theories that enable us to explain why this is the case. Further research in different places and over time would aid in testing the validity of our claims, as well as specifying the conditions under which visibility at party rallies matter.

Second, there are interesting and quite unexplored relationships between *clientelism and political participation*. In this book, I focus on three of these relationships:

(1) The relationship between clientelism and voter turnout. By distributing goods to poor voters in exchange for political participation, clientelistic parties could potentially have an effect on voter turnout. Assuming that voters turn out just to receive goods, we could argue that clientelism has a positive effect in increasing voter turnout by mobilizing voters who would otherwise stay home. In examining the effects of the use of clientelistic strategies of mobilization on voter turnout, scholars should also bear in mind differences between compulsory and noncompulsory voting, as well as differences in the enforcement of these laws. Assuming that clientelism does have an effect on voter turnout forces us to think carefully about its impact on the quality of democratic representation. After all, when voters turn out just because they will receive something in exchange, they are not providing any information about their policy preferences.

(2) The relationships among gender, political participation, and clientelism. Studying female participation in clientelistic networks, Auyero (2000) and I (Szwarcberg 2011) found important differences in *how* female and male politicians deliver goods to voters. Moreover, while our works focus on the performance of those who were delivering goods to voters, further studies should also examine the effects of gender in the relationships between those delivering the goods and those receiving these goods. Does a female politician deliver goods the same way to female and male voters? Does a male politician deliver the same goods to female and male voters? Focusing on the provision of public favors, Oliveros (2012) found that female patronage employees are more likely than men to be asked for favors. These empirical findings call for the development of theories that enable us to better comprehend these results. Answering these questions will help us to understand differences in gender and political participation in new democracies.

(3) The relationship between clientelism and political behavior. Studying the political careers of Argentine candidates, I found that their preferences to use clientelism are significantly shaped by their political participation during the military dictatorship in Argentina. Candidates who escaped the country, were persecuted, and/or who had several friends from their political group killed and/or disappear, were less likely to engage in clientelistic strategies than candidates who did not share these political experiences. Still, we need much more systematic studies in Argentina and beyond to understand the effects of political socialization and political experience on candidates' preferences to use clientelism.

Third, we should study if and how using clientelistic strategies of mobilization has an effect on voters' trust. Does the use of political clientelism make voters more or less likely (or indifferent) to trust political institutions? Specifically, it would be interesting to know if the use of political clientelism has an effect on voters' trust of political institutions, such as political parties, the party system, participation in elections, and the implications of these effects on political participation.

Fourth, we need to build theories and enhance our understanding of the relationship between *normative commitments and clientelism*. Few pieces examine in depth the effects that these practices have on the development of new democracies. The majority of contemporary work, mine included, simply states the advantages and disadvantages of the use of clientelistic strategies for democracy. Still, I am convinced that we need a more profound, theoretically rich, and systematic analysis of how scholars' commitments toward this phenomenon affect the study of it and what the consequences are of those biases in our findings. Beyond the importance of the academic exercise, this is key to designing effective public policies that could successfully contribute to improvements in the quality of life of the most vulnerable citizens in our polities.

Fifth and finally, we need to begin thinking about the relationship between *clientelism and corruption*. What are the differences and similarities between the two concepts? Is clientelism one particular practice of corruption? Answering these questions will contribute to our understanding of both phenomena. In addition, I believe that it would enable scholars working on these issues to share theoretical and empirical insights that could enable us to improve the quality of democracy and government.

Conclusion

This book explains the logic of perverse incentives that encourages candidates to use clientelism to mobilize poor voters to attend rallies and elections. Strategies of political mobilization that provide poor voters with benefits in exchange for their vote succeed in muting poor voters from expressing their political preferences: "As a normative ideal, democracy means political equality. Not only should all those affected be nominally included in decision-making, but they should be included on equal terms. All ought to have an equal right and effective opportunity to express their interests and concerns" (Young 2000: 23). Clientelism violates Robert Dahl's (1971, 1987) principle of equal consideration of interests: "during processes of collective decision-making, the interests of every person who is subject to the decision must (within the limits of feasibility) be accurately interpreted and made known" (1987: 86).

In 1999, Guillermo O'Donnell described an imaginary map of a country where areas colored blue designate districts with a high degree of functional and territorial presence of the state; green areas, where the territorial penetration is high but the presence is significantly lower in functional/class terms; and brown areas that are low or null in both dimensions. This imaginary map not only serves to describe and study the uneven political geography of clientelism, but it also helps theorize about different types of citizenship based on voters' everyday experiences with politics.

Voters living in blue areas build different linkages with their local, provincial, and municipal political representatives than do voters living in brown areas. Over time, the experience of living in brown areas translates to a completely different, and I would argue even radically different, understanding of the value of democracy. O'Donnell sensed this transition when he talked about the slow death of democracy:

> Democracies do not only suffer quick deaths, like an earthquake. They can also suffer, even more insidiously, a slow death, like a house eaten away by termites. A slow death is a long process of corrosion during which no one does anything because there are no spectacular episodes. But in three or maybe ten years, you wake up and realize that democracy is gone. I imagine it as a house that has had termites corroding its foundation. Up until last night it seemed perfect and the following morning a small wind blows it down.[8]

The consolidation of political clientelism in new democracies constitutes a solid sign of the slow death. The story of Laura and Mario described at the beginning of this book vividly illustrates the pernicious effects of the logic of perverse incentives. Understanding the unintended consequences of rewarding candidates based only on the number of voters they mobilize explains why a healthy baby boy became permanently handicapped.

Studying the design of social programs in Mexico, Diaz-Cayeros and his collaborators (2007) demonstrate that approximately 8,000 children would have been saved if the government had not used clientelism in designing and targeting antipoverty programs. The authors show that clientelism led to the deaths of innocent children who could have been easily saved if politicians had not used these programs for electoral purposes:

> The Zapatistas rose in arms with a variety of demands, among them, they called attention to the state's utter failure to provide

minimum social infrastructure that would prevent deaths from curable diseases such as diarrhea. The clever articulation of the Zapatistas' demands by Subcomandante Marcos made it transparent that poverty was linked to political corruption, government abuse, and lack of democratic accountability.

(223)

Clientelism matters because in buying the political participation of poor voters, the quality of political democracy suffers. And that suffering is visible and substantive in the life of innocent children who die from curable diseases or become handicapped for life. The awareness that clientelism kills is important for advancing changes which disassemble the logic of perverse incentives that encourages political candidates to use these strategies. Laura's son did not deserve to have his future handicapped because of politics, and when that is the result of a logic of incentives that encourages candidates to mobilize as many voters as possible without taking into account the consequences, even the winners lose.

Notes

1 Mobilizing Poor Voters

1. See Stokes (2007) and Hicken (2011) for similar definitions of *clientelism*.
2. I develop this argument in the Conclusions (Chapter 8).
3. I explore this logic of perverse incentives and its implications in Chapter 5.
4. I examine the origins and political careers of community organizers and paid and unpaid party activists in detail in Chapter 2, where I also study the use of municipal money to pay for their activities.
5. Although there are other local elected offices at the municipal level, school counselors (*consejeros escolares*), and auditors (*tribunales de cuentas*), these positions demand appointees to hold a degree in education, law, or accounting, restricting party bosses' ability to distribute these offices among brokers who in most cases lack a college education but are nevertheless effective in mobilizing voters.
6. The FPV is a faction of the Peronist Party. Both former President Néstor Kirchner (2003–2007) and current President Cristina Fernández de Kirchner (2007–present) were elected using the FPV Party label.
7. Aldo Rico and his *carapintadas* movement staged a series of barracks uprisings in 1987 during the presidency of Raúl Alfonsín; they demanded that the government end the trials of military personnel involved in the disappearance and torture of political detainees during the dictatorship.
8. The election took place on Sunday, April 9. Yet, given that no candidate received the required number of votes, the two candidates that received the most votes, Alan García from the American Popular Revolutionary Alliance (APRA) and Ollanta Humala from Union for Peru (UPP) competed again on Sunday, June 4. Alan García won the election.
9. I examine the case of Luis Juez and the New Party in detail in Chapter 8.
10. Beyond some petty theft, my first "bad experience" while conducting research in the Conurbano occurred exactly one day after I asked about the connections between local politicians and drug trafficking. The following afternoon, as I was walking on the street, the same street at the same hour I usually did during those months, someone, whom I did not know, hugged me from behind

and asked me to stop asking questions about drugs. "About politics ask whatever you want, but about drugs you stop asking questions." ("*De política pregunta lo que quieras, pero con las drogas no te metas.*") It was a quick and effective warning. My second bad experience took place the day of the election October 23, 2005, when I decided to stay longer than usual – late into the night – for the victory "celebrations" of the FPV in José C. Paz at the building of the mayor's *agrupación*. I am eternally grateful to Sergio for rescuing me. I have no doubt that were it not for him, my whole field research experience, as well as my life, would have been pretty different after that night.

2 The Microfoundations of Political Clientelism

1. Author interview, November 2005.
2. Author interview, September 2005. This and all subsequent translations from the Spanish are by the author.
3. Author interview, October 2005.
4. See also Bourdieu (1990).
5. Defining a structure of feeling, Auyero writes: "In conceptual terms, structures of feelings are 'social experiences in solution,' that is, cultural forms that have not yet precipitated out. In methodological terms, a structure of feeling is a 'cultural hypothesis.'" (2000: 211).
6. Author interview, April 2006.
7. See the International Institute for Democracy and Electoral Assistance (IDEA) for data about voter turnout for Argentina: http://www.idea.int/vt/country view.cfm?id=12
8. Half of the candidates in Buenos Aires were running to get elected or reelected, as the city council in the province is renewed by halves every two years. In Córdoba, on the other hand, candidates were campaigning to show their ability to turn out voters for the party to be considered for reelection in the upcoming election of 2009. In contrast to Buenos Aires, voters in Córdoba elect their mayors and councilors together every four years.
9. See Chapter 1 for a description and explanation of case selection. In contrast to councilors in the other selected municipalities, incumbent councilors in Malvinas Argentinas did not talk openly about almost anything, including their preferences to use clientelism. Chapter 6 examines this case in detail as one municipality that has been governed since its origins by the same mayor, who built a powerful machine and exercises an iron-grip control over every institution in the municipality, including the city council. Hence, I exclude the case of Malvinas in this analysis but discuss it substantively in other chapters.
10. Party networks are defined as *agrupaciones* that cluster neighborhood-level organizations. Chapter 3 examines in detail the construction of political, partisan, and social networks from the ground up, explaining how, when, and why party activists join these organizations and succeed or fail in mobilizing voters by using clientelism.
11. Author interview, April 2006.
12. Data collected from municipal authorities by the author.

13. Author interview, November 2005.
14. Author interview, September 2005.
15. The PAUFE is a right-wing political party whose founder, leader, and former mayor of Escobar (a municipality in Buenos Aires), Luis Patti, was police chief during the last dictatorship and who has since been convicted for the torture and disappearance of people during that period.
16. Author interview, November 2005.
17. Author interview, September 2005.
18. For instance, there is evidence that the mayor purposely restricted public transportation to the neighborhoods that were likely to support Néstor's candidacy (*La Hoja*, October 29, 2005).
19. Author interview, August 2005.
20. Author interview, August 2005.
21. Author interview, September 2006.
22. Author interview, December 2005.
23. Author interview, May 2006.

3 Building a Party Network: Political, Partisan, and Social Networks in Argentina

1. The majority of activists and voters live in houses that the Argentine census characterized as poor (see Table 1.1 in Chapter 1 for a detailed description of these indicators).
2. Author interview, September 2005.
3. Author interview, September 2005.
4. Author interview, October 2005.
5. Author interview, October 2005.
6. Author interview, October 2005.
7. Author interview, September 2005.
8. I examine the logic of perverse incentives, as well as its unintended consequences, in Chapter 5.
9. Author interview, September 2005.
10. Author interview, September 2005.
11. Author interview, September 2005.
12. Some parties also record information about the voter's family: number of children, ages, names, schools they are attending, and if they are receiving state aid. In some cases, parties even record the name of and information about the voter's employer.
13. Author interview, March 2000.
14. Author interview, March 2000.
15. Author interview, March 2000.
16. The document reads: "In accordance with the announcement made to all party members by Mayor Mario Ishii, president of the *Partido Justicialista* of Jose C. Paz and member of the National Council, I request that you notify all temporary public employees that it is obligatory without exception that they gather in the Plaza de Mayo tomorrow, Wednesday, June 18, 2008.

I also request that all tenured public employees of the municipality be invited to attend this event that aims to defend democracy and the established institutions." Source: Author's collection.

17. Author interview, April 2006.
18. Author interview, June 2006.
19. Author interview, October 2005.
20. Author interview, December 2005.
21. Author interview, September 2005.

4 Moral Hazard and Asymmetric Information Networks

1. To measure whether party candidates had failed or succeeded in meeting the party mayors' expectations in turning out voters at (1) rallies and (2) elections, I used the following question: "In evaluating the number of voters [name of the candidate] had mobilized to [(1) rallies, (2) the 2005 election], would you say that [he/she] had succeeded in meeting your expectations?" I expected party mayors to answer either yes or no, but surprisingly I found another answer for the case of party rallies. As reported in this chapter, for the case of party rallies, several mayors answered that candidates had exceeded (*sobrepasar*) their expectations.

2. Comparisons between the strategies pursued by candidates in Buenos Aires whose tenure was going to be renewed in two years and by those who were running for reelection and election in 2005 did not show dramatic differences. Neither did the strategies of candidates who were on the top of the closed list, at the cutoff point where candidates could either succeed or fail in getting elected, or even below the cutoff point where candidates were positive they were not going to get elected. This finding reinforces the argument advanced in this chapter that candidates have to constantly show their ability to turn out voters.

3. This description comes from an attendant at a rally in the province of Buenos Aires in 1996. My observations made almost ten years later support this testimony. Quoted in Otero (1997: 57).

4. Author interview, September 2005.

5. Quoted in Veiga (1998: 7).

6. *Olé*, October 22, 2006.

7. Author interview, March 2006.

8. Author interview, July 2009.

9. Chapter 1 provides an extensive review of the contributions and shortcomings of recent works in the discipline.

10. Author interview, May 2006.

11. The last names of these two councilwomen have been suppressed to ensure anonymity.

12. See *La Hoja*, August, September, and October 2001.

5 The Logic of Perverse Incentives

1. Author interview, September 2005.
2. Author interview, September 2005.
3. Author interview, September 2005.
4. Author interview, September 2005.
5. See http://www.youtube.com/watch?v=le2X30SZbhQ for some images and declarations.
6. See Chapter 4 for a vivid description of audience heterogeneity at party rallies.
7. Author interview, September 2005.
8. Author interview, September 2005.
9. Author interview, September 2005.
10. Author interview, November 2005.
11. Author interview, October 2005.
12. See author interview with Marcelo quoted in Chapter 3.
13. Author interview, September 2005.
14. Figure 3.3 shows an official government document requesting public employees' participation at a party rally in José C. Paz.
15. Author interview, September 2005.
16. Quoted in *La Hoja*, September 3, 1999.
17. "Since 1983 the average reelection rate for the Chamber of Deputies has been twenty percent, ranging from a high of twenty-nine percent in 1985 to a low of fifteen percent in 1995" (Jones et al. 2002: 658).
18. Author interview, September 2005.
19. Author interview, June 2006.
20. Author interview, September 2005.
21. Author interview, September 2005.
22. Phone conversation with *La Hoja* investigative reporter, Fabián Domínguez, April 2013.
23. In commenting on this candidate's actions, a party activist told me: "To be in politics you have to be willing to turn a blind eye, but yes, in this case [referring to the actions described here], I don't know, I guess that you also have to have the stomach" [*tenes que tener estómago*]. Author interview with a party activist in San Miguel, October 2005.
24. This conversation took place at an informal meeting with reporters during a political campaign. September 2005. *Radio Mitre*.
25. Author interview, September 2005.

6 Scaling Up

1. See Chapter 1 for a detailed description and descriptive statistical data about the Conurbano.
2. Exceptions include Beck Fenwick (2010), which is examined in detail in the following section.
3. Weitz-Shapiro defines and measures clientelism as a method of distribution focusing on "whether or not local executives (mayors) are personally

involved in the selection of beneficiaries for a large food distribution program across a sample of over 120 small and medium-sized Argentine municipalities" (2012: 569).

4. Table A.1 in the appendix to this chapter lists the names of the municipalities, the number of voters (from the highest to the lowest), the percentage of voters in each municipality, and the electoral section number.

5. The number of observations varies given the creation and disappearance of some municipalities over time. Some municipalities have elections more or less frequently given specific contexts: deaths, corruption scandals, and so on.

6. In 1999, the UCR together with Peronist candidates who did not agree with the political program of Peronist President Carlos Menem formed the Alliance *(Alianza)*. The electoral coalition was thus composed of Radical and Peronist candidates. The number and prominence of Radical and Peronist candidates varied in each municipality given the historical representation of each force and the specificities of the electoral context. In the province of Buenos Aires, as in other provinces, the Alliance was made up of mostly Peronist candidates in some municipalities, mostly Radical candidates in others, and a fair mixture of both parties in municipalities where the distribution of voters' preferences had been historically even. Juan Abal Medina (2009) provides an excellent overview of the creation and problems of the coalition. Assuming that the Alliance was not Peronist, I found that 54.64 percent of mayors elected in Buenos Aires are Peronist. If, however, we assume that the Alliance was indeed Peronist, the number rises to more than 60 percent.

7. Author interview, October 2005.

8. Author interview, December 2011.

9. See note 6 for a description of the *carapintadas* movement.

10. Author interview, December 2005.

11. Author interview, November 2005.

7 Mobilizing Poor Voters

1. Author interview, January 2006.

2. Author interview, January 2006.

3. See Suárez Bustamante (2003); Alcázar et al. (2003); and Alcázar (2007) for more information about the Glass of Milk program.

4. Author interview, March 2006.

5. Quoted in Muñoz (2013: 67). Personal interview with a former councilman of Santiago district, Cusco, May 24, 2010.

6. For Magaloni (2006), voter dissatisfaction is a key variable in explaining the PRI's electoral defeat in 2000.

8 Conclusions

1. *"Como tanta otra tristeza a la que te acostumbras."* The words belong to an Argentine rock band, Patricio Rey y sus Redonditos de Ricota.

2. See Stokes (2007) for a thorough discussion.
3. For instance, in my own work about illegal protests in new democracies (Szwarcberg 2004b), I ask why individuals from little-known provincial communities (Cutral-Co, Plaza Huincol, Tartagal, and Mosconi) who have been experiencing unemployment since the introduction of neoliberal reforms in the 1990s decided to protest in June 1996 and not, for instance, before Menem's reelection.
4. See Chapter 3 for a detailed analysis and criticism of Levitsky's (2003) argument.
5. Moreover, contrary to the forecast that voters would support Luis Juez for mayor but vote for Radical representatives, voters did not split their tickets. As a result, the elected mayor's support for his party's ballot led to its victory in four electoral sections, challenging the expectation that national and provincial figures would determine the success of the ballot. In this case it was Juez, the local candidate, who most greatly influenced the party's success, and not vice versa.
6. See note 6 in Chapter 6 for a description of the Alliance.
7. The article's full title is "Local Battle: One Tough Mayor Shows Argentina How to Clean House; while Corruption Still Hobbles Latin American States, a Few Cities Get Results"; on web: "Mr. Sabbatella's Rent." Matt Moffett, *Wall Street Journal* (Eastern edition), July 1, 2003, p. A1.
8. Interview of Guillermo O'Donnell by Horacio Verbitsky (2000). Translated from the Spanish by the author.

References

Abal Medina, Juan. 2009. "The Rise and Fall of the Argentine Centre-Left: The Crisis of Frente Grande." *Party Politics* 15(3): 357–75.

Acemoglu, Daron, and James A. Robinson. 2012. *Why Nations Fail: The Origins of Power, Prosperity and Poverty*. New York: Crown Publishers.

Alabarces, Pablo, and María Graciela Rodríguez. 1996. *Cuestión de Pelotas: Fútbol, Deporte, Sociedad, Cultura*. Buenos Aires: Atuel.

Alcázar, Lorena. 2007. *Por qué no Funcionan los Programas Alimentarios y Nutricionales en el Perú? Riesgos y Oportunidades para su Reforma*. Lima: Grupo de Análisis para el Desarrollo.

Alcázar, Lorena, José Roberto López, and Erik Wachtenheim. 2003. *Las Pérdidas en el Camino. Fugas en el Gasto Público: Transferencias Municipales, Vaso de Leche y Sector Educación*. Lima: Grupo de Análisis para el Desarrollo.

Ansión, Juan, Alejandro Dierz, and Luis Mujica (eds.). 2000. *Autoridad en Espacios Locales*. Lima: Fondo Editorial PUCP.

Ansolabehere, Stephen, and James M. Snyder Jr. 2003. "Why Is There So Little Money in U.S. Politics?" *Journal of Economic Perspectives* 17(1): 105–30.

Auyero, Javier. 2000. *Poor People's Politics: Peronist Survival Networks and the Legacy of Evita*. Durham, NC: Duke University Press.

   2003. *Contentious Lives: Two Argentine Women, Two Protests, and the Quest for Recognition*. Durham, NC: Duke University Press.

   2012. *Patients of the State: The Politics of Waiting in Argentina*. Durham, NC: Duke University Press.

Bates, Robert H. 1998. *Analytic Narratives*. Princeton, NJ: Princeton University Press.

Bayard de Volo, Lorraine, and Edward Schatz. 2004. "From the Inside Out: Ethnographic Methods in Political Research." *Political Science & Politics* 37(2): 267–71.

Beck, Linda. 2008. *Brokering Democracy in Africa: The Rise of Clientelist Democracy in Senegal*. New York: Palgrave Macmillan.

Bischoff, Efrain U. 1995. *Historia de Córdoba*. Buenos Aires: Editorial Plus Ultra.

Bourdieu, Pierre. 1990. "The Scholastic Point of View." *Cultural Anthropology* 5(4): 380–91.

1997. *Practical Reason: On the Theory of Action.* Stanford, CA: Stanford University Press.

2000. *Pascalian Meditations.* Stanford, CA: Stanford University Press.

Bruhn, Kathleen. 1997. *Taking on Goliath: The Emergence of a New Left Party and the Struggle for Democracy in Mexico.* University Park: Pennsylvania State University Press.

Brusco, Valeria, Marcelo Nazareno, and Susan C. Stokes. 2004. "Vote Buying in Argentina." *Latin American Research Review* 39(2): 66–88.

Calvo, Ernesto, and María Victoria Murillo. 2004. "Who Delivers? Partisan Clients in the Argentine Electoral Market." *American Journal of Political Science* 48(4): 742–57.

2005. "The New Iron Law of Argentine Politics? Partisanship, Clientelism, and Governability in Contemporary Argentina." In *Argentine Democracy: The Politics of Institutional Weakness,* edited by Steven Levitsky and María Victoria Murillo. University Park: Pennsylvania State University Press, pp. 207–28.

2013. "When Parties Meet Voters: Assessing Political Linkages Through Partisan Networks and Distributive Expectations in Argentina and Chile." *Comparative Political Studies* 46(7): 851–82.

Canton, Darío, and Jorge Raúl Jorrat. 2003. "Abstention in Argentina Presidential Elections, 1983–1999." *Latin American Research Review* 38: 187–201.

Carreras, Sergio. 2004. *El reino de los Juárez: medio siglo de miseria, terror y desmesura en Santiago del Estero.* Buenos Aires: Aguilar.

Case, Anne. 2001. "Election Goals and Income Distribution: Recent Evidence from Albania." *European Economic Review* 45: 405–23.

Chandra, Kanchan. 2004. *Why Ethnic Parties Succeed: Patronage and Ethnic Head Counts in India.* New York: Cambridge University Press.

Chong, Dennis. 1991. *Collective Action and the Civil Rights Movement.* Chicago: University of Chicago Press.

Christakis, Nicholas A., and James H. Fowler. 2009. *Connected: The Surprising Power of Our Social Networks and How They Shape Our Lives.* New York: Little, Brown and Co./Hachette Book Group.

Chubb, Judith. 1981. "The Social Bases of an Urban Political Machine: The Case of Palermo." *Political Science Quarterly* 96(1): 107–25.

Cleary, Matthew. 2007. "Electoral Competition, Participation, and Government Responsiveness in Mexico." *American Journal of Political Science* 51(2): 283–99.

Collier, Ruth Berins, and David Collier. 1991. *Shaping the Political Arena: Critical Junctures, the Labor Movement, and Regime Dynamics in Latin America.* Princeton, NJ: Princeton University Press.

Cornelius, Wayne A. 1996. *Mexican Politics in Transition: The Breakdown of a One-Party-Dominant Regime.* San Diego: UCSD – Center for US-Mexican Studies.

2004. "Mobilized Voting in the 2000 Elections: The Changing Efficacy of Vote Buying and Coercion in Mexican Electoral Politics." In *Mexico's Pivotal Democratic Election,* edited by Jorge I. Domínguez and Chappell Lawson. Stanford, CA: Stanford University Press, pp. 47–66.

Cornelius, Wayne A., Todd A. Eisenstadt, and Jane Hindley. 1999. *Subnational Politics and Democratization in Mexico*. San Diego: University of California, San Diego.

Cotler, Julio, and Romeo Grompone. 2000. *El Fujimorismo: Ascenso y Caída de un Régimen Autoritario*. Lima: IEP Ediciones.

Cox, Gary W. 2010. "Swing Voters, Core Voters, and Distributive Politics." In *Political Representation*, edited by Ian Shapiro, Susan C. Stokes, Elisabeth Jean Wood, and Alexander S. Kirshner. New York: Cambridge University Press, pp. 342–57.

Cox, Gary W., and Matthew D. McCubbins. 1986. "Electoral Politics as a Redistributive Game." *Journal of Politics* 48(2): 370–89.

Dahl, Robert. 1971. *Polyarchy: Participation and Opposition*. New Haven, CT: Yale University Press.

1987. *Democracy and Its Critics*. New Haven, CT: Yale University Press.

Dahlberg, Matz, and Eva Johansson. 2002. "On the Vote Purchasing Behavior of Incumbent Governments." *American Political Science Review* 96(1): 27–40.

Diaz-Cayeros, Alberto, Federico Estévez, and Beatriz Magaloni. 2007. "Strategies of Vote Buying: Democracy, Clientelism and Poverty Relief in Mexico." Unpublished manuscript. Stanford University.

Dixit, Avinash, and John Londregan. 1996. "The Determinants of Success of Special Interests in Redistributive Politics." *The Journal of Politics* 58(4): 1132–55.

Eaton, Kent. 2004. *Politics beyond the Capital: The Design of Subnational Institutions in South America*. Stanford, CA: Stanford University Press.

Elster, Jon. 1985. *Making Sense of Marx*. New York: Cambridge University Press.

Falleti, Tulia. 2005. "A Sequential Theory of Decentralization: Latin American Cases in Comparative Perspective." *American Political Science Review* 99(3): 327–46.

2010. *Decentralization and Subnational Politics in Latin America*. New York: Cambridge University Press.

Fenwick, Tracy Beck. 2010. "The Institutional Feasibility of National-Local Policy Collaboration: Insights from Brazil and Argentina." *Journal of Politics in Latin America* 2: 155–83.

Foucault, Michel. 1977. *Discipline and Punish: The Birth of the Prison*. New York: Pantheon Books.

Fox, Jonathan. 1994. "The Difficult Transition from Clientelism to Citizenship." *World Politics* 46: 151–84.

Frederic, Sabina. 2004. *Buenos vecinos, malos políticos: moralidad y política en el Gran Buenos Aires*. Buenos Aires: Prometeo Libros.

Gans-Morse, Jordan, Sebastián Mazzuca, and Simeon Nichter. 2014. "Varieties of Clientelism: Machine Politics during Elections." *American Journal of Political* 58(2): 415–32.

Gay, Robert. 2006. "The Even More Difficult Transition from Clientelism to Citizenship: Lessons from Brazil." In *Out of the Shadows: Political Action and the Informal Economy in Latin America*, edited by Patricia Fernández-Kelly and Jon Shefner. University Park: Pennsylvania State University Press, pp. 195–218.

George, Alexander L., and Andrew Bennett. 2005. *Case Studies and Theory Development in the Social Sciences*. Cambridge, MA: MIT Press.

Gerring, John. 2001. *Social Science Methodology: A Critical Framework*. New York: Cambridge University Press.

2007. *Case Study Research*. New York: Cambridge University Press.

Gervasoni, Carlos. 2010. "A Rentier Theory of Subnational Regimes: Fiscal Federalism, Democracy, and Authoritarianism in the Argentine Provinces." *World Politics* 62(2): 302–40.

Gibson, Edward L. 2004. *Federalism and Democracy in Latin America*. Baltimore, MD: Johns Hopkins University Press.

2005. "Boundary Control: Subnational Authoritarianism in Democratic Countries." *World Politics* 58: 101–32.

2012. *Boundary Control: Subnational Authoritarianism in Federal Democracies*. Cambridge: Cambridge University Press.

Gibson, Edward L., and Ernesto Calvo. 2001. "Federalism and Low-Maintenance Constituencies: Territorial Dimensions of Economic Reform in Argentina." *Studies in Comparative International Development* 35(3): 32–55.

Giraudy, Agustina. 2009. "Subnational Undemocratic Regime Continuity after Democratization: Argentina and Mexico in Comparative Perspective." PhD Dissertation. Department of Political Science, University of North Carolina at Chapel Hill.

Gonzalez-Ocantos, Ezequiel, Chad Kiewiet de Jonge, Carlos Meléndez, Javier Osorio, and David W. Nickerson. 2012. "Vote Buying and Social Desirability Bias: Experimental Evidence from Nicaragua." *American Journal of Political Science* 56(1): 202–17.

Grabia, Gustavo. 2009. *La Doce: la verdadera historia de la barra brava de Boca*. Buenos Aires: Sudamericana.

Greene, Kenneth F. 2007. *Why Dominant Parties Lose: Mexico's Democratization in Comparative Perspective*. New York: Cambridge University Press.

Gutiérrez, Tomás S. 2000. *El 'Hermano' Fujimori: Evangélicos y Poder Político en el Perú del '90*. Lima: Archivo Histórico del Protestantismo Latinoamericano.

Hicken, Allen. 2011. "Clientelism." *Annual Review of Political Science* 14: 289–310.

Hilgers, Tina. 2005. "The Nature of Clientelism in Mexico City." Paper prepared for the Canadian Political Science Association Annual Conference. June 2–4, 2005, London, Ontario (pp. 1–49).

2008. "Causes and Consequences of Political Clientelism: Mexico's PRD in Comparative Perspective." *Latin American Politics and Society* 50(4): 123–53.

2012. *Clientelism in Everyday Latin American Politics*. New York: Palgrave Macmillan.

Holzner, Claudio A. 2010. *Poverty of Democracy*. Pittsburgh: University of Pittsburgh Press.

James, Daniel. 1988. *Resistance and Integration: Peronism and the Argentine Working Class, 1946–1976*. New York: Cambridge University Press.

Jones, Mark P., Sebastián Saiegh, Pablo T. Spiller, and Mariano Tommasi. 2002. "Amateur Legislators-Professional Politicians: The Consequences of Party-Centered Electoral Rules in a Federal System." *American Journal of Political Science* 46(3): 356–69.

Kalyvas, Stathis N. 2006. *The Logic of Violence in Civil War*. New York: Cambridge University Press.

King, Gary, Robert O. Keohane, and Sidney Verba. 1994. *Designing Social Inquiry: Scientific Inference in Qualitative Research*. Princeton, NJ: Princeton University Press.

Kitschelt, Herbert. 2000. "Linkages between Citizens and Politicians in Democratic Polities." *Comparative Political Studies* 33(6–7): 845–79.

Kitschelt, Herbert, and Steven Wilkinson. 2007. *Patrons, Clients, and Policies: Patterns of Democratic Accountability and Political Competition*. New York: Cambridge University Press.

Knoke, David. 1990. *Political Networks: The Structural Perspective*. New York: Cambridge University Press.

Kuran, Timur. 1991. "Now Out of Never: The Element of Surprise in the East European Revolution of 1989." *World Politics* 44(1): 7–48.

Langston, Joy. 2001. "Why Rules Matter: Changes in Candidate Selection in Mexico's PRI, 1998–2000." *Journal of Latin American Studies* 33(3): 485–511.

Levitsky, Steven. 2001. "An Organized Disorganization: Informal Organization and the Persistence of Local Party Structures in Argentine Peronism." *Journal of Latin American Studies* 33(1): 29–66.

   2003. *Transforming Labor-Based Parties in Latin America: Argentine Peronism in Comparative Perspective*. New York: Cambridge University Press.

   2013. "Peru: The Challenges of a Democracy without Parties." In *Constructing Democratic Governance in Latin America*, edited by Jorge I. Dominguez and Michael Shifter. Baltimore, MD: Johns Hopkins University Press, pp. 282–315.

Levitsky, Steven, and Max Cameron. 2003. "Democracy without Parties? Political Parties and Regime Change in Fujimori's Peru." *Latin American Politics and Society* 45(3): 1–33.

Levitsky, Steven, and María Victoria Murillo. 2005. *Argentine Democracy: The Politics of Institutional Weakness*. University Park: Pennsylvania State University Press.

   2008. "Argentina: From Kirchner to Kirchner." *Journal of Democracy* 19(2): 16–30.

Lieberman, Evan S. 2005. "Nested Analysis as a Mixed-Method Strategy for Comparative Research." *American Political Science Review* 99(3): 435–52.

Lindbeck, Assar, and Jorgen Weibull. 1987. "Balanced Budget Distribution as Outcome of Political Competition." *Public Choice* 52(3): 273–97.

Lipset, Seymour M. 1959. "Some Social Requisites of Democracy: Economic Development and Political Legitimacy." *American Political Science Review* 53: 69–105.

Lohmann, Susanne. 1994. "The Dynamics of Informational Cascades: The Monday Demonstrations in Leipzig, East Germany, 1989–91." *World Politics* 47(1): 42–101.

Magaloni, Beatriz. 2006. *Voting for Autocracy: Hegemonic Party Survival and Its Demise in Mexico*. New York: Cambridge University Press.

Magaloni, Beatriz, Alberto Diaz-Cayeros, and Federico Estévez. 2007. "Clientelism and Portfolio Diversification: A Model of Electoral Investment with Applications to Mexico." In *Patrons, Clients, and Policies: Patterns of Democratic Accountability and Political Competition*, edited by Herbert Kitschelt and Steven Wilkinson. New York: Cambridge University Press, pp. 182–205, chap. 8.

Mainwaring, Scott, and Timothy R. Scully (eds.). 1995. *Building Democratic Institutions: Party Systems in Latin America*. Stanford, CA: Stanford University Press.

Montero, Alfred, and David Samuels (eds.). 2004. *Decentralization and Democracy in Latin America*. Notre Dame, IN: University of Notre Dame Press.

Moore, Barrington. 1966. *Social Origins of Dictatorship and Democracy*. Boston: Beacon Press.

Mora y Araujo, Manuel, and Ignacio Llorente. 1980. *El Voto Peronista*. Buenos Aires: Editorial Sudamericana.

Muñoz Chirinos, Paula. 2013. "Campaign Clientelism in Peru: An Informational Theory." PhD Dissertation. Department of Political Science, University of Texas at Austin.

Nichter, Simeon. 2008. "Vote Buying or Turnout Buying? Machine Politics and the Secret Ballot." *American Political Science Review* 102(1): 19–31.

O'Donnell, Guillermo (ed.). 1999. *On the State, Democratization, and Some Conceptual Problems: A Latin American View with Some Postcommunist Countries*. Notre Dame, IN: University of Notre Dame Press.

O'Donnell, Guillermo A., and Philippe C. Schmitter. 1986. *Transitions from Authoritarian Rule: Tentative Conclusions about Uncertain Democracies*. Baltimore, MD: Johns Hopkins University Press.

O'Donnell, María. 2005. *El Aparato: Los Intendentes del Conurbano y las Cajas Negras de la Política*. Buenos Aires: Aguilar.

Oliveros, Virginia. 2012. "Public Employees as Political Workers: Evidence from an Original Survey in Argentina." PhD Dissertation. Department of Political Science, Columbia University.

Ollier, María Matilde. 1998. *La creencia y la pasión. Privado, público y político en la izquierda revolucionaria, 1966–1976*. Buenos Aires: Siglo XXI.

Ostiguy, Pierre. 1998. "Peronism and Anti-Peronism: Class-Cultural Cleavages and Political Identity in Argentina." PhD Dissertation. Department of Political Science, University of California at Berkeley.

Otero, Daniel. 1997. *El Entorno: La Trama Intima del Aparato Duhaldista y sus Punteros*. Buenos Aires: Nuevo Hacer.

Pachirat, Timothy. 2009. "The Political in Political Ethnography: Dispatches from the Kill Floor." In *Political Ethnography: What Immersion Contributes to the Study of Power*, edited by Edward Schatz. Chicago: University of Chicago Press, pp. 143–62.

Panebianco, Angelo. 1988. *Political Parties: Organization and Power*. Cambridge: Cambridge University Press.

Panfichi, Aldo, and Omar Coronel. 2012. "Cambios en los Vínculos entre la Sociedad y el Estado en el Perú: 1968–2008." In *Cambios Sociales en el*

Perú 1968–2008, edited by Orlando Plaza. Lima: Centro de Investigaciones Sociológicas, Económicas, Políticas y Antropológicas, pp. 73–106.

Piattoni, Simona (ed.). 2001. *Clientelism, Interests, and Democratic Representation: The European Experience in Historical Perspective.* Cambridge: Cambridge University Press.

Posner, Daniel N. 2005. *Institutions and Ethnic Politics in Africa.* New York: Cambridge University Press.

Putnam, Robert D. 2000. *Bowling Alone: The Collapse and Revival of American Community.* New York: Simon & Schuster.

Riordon, William L. [1948] 1995. *Plunkitt of Tammany Hall: A Series of Very Plain Talks on Very Practical Politics.* New York: Penguin.

Rosas, Guillermo, and Kirk Hawkins. 2007. "Turncoats, True Believers, and Turnout: Machine Politics in an Australian Ballot System." Unpublished manuscript. Washington University in St. Louis and Brigham Young University.

Sahlins, Marshall D. 1977. "Poor Man, Rich Man, Big-Man, Chief: Political Types in Melanesia and Polynesia." In *Friends, Followers, and Factions,* edited by Steffan W. Schmidt, Laura Guasti, Karl H. Landé, and James C. Scott. Berkeley: University of California Press, pp. 220–31.

Sanchez, Omar. 2009. "Party Non-Systems a Conceptual Innovation." *Party Politics* 15(4): 487–520.

Schady, Norbert R. 2000. "The Political Economy of Expenditures by the Peruvian Social Fund (FONCODES), 1991–95." *American Political Science Review* 94(2): 289–304.

Schaffer, Frederic Charles. 2007. *Elections for Sale: The Causes and Consequences of Vote Buying.* Boulder, CO: Lynne Rienner Publishers.

Scott, James C. 1969. "Corruption, Machine Politics, and Political Change." *American Political Science Review* 63(4): 1142–58.

Semán, Pablo. 2004. *La Religiosidad Popular: Creencias y Vida Cotidiana.* Buenos Aires: Capital Intelectual.

Shefter, Martin. 1977. "Parties and Patronage: England, Germany, and Italy." *Politics and Society* 7(4): 403–51.

Simpser, Alberto. 2013. *Why Governments and Parties Manipulate Elections: Theory, Practice, and Implications.* New York: Cambridge University Press.

Snyder, Richard. 2001. "Scaling Down: The Subnational Comparative Method." *Studies in Comparative International Development* 36(1): 93–110.

Stokes, Susan C. 2005. "Perverse Accountability: A Formal Model of Machine Politics with Evidence from Argentina." *American Political Science Review* 99(3): 315–25.

2007a. "Is Vote Buying Undemocratic?" In *Elections for Sale: The Causes and Consequences of Vote Buying,* edited by Frederic C. Schaffer. London: Lynne Rienner Publishers, pp. 81–99.

2007b. "Political Clientelism." In *The Oxford Handbook of Comparative Politics,* edited by Carles Boix and Susan C. Stokes. New York: Oxford University Press, pp. 604–27.

2009. "Pork, by Any Other Name ... Building a Conceptual Scheme of Distributive Politics." Unpublished manuscript. Yale University.

Stokes, Susan C., Thad Dunning, Marcelo Nazareno, and Valeria Brusco. 2013. *Brokers, Voters, and Clientelism: The Puzzle of Distributive Politics.* New York: Cambridge University Press.

Suárez Bustamante, Miguel. 2003. *Caracterización del Programa Vaso de Leche.* Lima: Dirección de General de Asuntos Económicos y Sociales del Ministerio de Economía y Finanzas.

Svampa, Maristella (ed.). 2000. *Desde Abajo.* Buenos Aires: Biblos-UNGS.

Svampa, Maristella, and Sebastián Pereyra. 2003. *Entre la Ruta y el Barrio.* Buenos Aires: Editorial Biblos.

Szwarcberg, Mariela. 2004a. "Feeding Political Loyalties: Clientelism in Argentina." Unpublished manuscript. University of Chicago.

   2004b. "Bringing the Stones Back In: Illegal Protests in New Democracies." Unpublished manuscript. University of Chicago.

   2009. "Making Local Democracy: Political Machines, Clientelism, and Social Networks in Argentina." PhD Dissertation. Department of Political Science, University of Chicago.

   2011. "Empowering Poor Women: The Unexpected Effects of a Welfare Program in Argentina." *Women's Policy Journal of Harvard* 8: 13–21.

   2012a. "Revisiting Clientelism: A Network Analysis of Problem-Solving Networks in Argentina." *Social Networks* 34(2): 230–40.

   2012b. "Uncertainty, Political Clientelism, and Voter Turnout in Argentina: Why Parties Conduct Rallies in Argentina." *Comparative Politics* 45(1): 88–106.

   2013. "The Microfoundations of Political Clientelism: Lessons form the Argentine Case." *Latin American Research Review* 48(2): 32–54.

   2014. "Political Parties and Rallies in Latin America." *Party Politics* 20(3): 456–66.

Tanaka, Martín. 1999. "La Participación Social y Política de los Pobladores Populares Urbanos." In *El Poder Visto Desde Abajo: Democracia, Educación y Ciudadanía en Espacios Locales,* edited by Martín Tanaka. Lima: IEP, pp. 103–53.

   2005. *Democracia sin partidos, Perú, 2000–2005: los problemas de representación y las propuestas de reforma política.* Lima: Instituto de Estudios Peruanos.

Torre, Juan Carlos. 2005. "Citizens versus Political Class: The Crisis of Partisan Representation." In *Argentine Democracy: The Politics of Institutional Weakness,* edited by Steven Levitsky and María Victoria Murillo. University Park: Pennsylvania State University Press, pp. 165–80.

Vaca Narvaja, Hernán. 2001. *El Candidato: Biografía no Autorizada de José Manuel de la Sota.* Buenos Aires: Editorial Sudamericana.

Vargas Llosa, Mario. [1993] 2005. *El pez en el agua.* Lima: Alfaguara.

Veiga, Gustavo. 1998. *Donde manda la patota: barrabravas, poder y política.* Buenos Aires: Agora.

Verbitsky, Horacio. 2000. "La muerte lenta" (interview of Guillermo O'Donnell). *Página/12.* October 15, pp. 12–13.

Wantchekon, Leonard. 2003. "Clientelism and Vote Behavior: Evidence from a Field Experiment in Benin." *World Politics* 55(3): 399–422.

Weeden, Lisa. 2009. "Ethnography as Interpretative Enterprise." In *Political Ethnography: What Immersion Contributes to the Study of Power*, edited by Edward Schatz. Chicago: University of Chicago Press, pp. 75–93.

2010. "Reflections on Ethnographic Work in Political Science." *Annual Review of Political Science* 13(1): 255–72.

Weitz-Shapiro, Rebecca. 2012. "What Wins Votes: Why Some Politicians Opt Out of Clientelism." *American Journal of Political Science* 56(3): 568–83.

Welhofer, Spencer E. 1979. "Strategies for Party Organization and Voter Mobilization: Britain, Norway, and Argentina." *Comparative Political Studies* 12(3): 169–204.

Wilkinson, Steven. 2004. *Votes and Violence: Electoral Competition and Ethnic Riots in India*. New York: Cambridge University Press.

Young, Iris Marion. 2000. *Inclusion and Democracy*. New York: Oxford University Press.

Zarazaga, Rodrigo S. J. 2014. "Brokers Beyond Clientelism: A New Perspective through the Argentine Case." *Latin American Politics and Society* 56(3): 23–45.

Index